YOM KIPPUR
a go-go

YOM KIPPUR
a go-go

MATTHUE ROTH

CLEIS
PRESS

Published in the United States by Cleis Press Inc., P.O. Box 14697, San Francisco, California 94114.

Printed in the United States.
Cover design: Scott Idleman
Cover photo: Mark Douet/Getty Images
Text design: Frank Wiedemann
Logo art: Juana Alicia
First Edition.
10 9 8 7 6 5 4 3 2 1

The title "Most Unsuitable Suitable Husband In the World, Ever" was co-opted from Tanuja Hidier's *Born Confused,* Scholastic/PUSH Books. One line in "Cautious of Kashrus" was sampled from Michelle Tea's book *Valencia.* Lyrics from "Egg" and "Robbin' the Bank" by Up With Hope, Down With Mayonnaise.

Library of Congress Cataloging-in-Publication Data

Roth, Matthue.
   Yom Kippur a go-go : a memoir / by Matthue Roth.—1st ed.
      p. cm.
   ISBN 1-57344-219-4 (pbk. : alk. paper)
   1. Roth, Matthue. 2. Roth, Matthue—Homes and haunts—California—San Francisco. 3. Mission District (San Francisco, Calif.)—Social life and customs. 4. Mission District (San Francisco, Calif.)—Biography. 5. Authors, American—21st century—Biography. 6. Jewish authors—United States—Biography. 7. Judaism and literature—United States. I. Title.
   PS3618.O863Z478 2005
      813'.6—dc22
                        2005011691

b"h

for my family, born and found

acknowledgments

Thanks to my ridiculously supportive parents, who will read this even though I tell them not to. My sister, who makes sure I'm still getting outside. Cuz and especially Grandmom. Itta—you're my superhero. Thanks for saving me from those burning buildings. Jenny Traig, Daphne Gottlieb, and Shawna Kenney for showing me how to do it. Yael/Zack/Liz/Cara/Steph/Harbeer for early edits. Miyabi and Pinhas for translations. Dom and Coltrane, you're my escape crew. And thanks to my friends, who saw me ripping my heart out and pitched in a hand to help. K'vetch, and anyone who's ever read there. The Berkeley slam kids. Jen Joseph. Paradise Lounge. The whole San Francisco open mic scene. Ewert, for seeing gemara in my editing arrows. Horehound. West. Mark and Positive Force DC. The LL. Kris. Sarah. JewishFashionConspiracy.com. The San Francisco Literation Front. Levithan. Langers. Potashes. Freundels.

David Sacks. Violet. My eternal roommate Aaron. Sherilyn and Katrina, for being their big bad goth fuzzy bunny selves. To Chris and Diane, for keeping me on time and on track. To Gedalia, for teaching me to see the goodness in every person. To Felice Newman and Frédérique Delacoste at Cleis Press. And thanks to Kirk, for bravery.

contents

1

battlefront

The World Bank held its annual summit that week, and Washington braced for the worst. They shut down the Capitol, the White House, and the Smithsonian museums, and any tours that hadn't been canceled were escorted by hulking security troops. Police officers were working eighteen-hour shifts. The president went on TV and said he was calling in the National Guard, but weren't they in Washington already? The first World Bank riots, the previous autumn in Seattle, saw the largest domestic protest in U.S. history. Gas bombs, rubber bullets, anarchists picking fistfights with the police, nose to nose. All the rich-kid activists in Washington used their frequent-flyer miles to fly there and participate firsthand. The rest of us were unspeakably jealous. We called them sellouts for months afterward. Now, the next phase of the riots was happening in Washington, D.C.

It was practically in my backyard.

I was in Washington that year, living on a very big scholarship from a very big university. The university, with its rich North Jersey political science majors and Pepsi-sponsored welcome seminars, was everything terrible we hated about America. Its president, a blubbery iceberg of a man in a walrus moustache and too-tight neckties, was the kind of guy who would cancel funding for the rape awareness group because he said it made the school look bad. He was also given to making lame jokes about the cost of tuition—you know, like If You Have To Ask.

Our school president welcomed the World Bank conference with open arms. Like good activists, we were devastated, although in retrospect his enthusiasm fueled our fire like nothing else could. The university had paid for our housing and education, and encouraged us to leave our hometowns and move to D.C. Now we would use everything they'd given us to strike back. The conference started on Sunday. Activists planned to make human chains around crucial buildings on Saturday afternoon.

The National Guard tanks rolled in on Friday morning.

The air was tense and the city was jumpy. Regular citizens, the kind who didn't wear combat fatigues and handkerchiefs over their faces, were jumpy.

The entire city held its breath.

I was gearing up for the best weekend ever. Dubbing mixtape soundtracks, making plans with friends, picking out my best T-shirts—the ones that started conversations, that made strangers walk up and say to me, "Damn, where did you get *that* from?" Riots, intrigue, the National Guard, hot activist girls in combat gear coming from across the country for the weekend. You knew there were going to be some good parties.

The streets would be closed off to traffic, just like the Fourth of July. Bands were scheduled to play nonstop concerts all along the paved-over quadrangles near the Washington Monument. The entire weekend was a punk-rock paradise. I was stoked as hell.

Only, the riots started on Shabbos.

I had just decided to become Orthodox. I had left Washington for a semester, come back, started hanging with the religious kids, and then, one day in late fall, I realized I was keeping kosher, scheduling my jobs so I didn't work on Saturdays, and I hadn't skipped synagogue in longer than I could remember. I was going through a geek phase, and, as geeks went, Orthodox kids were the absolute geekiest. The laws were so strict that it would be impossible *not* to rebel. In a religion that dictated the order of putting your shoes on, there had to be some pretty heavy partying going on to supplement all the rules.

Plus, they had six thousand years of history as backup. They had to be doing *something* right.

Maybe I was feeling insecure about life, the uncertainty that followed college. Maybe I was just that rebellious, and all the usual rebellions had already been played out.

So suddenly, I was Orthodox. Learning how to be Orthodox was like learning to walk again, maybe like learning to walk on the moon. My house, which I shared with Yuri, had two sets of dishes. Our light switches had little metal covers so you wouldn't accidentally turn a light off on Shabbos. Our alarm clock went off every day at 6:45 A.M., a ten-minute shower before we had to say the morning prayers. Everybody I knew slept till 11:00, or ten minutes before class, whichever came first. The first time I got challenged for being Orthodox—by some vegan straightedge kid at a hardcore show, *You can't be serious, Matt, that shit is so misogynistic*—I shoved the 6:45 A.M.

Two sets of dishes. One for meat, one for dairy. Actually, we had two and a half sets, because my roommate was especially anal and wanted to have neutral dishes, too—nonmeat and nondairy.

thing in his face. "YOU TRY WAKING UP AT SIX FUCKING FORTY-FIVE IN THE MORNING EVERY MORNING, *THEN* YOU CAN TALK SMACK ABOUT BEING FUCKIN' ORTHODOX."

Fuckin' Orthodox. My religious friends always flinched when they heard me talk, but somewhere deep inside I think they understood. They humored my secular side. They thought I'd grow out of it.

The activists did not humor me. They were all into Buddhism and Hinduism, but conventional religion, even one with a history as quirky and working-class as Orthodox Judaism, was too close to home. Plus there was this whole Palestine deal—I was wearing a yarmulke, so I was a Jew, and to them, being a Jew meant I supported Israel, and supporting Israel meant I hated Arabs. In their book, I was already a racist and a proto-American oppressor.

But even though I hadn't been to a rally in two months—even though I was on the outs with the truly dedicated—this was going to be the mother of all protests.

I wouldn't miss it for the world.

All week, the campus buzzed, like New Orleans before Mardi Gras, or like the Christian world on Christmas Eve. Then, late Friday afternoon, everything slowed down. Kids blowing soap bubbles on the lawns turned to stone, slow-motion, timelessly retro. The businessmen walking home stopped in their tracks for five whole seconds, entire blocks frozen, people straining their heads to watch the streaking purple clouds in the sky. It almost made you want to believe in God. White marble buildings bathed in an electric orange sunset, the kind of quiet, tranquil beauty of the Smithsonian museums at closing time. The world settled into an uneasy peace.

Gavin picked me up at my apartment on the way to services. "Can you believe this shit?" he said, sweeping his hand toward the Washington Monument.

Gavin was my first Orthodox friend. He used to be in a frat, but they kicked him out because he signed everyone up for the Young Republicans email list and the frat president's dad was a Democratic congressman. Gavin was the type of kid who called problems *setbacks*. But when you asked him what he was thinking and he shrugged and said *nothing* and you both turned back to the TV, it was the most reassuring thing in the world.

We walked in silence, cutting across the campus quad to the Jewish Student Center.

In the pigeon-colored basement, the handful of Orthodox kids sat in bored, contemplative silence, reading the Song of Songs, studying the week's Torah portion, or talking campus politics. Beryl, a senior, sat alone in a corner, watching the vanishing sunlight, glancing at his watch every other second, whispering in Shifra's ear about how we needed to start on time. Shifra was the president of the Orthodox Student Union and she was the one who bugged everyone to come earlier. Yehoshua, who'd been doing the Orthodox thing for almost a year and was totally absorbed—he was even starting to wear a black hat—sat with Daniel, who had just started keeping Shabbos and was still asking questions like *Why do I need to wear a yarmulke all the time?* We were probably at the same level, but I was better about pretending I knew what was going on. The sun lingered on the horizon, danger-

The Jewish Student Center was a combination of a synagogue, a cafeteria, a meeting hall, and a hangout space. Nobody really hung out there, but the staff were forever engaged in a struggle to throw more elaborate and good-naturedly ironic events there—things like retro disco dances and "must see TV" parties. God bless 'em; when nobody showed up, the administrators just tried something else, or tried harder.

ously close to setting. We still only had nine men, one short of the ten-person quorum that we needed to pray.

At the last possible minute, this kid Evan, who wasn't Orthodox but sometimes prayed with us, ran down the stairs. Behind him trailed a girl in a long skirt. Usually we were good at asking questions about new people—that's a lie, we were fanatical about it—but that day, we were a minute away from running out of afternoon.

Beryl banged on the podium. He started to pray in the loudest murmur he could manage, and we leaped to attention. He shouted out the first words of Kaddish, the Aramaic syllables twisting around each other in a fine, coagulated mush. We yelled *Amen!* like we meant *Danger!* Outside there might be a war going on, but inside, we were fire and light.

After praying came dinner. All the people from all the services came together: the Conservative kids in their pointy sweatshop yarmulkes, the Reform kids with no yarmulkes at all. The Orthodox kids clustered around one narrow table in a corner, whispering the prayers as the rest of the community sang some cheesy Jewish song that everyone vaguely remembered from when they were ten years old, like "Hinei Ma Tov" or "Shabbat Shalom," in smarmy campfire voices. The girl in the long skirt looked lost, alone among the clusters of cliques. I went up to her and said—quietly, so she could pretend I wasn't talking to her if she wanted to—that she could sit with us.

Shifra, the maternal one among us, smiled at me approvingly.

Some cheesy Jewish song. We sang "Shalom Aleichem"—we did each verse three times, not just once, the way the rest of Hillel did, and never to the tune of Billy Joel songs like they did. And then we did "Eishes Chayil," "A Woman of Valor," which was long and entirely in Hebrew. None of the non-Orthodox people even knew where to begin on that one.

It wasn't that we thought we were closer to God than everybody else, or that we were necessarily more righteous people. At one time or another, the single most religious kid in the world has bit into a Snickers bar without remembering to say the prayer over it.

What made us Orthodox Jews different from everyone else was that we tried to be better. We took on new stringencies, learning new laws to follow. Maybe it did bring us closer to God, and maybe it didn't, but in our minds, we were always trying to get closer. Like discovering your first indie band that no one else in school has heard of, it made us different. It made us special.

And that was why we said our additional prayers, sat separately at meals, prayed when we woke and before we fell asleep at night and every single minute we spent alone—we did it all for God. The reason we wore yarmulkes, and the reason we let our fringes hang out and trail on our seats instead of tucking them into our pants, had nothing to do with God. That was because we wanted to represent. If we were gonna be different, we were gonna be different with *pride*.

Over dinner, between Shifra and Beryl and Yehoshua and me, we were able to coax out the girl's story. Her name was Ilyana and she wasn't religious, although she grew up praying at a Chabad synagogue. Chabad are these Hasidic Jewish missionaries who set up synagogues in small towns without a large Jewish community, and they do services and Shabbos dinners for anyone who wants to come. She'd grown up in Oklahoma City, in the only Jewish family in her neighborhood, and this year she was a freshman. Oklahoma City was a long way from Washington. "I walked into the Conservative service, but it felt all forced," she said with a shrug. "I didn't think I'd start coming to services here in Washington. I guess I just missed feeling comfortable."

"Oh, honey," said Shifra. "You can feel comfortable with us."

"Were you at the School of Assassins rally at the Capitol?" Ilyana asked abruptly, staring at me head-on.

"Yeah," I said. "Didn't you speak at the Free Trade to Mexico thing on Sixteenth Street?"

"Seventeenth," she said. "Sixteenth Street was the week before, for Free Tibet."

"Were you at Free Taiwan too?"

"Yeah! What about the Peace for Prostitutes benefit?"

"Positive Force?"

"The Punk Rock Inaugural Ball with Boy Sets Fire?"

"I DJ'd it!" I said.

We were friends immediately.

The other kids at the table, the Orthodox kids, shifted in their seats. I told them it was okay, rallies were all about saving poor people and making the world better. I wanted them to understand my rallies. I mean, Jews were the original outsiders. It should totally make sense.

I surveyed the perplexed faces around the table. Beryl looked unconvinced. But Gavin, the most right-wing person at the table, was overjoyed. He kept asking her questions like *Do you ever buy clothes from the Gap?* and *What happens if we don't use cheap Indonesian labor to make Starbucks coffee, would you really pay fifteen dollars for a cup of coffee?* Ilyana was smarter; she told him that all her clothes were from thrift stores and she didn't drink coffee because she got headaches from caffeine. I think they approved of each other, though.

That night a bunch of us walked along the pale white pavement between monuments, the Lincoln winding along to the Jefferson, the spooky World War II memorial with stones that jutted out of the ground. We lost each other in the maze of rock, Shifra and Yehoshua hiding behind walls that abruptly formed and sloped away. Then Gavin brought us to a party at the Jewish frat house, which wasn't shomer Shabbos—there was going to be music playing, he warned us. Shifra and Beryl said they were going home, but Ilyana and the rest of us followed him.

I fluctuate between being party-positive and party-negative. It might possibly be the most controversial question among Orthodox kids at secular colleges nationwide: *Do you turn yourself off for Shabbos or don't you?* Friday nights are the biggest social night of the week. Free beer, people you don't know, and for me, with my constant jobs, the only time I had to see friends. We weren't going to actively break Shabbos—we wouldn't touch the CD player or ride an elevator or drink beer if it came from a refrigerator with the light on, but there was a keg to drink out of, and we could just stand and schmooze and catch up with the social scene that we'd been neglecting.

The party was crowded, shoulder-to-shoulder. Ilyana and I traded looks, like, *I can't believe it's the night before the rally and we are here.*

At once I ran into a group of hardcore kids. They lived across the street and the noise from the party was keeping them awake, they told me, so to protest they came over and ate all the potato chips. I asked them how long they'd been here. They said two hours, so far.

I left them trying to start up a mosh pit in the living room and wandered into the kitchen, where Ilyana and the Orthodox kids were. There were Jello shots, and Gavin was insisting that his frat brother show him the Jello box. Finally they dug it from the trash, tossing beer cans

Constant jobs. I had four jobs: a shitty job at a coffee shop, hauling medical books for a medical supply store downtown, teaching Hebrew to fourth-graders in Alexandria, and typing up memos and rules for the neighborhood rabbi.

and red plastic cups to the floor. Gavin took one cursory look at the ingredients. "It's kosher," he said. He closed one chubby hand around a Dixie cup filled with jiggly red liquid and tossed it back.

Ilyana giggled. "That means it's vegetarian, too?" she asked, downing a green one herself.

"For Christ's sake! Animals don't feel pain!"

"Why the fuck are you swearing by Christ?" Ilyana asked, nonchalantly, flirtily.

When I left, they were still trading shots.

The next morning, I got to shul early. I went to the downstairs service, where they pray quickly and efficiently, like robots. The entire early service was small, maybe twelve or thirteen men, plus a few old women who stood off to the side and prayed in an assembly-line buzz. Most weeks I was the youngest one there by at least ten years, maybe twenty. The pace was so fast that it hooked you into paying attention to the words, made you want to catch them before they sailed by. It also forced me, in my phlegmy stammering Hebrew, to not spend hours stumbling over each word. It was like learning to speak a foreign language in a country where they don't speak anything else.

The Torah reading flowed swiftly, slid straight into the additional service for Shabbos, which we breezed through like extra credit problems at the end of a math test. When I looked up from my book at the end of services, Gavin was grinning at me wickedly.

I freak out when I'm late to synagogue, trying to catch up and say every word of the prayers, but Gavin was easier on himself. He got to shul ten minutes before the

Shul, aka synagogue. They mean the same thing, but we use both words in different contexts. I'd break it down for you if there were any concrete grammatical rules, but there aren't. It's a Jew thing. It's a different lanaguage—one way or another, you just learn to speak it.

end of services, did the prayers you absolutely need to say, and finished by the time they brought out the steaming bowl of chollint.

We clustered around the table with the middle-aged men, fidgeting in the breezy restlessness that follows the bustle of praying. This guy Joseph, who was in his early thirties but let the old men order him around, carried out the chollint. He ladled it out to the old men, one potato-filled spoonful at a time. Since we were the youngest, we got served last. "What the hell happened to you last night, Matt?" Gavin hissed at me while we were waiting.

I shrugged. "I got too Orthodox to stay."

Gavin looked like he couldn't decide if I was joking or not.

"But that's not important. What happened to *you* last night?" I needled.

Gavin raised his eyebrows, but he wouldn't say a word until we were out on the street.

"Where should we start?" he asked.

"What are we starting?" I said.

"You're not going to pass up the protests, are you?" The light changed and Gavin crossed the street, heading toward Pennsylvania Avenue and the White House. "Don't tell me you're too Orthodox for *that.*"

The white WALK sign started flashing red, and I scurried after him. "What do you mean?" I asked, ripping off my tie and jamming it into my pocket. "I thought you hated this stuff."

Gavin looked exasperated.

"I hate liberals," he said. "But I *love* protests."

You absolutely need to say. Ashray, the prayers before the Sh'ma, and the Amidah.

Chollint. A traditional Jewish stew composed of barley, beans, potatoes, vegetables, spices, and—usually, but not in the case of our local synagogue—meat.

Most Shabboses, we stay in the neighborhood. Usually on Saturdays, we go to synagogue and hang around the cake table downstairs until somebody invites us over for lunch. By the time we're done eating the inevitable four course meal—challah and Israeli salads and soup and ku-gels and knishes and meat and dessert—it's late afternoon and there's barely time to run back to synagogue to do the sunset services and close out Shabbos. When you live inside the Jewish community, even a Jewish community as small as Washington's, you become sheltered; you start to exist in a bubble of Shabbos that never gets popped.

Walking down Pennsylvania Avenue took forever, and I kept almost forgetting that I couldn't hit the but-ton on the traffic pole that would make the light change quicker. Gavin wrapped one hand around the pole and I jumped to swat it away. He swung around the pole, like Fred Astaire, flinging his hand out against the blue sky.

I bugged him to tell me about Ilyana and the rest of last night. We were nearly in front of the White House now, and huge crowds of kids were spurting up around us. Some were sweaty and dreadlocked and in riot gear like a rap-metal band, but most were just ordinary kids in T-shirts and jeans. Police were everywhere, black clumps of uniforms mixed into the colorful crowd. At Wash-ington Circle Gavin made a sudden left onto K Street. "What gives?" I whined, "I thought we were going to check out the protesters—"

"I don't feel like talking about it with people around," Gavin said. "We were flirting and drinking and Yehoshua

Invites us over for lunch. One of the commandments of Shabbos is to have a number of festive meals. Saturday lunch isn't as ritualized and formal as dinner on Friday night, but (a) it's still a grand-magnitude feast and (b) it's still a commandment. Eating all this food that be-longed to other people is a little bit embarassing and a little uncom-fortable. But when we reframe it as a commandment brought down from God, it's easier to dig in and pig out without residual guilt.

started drinking, too, and you know how he can put anyone under the table? He can. Only, Ilyana is half Russian, she starts talking about how her father started her on vodka when she was five, and she can hold more alcohol than anyone she's ever met—than any *guy* she's ever met, she says. And before you know it, she and Yehoshua are engaged in the drinking match of the century. Everyone is crowded around them. Anyway, they start drinking—she matches him shot for shot—and they don't stop till way after everybody else clears out."

"And then what happened?" I asked.

"And then I went home to go to bed. I don't ask questions. I'm Orthodox," Gavin snapped. We hit the end of the block and he sailed right. We turned the corner and we were back in the sea of people, that smelly oasis of organic deodorant and pot and sweaty T-shirts, all here to show corporate America who was boss.

Gavin and I swapped looks. We really did know who The Boss was, but it didn't really fit into the paradigm of these activist kids and oil companies and the president.

Together, we cruised the crowd. I can't explain why I needed to be there with Gavin, but at that moment, he was the only companion I ever wanted to have. As conservative and close-minded as Gavin was, he was the most likely to be seduced by the fun.

Across the street from the White House, a man dressed as the Lorax from Dr. Seuss danced around on the closed-off part of Pennsylvania Avenue. Sporadically he ran up to the fence and shook his fist and yelled, "Hey, you bastards! I speak for the trees!" To his right was the biggest hackey-sac ring I'd ever seen, twenty or thirty hippies in baggy jeans, kicking around beanbags, rolling them, hands-free, up and down their bodies. It wasn't a protest so much as a celebration, but I'd be wrong to say it wasn't both. It was a circus revolution.

Around the White House, it was more circus than revolution; you had to get closer to the World Bank buildings to see the blocks of people chained up. Kids were duct-taping their arms together inside cardboard tubes, forming barricades around all the major buildings. The kids around here looked less Joker and more Batman, determined and afraid. The coordinators swarmed all over, barking instructions into megaphones, pulling the duct tape tight. I was wondering how they would manage to eat, and then I saw one girl feeding another with her bare hands, shoveling rice into her friend's mouth and licking the other girl's fingers clean. I kept walking. Gavin caught my arm. "Hold on," he said. "I want to watch the activism in action."

I walked away from him, down the block, losing myself in the sea of kids. With my tie off and my shirt pulled out, I looked like another kid like everyone else, here to witness the spectacle and maybe be a part of it. I fit somewhere between these new laws I was trying to follow and this new regime we were trying to topple.

I found Ilyana among the chained protesters in front of the massive dioramas and revolving doors. Behind the glass of the World Bank building a few peons scuttled in and out of elevator doors. To them, we didn't exist.

The purpose of the human chains was to stop the limousines that carried the ambassadors and honchos of World Bank–related companies from driving through. If the entrances were completely surrounded by people, the theory went, then all the CEOs would have to walk through like ordinary people, and then we could yell at them. Ilyana had the biggest megaphone of anyone, a Rage Against the Machine shirt with the sleeves torn off, a skull-and-bones bandanna around her head. She was ordering people around. "Don't let those arms down!" she barked through the megaphone. "Pretend the lives of African children depend on you and your scrawny-ass arms! Yeah, that's right! Up! *Up!*" she shouted.

"Who made you king?" I said from behind her. She saw it was me and lowered the megaphone.

"Arbitrary decision," she said. "I'm good at king."

"You seem like a natural."

"You here to join the chain gang?" she asked me, and the megaphone picked up an edge of her voice and squealed. I winced, realizing that talking to her was making her violate Shabbos through the electric megaphone current. She saw me wince and turned the megaphone off. My belly sunk further.

"Today it's Shabbos, I can't," I told her. "But first thing when the sun goes down—"

"You know, it doesn't matter tomorrow, right?" Ilyana said. "None of this is going to matter. Not the yelling, not the barricades, nothing. They'll shuttle in the dignitaries, one way or another. Today, we're posing for the camera crews. That's the part the world will see. That's the part that counts."

"I know. That makes me feel so much better it hurts."

She tapped my shoulder. "Nobody's fault but your own, my friend."

There were all these things unspoken in the air. Dinner and the frat party last night seemed about a million years away. It was the only thing we'd ever done together. You know how you can meet someone, and there's something, seemingly insignificant, that makes you recognize a kindred spirit? Well, something about Ilyana made me feel that way about her. In the middle of this muddled, murky world of Orthodoxy, where I totally believed in the religion but I didn't have any actual friends, I felt connected to her. I wanted to hold onto her.

"At least you got a Shabbos dinner out of it, right?" I said at last.

Ilyana's voice dropped a notch. Her head slouched forward as if we were in a huddle, and her blue eyes took mine and stared right inside.

"Matt," she said, "I like you. But those Orthodox boys, they're absolute assholes."

Ilyana took a breath.

Then she told me how Yehoshua had followed her home. The minute she shut the door, he was on her like a thirsty baby. They necked and bit each other's skin and kissed with those hungry open-mouth kisses like they'd never hooked up with another human being before. They twisted into each other and dry-humped and then Ilyana asked him about keeping Shabbos, and he started explaining Jewish stuff to her, and they talked in that dazed and drunken state for an hour.

When he left, Ilyana walked him home across the campus green, and when he said goodnight he wouldn't even hug her. "Shit," she demurred. "Hypocrisy burns me more than anything. In my bedroom he kept trying to hike my skirt up but in public, he wouldn't even shake my hand. I wanted to take everything back in that one-second vortex. And I just couldn't, you know? Your religion has got a lot to answer for."

"Don't confuse Yehoshua with Judaism," I said. "They're not the same. They don't even have the same nose."

"Yeah, well, it still sucks," fumed Ilyana.

She crossed her arms over the Rage logo on her chest.

"Would it help if I said he's not a very good Jew at all?"

"Marginally." She looked trepidatious.

"Come on. If I told you every activist I've seen who buys cigarettes and eats at McDonald's—"

"I don't do any of that shit," Ilyana said. Her eyes glinted, though, like she knew what I was talking about.

"Tell me this is not the last time I'll ever see you."

"It's not the last time you'll ever see me."

"Good," I said.

"I mean," she said, "aren't you gonna be out here first thing tomorrow?"

Meanwhile, Gavin had found us. He was ranting about some activists he'd seen who hung up a flag upside down. "That's not free speech," he said. "They weren't speaking or anything. That's just sad, is what it is."

Ilyana laughed, although I could see she was trying not to.

The next day was the rally, and it was every bit as spectacular as I'd hoped. I woke up early, just as the sun peaked on the horizon. It took me almost an hour to say the morning prayers. My Hebrew was like an old record, dust still caught between the grooves. I was uneasy speaking these words I hadn't even written. So I shouted them out like my favorite punk rock song, Fugazi, the Dismemberment Plan, Aretha Franklin, shokeling my body back and forth like it was being rocked by a windstorm.

Then I was on the street, ebullient and buoyed, feeling like God was on my shoulder and like I could rock any house I wanted to. The streets crawled with kids in battle gear, paint-stained shirts and sweatpants, bandannas around their heads. All the buildings were closed. There were all these old Greek buildings with lots of pillars on the blocks around the White House. They all belonged either to the university or to one of those secret societies, Mason-like organizations of aged Republicans who had cocktail hour right when we were leaving classes.

Shokeling. If praying was jamming and synagogue was a rock club, then shokeling would be moshing. Shake your body back and forth (some people twist left to right), moving with the rhythm of the words you use to pray—that's shockeling.

I met up with my best friend, Janelle. She had stayed home writing comic book scripts yesterday instead of going to the rally. We walked around like tourists after the Apocalypse. Janelle's friend Dustin, a freshman, ran up to us. He was an anarchist—a native of the protest zone. He pointed out the World Bank headquarters blockade, the rebuilt human chains, the protester headquarters where they were giving away free vegan food and Gatorades. We stood on the intersection of H Street and 17th, right in front of the White House. We could see everything.

"So what do we do," Janelle asked, "stand around and wait for cars to try and roll through us?"

"Or for the police to ask us politely?" I added.

Dustin's eyes got suddenly alert. The air changed, like right before a storm. "What's up?" I asked.

"Did you bring mmmfle?" he asked. The second half of his sentence got swallowed by the bandana he pulled over his nose and mouth.

I opened my mouth to ask what.

Dustin grabbed Janelle's forearm and lunged forward.

Tear gas sprung up around us like sudden walls of mist. I didn't know what it was at first, just the air turning gray fast. The smoke caved in. I couldn't see anything. I breathed in. It tasted like fire. Dustin was no longer next to me. Everyone had slipped away. I gasped for air. The gas scraped the walls of my lungs. My skin felt toxic from the inside. I wondered if this was what dying felt like.

Hands yanked at my shirt, tore at me, literally trying to pull me down, stretching the fabric away from my chest. Somewhere, one of those greasy diplomats had given an order to a police commander who'd passed it down to his officers, and those very officers were at this moment trying to eject me from the street. Me—who always tried to be friends with all the kids in high school, the geeks as well as the bullies. They were throwing canisters of gas at *me*.

I dropped to the ground. The gas was lighter there. I breathed sharply. My throat and my eyes and nostrils still raged, but the gas didn't burn as badly now. My lungs started to close. Not breathing felt better. My head started to go light.

A palm hit into my cheek. The blow was sharp and loud. "Let's go!" a voice barked, and I felt the breath of words on my face.

My eyes shot open.

The sunlight stunned me. I wanted to shut them again and lie down on the asphalt.

"Come on," he said. "Follow me. They don't spray tear gas to convince you to stay put."

A block away, we detoxed, five or six of us, gulping large breaths of air to fill back our lungs. My body was screaming. It wanted me to breathe all at once. A tall blond man rubbed my back, relaxing my muscles. "Slowly," he cautioned. "Otherwise, your body won't know what to do and you'll throw up."

Like in an instructional video, I heard retching behind me.

Mark was this kickass activist, the same age as my parents but with a spirit that was wild. The air rushed in, and I started to choke. Mark patted me on the back, rubbing around the spine to steer my breathing back to normal. We were catching our breath, feeling our chests inflate and return to normal. I fell against the foundation wall, a red colonial brick thing that made me think of Gettysburg. We didn't say anything but we watched each other sweating and straining, slowly getting our balance back, feeling the sun beat down some vitamin D on us.

Mark watched me wobble away, making sure I was good to go. He told me not to get too close again, that

I had already earned my scars for today. Around the corner, I ran into Ilyana, ordering people right and left. She saw my bloodshot eyes and shaky disposition, noting them approvingly. "Now you're one of us," she said, laying a hand on my shoulder.

2

retreat

Rabbi Samborra lectured Monday night at the Jewish Student Center, and a surprising number of kids showed up. Rabbi Samborra had a congregation in Silver Spring, where all the highly religious Jews lived. His weekly peregrinations to Washington, D.C.—and to Foggy Bottom, at that, the sports bar–intensive part of the city where our college is located, and which people say was named after the foamy drizzle at the bottom of a beer mug—would make another rabbi's blood run cold and his stomach go clammy.

Not Rabbi Samborra. People say he was descended from the Baal Shem Tov, the founder of Hasidic thought, and he has all these intense stories about rabbis who could shoot fire from their eyes and what happened between the lines of Bible stories. In Hebrew School, we used to whisper how Ruth and Naomi were gay and speculate about how Adam and Eve learned to have sex—all the stuff that God forgot to print in the Torah. There are official stories like those, slightly more legit ones, called Midrashes. Rabbis have been writing them for hundreds of years. There are volumes and volumes of books filled with Midrashes—vivid stories about Zipporah and Noah's clothing ensembles, dry explanations of the foods that Avraham cooked for the angels who visited him in the desert, the biggest pet peeves of Moses's father-in-law.

But Rabbi Samborra was like a miracle worker. We Orthodox kids, especially the newly Orthodox ones, loved him like a pop star. We brought him innumerable plastic four-ounce cups of water, we scribbled down everything he said, and we talked through his lessons over lunch in the kosher cafeteria for the rest of the week.

We inhabited the Jewish Student Center, much to the annoyance of the staff there, like a gonorrheal virus that fades away but keeps coming back. We ate there, we prayed there every afternoon, and on Shabbos, we basically lived there for the entire twenty-five hours. The staff were secular Jews who didn't eat pork and went to synagogue for the big holidays. Other than that, their Jewishness was relegated mostly to pickles and Brooklyn accents. They stayed open late for our meetings and hang-out sessions, but somewhere in their selfless souls they must have wished they could zap their nonkosher lunches in the building's microwave or watch the big-screen TV on Friday nights in the student lounge.

There weren't a lot of Orthodox students at our university, but we were good at being visible. In some ways,

Twenty-five hours. In the Jewish calendar, days begin at sunset. But Shabbos and holidays have a special holiness attributed to them, and they begin as the sun starts to set and don't end until we can see three stars in the sky—which, all told, takes about twenty-five hours.

the Jewish Student Center people tolerated us, but they also relied on us. When, post–Yom Kippur, the rest of the student body stopped caring about being Jewish, there we were, singing our Jewish songs, chairing discussion groups for every minor fast day. So the words of Rabbi Samborra held us together. For better or worse, they cemented the Jewish community at the university.

Rabbi Samborra attracted more than just the Orthodox crowd. Some Reform kids, refugees from the Jewish Public Service Club, would come, plus maybe a Conservative or two, but the most inexplicable were the frat boys and student government girls who showed up. They'd never done anything that was Jewish since their Bar Mitzvahs and, suddenly, they were addicted to this wacky Lithuanian rabbi discussing medieval rabbinic disputes and telling Bible stories. Month after month, regular as a period, they showed up like zealots. Three guys from the basketball team, stocky, with haircuts like they'd just gotten electrocuted. Tal, the secular Israeli who tried to argue all the time until he shut up and listened and started getting off on Rabbi Samborra's trippy medieval stories. This girl Kayla, who talked like a hippie but dressed in prim, polka-dot dresses and frilled-up shirts, as though she'd just stepped out of a black-and-white movie. All the Orthodox guys stared at her cleavage, and I think Beryl even spoke to Rabbi Samborra to ask her to leave, but the rabbi replied, stern as salt, that the class was open to anyone who wanted to learn, and Kayla was wearing modest clothes, elbows and knees covered, and the nonobservant kids didn't seem distracted.

They listened, as intensely as us yarmulke-wearers, as Rabbi Samborra described how Avraham, with his two wives, wasn't a master so much as a servant of both, and how it was a physical and spiritual strain to keep them both satisfied, because he knew that the women would play as important a role in history as he would.

Rabbi Samborra stopped talking, taking a sip of water, draining the entire two-fingers-tall cup. He looked up, noticed a hand waving. It was one of the frat hands.

"Yes, Christopher?" he said, pronouncing the name as reverently as if he'd said *Shmuel* or *Elijah*. The Orthodox kids had a hard time taking anyone with an English name seriously. When Christopher spoke, Beryl and Yehoshua cracked mawkish sneers at each other.

"This is kind of a stupid question, but…."

"There *are* no stupid questions, Christopher."

Christopher tugged the brim of his white baseball cap nervously. "There's these two girls I'm hooking up with, and I was wondering, do you think Avraham told his wives, Sarah and, umm, Hagar, about each other?"

And Rabbi Samborra, without batting an eye, replied that, while one should never embarrass or bring harm to a person either by sharing or concealing hurtful information, our own Holy Forefathers were able to build meaningful, sacred relationships with more than one woman only by the grace of a caring and miraculous God, Blessed is the Name, and we should scrupulously aim for openness and honesty in all our interpersonal dealings.

Rabbi Samborra was a breath of fresh air. More religious and more stringent than any of us—he wore a black hat, bought more strictly inspected meat, and lived in a more religious area than us—he was our prophet. For the baal teshuva kids, the ones who had just become religious, Rabbi Samborra was the tradition they had never had. For the kids who had grown up observant, he was the home they missed, but without the oppressive, monolithic culture that told them how to decorate their bedrooms and don't be late to synagogue.

For me, Rabbi Samborra was both. He reminded me

of my parents' cool friends, the ones who never talked down to me or treated me like a kid. He was one of those ultra-Orthodox people who never forgot that he wore that black hat for God, not for show. I'd grown up observant, but the mellow kind of observant that warned you to watch what foods you ate at nonkosher friends' houses, and allowed you to drive to synagogue when it rained on Saturday mornings. In youth group, we were told that religion was not about things we enjoyed or things that made us feel good. At fifteen, I called the group leader a fascist and walked out.

Now, I was twenty-one years old and I was coming back. I was doing it on my own terms—I skipped the prayer that says, "Thank You, God, for not making me a woman," and I sat as far away as I could from the mechitza, the barricade that excludes women from the service.

I studied with Rabbi Lavigne, the Orthodox rabbi in Washington proper, who was the antithesis of Rabbi Samborra. He was practical, gruff, and kind of a practical joker, yet he always had a businesslike countenance when it came to Judaism. You didn't approach him to ask about the mystical properties of Avraham's two wives. You asked Rabbi Lavigne where it says that Jews can't be polygamous (the Takana of Rabbi Gershom, circa 1300) or what verse Sarah dies in (Genesis 23:2) or whether Jewish law says you can close a business deal when you've been drinking at a frat party (No). Laws of mechitza were the first thing he ever taught me. I was all ready to launch the über-feminist attack. In Youth Group, they had told

---

Barricade that excludes women. In most synagogues—in the good ones, at least—the mechitza runs straight down the center of the room, more like a volleyball net than a barricade. In fact, the really high mechitzas, the ones that women can't see over, are forbidden by Jewish law. You're always supposed to be able to see the Torah being lifted, and that usually happens on the men's side.

us that mechitzas stopped you from getting distracted by women, so that you felt more comfortable. Rabbi Lavigne shook his huge head, *no*. "The mechitza is *supposed* to make you uncomfortable, Matt," the rabbi told me. "Comfort is being around other people. The going theory is, man or woman, you retreat into your prayers for comfort."

Retreat. I was all about retreat in those days. Rabbi Lavigne taught Orthodox Judaism as a system, like metric or Pilates—you use it to get things done. I was overwhelmed by the secular world, not fitting in sometimes, and sometimes fitting in too well. Surrendering to the laws of my ancestors seemed like an easy way to make sure I was doing the right thing.

They say religion is the last refuge of the incontinent, and it's true. No matter how fucked up your life gets, God—the abstract idea, your first imaginary friend—is there to catch you. Local synagogues will always let a stranger off the street inside to pray, and most of the time they will say blessings for you in synagogue and take you home to dinner afterward, but their welcoming arms will only hold you so long if you keep smelling as bad as you did in the secular world.

And so it was that I found myself at the table of the Jewish Student Center student lounge, nine o'clock on a Monday night, listening to an elf-sized man with a pointy red beard and a cuffed black hat talking about nudity. Ester, the president of the Orthodox Student Union, was blushing a vibrant purple. The black-hat boys were trying to not look quite so excited. The frat boys scratched at their stubble listlessly.

"Adam and Eve—whom we call Hava—didn't *know* they were nude! From the beginning, Man was selected above the other creatures to perform God's commandments. We have an additional level of consciousness. We can remember, we can talk, we can walk upright naturally. We have an additional soul that animals don't have; it's called a *neshama*. What was the first thing Hava realized after she ate the apple? She was naked!" Rabbi Samborra slammed the table with his palm. "Naked! And she knew something was wrong with that. And she couldn't take being alone in her sin, so she came to Adam, knowing she was in sin, and he ate too. Only then did they realize, they were sinning together. And together they sewed leaves to make clothes to cover their nakedness. Now, of course Man has the capability to sin, and to make others sin, through it. But Man can also fulfill God's holy commandments, and help others to do the same. We all have this power. Now, what do you want to do with it?"

Monday night. The jocks looked tired, exhausted after the weekend parties and staying up late, and they were probably still a little hungover. The Orthodox kids' eyes gleamed. Friday night was their big night, and then Saturday night was the end of Shabbos, when you walked home from synagogue and washed dishes and maybe rented a movie. If you did Shabbos well, you should be thoroughly wiped out for the rest of the weekend.

I didn't do Shabbos well. I mean, I tried. But, by the twenty-third hour Saturday afternoon, you're singing Jewish folk songs in synagogue and thinking about the CD you just bought that you can't wait to listen to. Before I got religious, Friday night was the big party night. Now that God had taken away Fridays, I had to get it all out on Saturday nights. I loved my newfound Orthodox community, but I was getting tired of their resistance to getting down.

That Saturday, I had gotten tickets to the They Might Be Giants show.

I went alone. I was going alone to concerts a lot those

days. I left before Shabbos ended, so I left my wallet at home and walked. The 9:30 Club was an hour's walk from my apartment. That was okay, I didn't have anything else to do. Leaving for the show while it was still Shabbos was kind of Orthodoxically sketchy. I told someone about it at synagogue, to see if they'd pick a fight with me. The couple I told, these mild-mannered Democratic party workers in their late twenties, looked horrified. "You're going to walk through *that* area?"

I was horrified right back. I used to *live* in that area. It was mostly working-class black families. It resembled Northeast Philadelphia, where I'd grown up, more than any other part of Washington.

The walk was beautiful, the stale monolithic office buildings all turned a gleaming orange against a vibrant blue sky. It felt unreal, the colors changing every minute, like an instantly nostalgic Pop Art cartoon. I took the diagonal state streets, a maze of shortcuts and detours that Pierre L'Enfant, the original architect of Washington, D.C., designed to protect the city from invasion by enemy tanks. They carried me with an old, comfortable familiarity. When I hit 14th Street and my old neighborhood, the air popped and smelled like sea salt and curry, sizzling fried fish, and a smoky haze of baby back ribs. People appeared on the street, draped against brick walls and hanging out. Kids played basketball in the streets. In the part of D.C. where I lived now, we didn't even have teenagers.

There used to be this cool little coffee shop across the street from the 9:30 Club. Now it was a shop for nappifying white kids' hair. The same people ran it, a southern family with accents as thick and impenetrable as chollint. I debated stopping in and saying hi. The sky blazed, the sun lingering in that early autumn time-stop. I didn't. Cheating once in a night already had me rattled; entering an actual place of business on the Day of Rest felt like an avalanche. Right then, I wanted to avoid contact with other human beings. I felt like any conversation could turn into a confession.

So I ran inside the club.

The entire ground floor was a pit, people crammed against each other, a maze of potbellies and breasts. Shoulders and elbows jabbed at me. Professional-looking men hustled drinks from the bar and brought them back to their girlfriends. I felt Shabbos end with a puff of smoke.

The opening bands played, sparkled, faded out. What makes bands book other bands that sound like worse versions of themselves? I wondered. I moved through the crowd between sets, saying hi to people I knew vaguely, from school and the café I worked at, ducking questions like Why did they never see me anymore? I kept glancing at the stage as though I couldn't wait for the next band to come on. The more I feigned indifference, the more I started to get a chill, thinking of the actual band. They Might Be Giants was the first band I'd ever seen live. So geeky they were cool. So cool they were geeky.

I stood near stage left talking to Donny, who was there with his new lesbian girlfriend. He was the perfect kid to have a lesbian girlfriend, shy and reserved and more considerate than a slave. He was the kind of kid who asked if it was okay before he sneezed. The girlfriend was small and in the very beginning stages of butch—stone-washed denim jacket, short pixie haircut. They held hands nervously, like they'd never done it before. They were great to talk to, so tentative and real. I remembered what it was like to be part of other people's lives.

Finally the band broke onstage. John Flansburgh wore a plaid pocket protector–ready shirt and heavy rimmed glasses and carried his guitar on a space-alien strap, John

Linnell behind him with his tuba, his hair in a bowl cut and wearing a baggy T-shirt. The drummer leaped right into a beat and the crowd started shokeling.

Dancing at a They Might Be Giants concert is a spiritual experience, the kind you have at synagogue where you look around and realize everyone looks dorkier than you and you realize, by proxy, that it is socially acceptable to look dorky. I was only just learning how to dance for real. In high school we used to go to metal shows, where you danced by default, throwing your body into a crowd and getting thrashed from one end of the dance floor to the other. Around me, boys were skanking. Boys were pogo dancing. My ass shook. My shoulders rolled back. I was feeling out the way my body moved, throwing my arms into motion, finding the muscles that made my hips move.

The band blasted through "Birdhouse in Your Soul" and "Istanbul" and "No One Knows My Plan" and then the staticky staccato-guitar intro of "Ana Ng" came on, which was metallic and electro-beat and almost intolerably danceable. In front, the kids who knew all the words were starting to pogo. I got ready, jumped, laughed into a deep grind with myself. I looked like an ass. Everyone looked like an ass. I loved it.

These are the reasons I go to shows alone. So I won't have to talk through the opening bands if they're good. So I can think, or not think, depending on my mood. In these moments, it's just me and the band, and everybody else on the dance floor evaporates in translucence. When I danced these first uncertain steps, I was jamming with the band, I was becoming my own part of the concert. And when I wanted to switch reality back on, I could watch all the dancers and check out girls and pretend they weren't checking me out right back. There was this girl in a '50s polka-dot dress who looked like a punk-rock

Audrey Hepburn, lost marble eyes and short blue hair held back in a scarf, alternately rocking out on an air guitar and standing coolly composed, head nodding with the beat. Eventually we were dancing opposite each other, one eye on the band's antics, one eye tracking our own frenzied dance.

The song ended. Both Johns were onstage, sweating their weight away. They danced all over the stage. They danced like Looney Tunes. One horn player did a split while a tuba encased his body. They never let more than a second interrupt the set.

In one of those seconds of silence, I felt a hand on my shoulder.

"Hey, Matt," she said. "It's good to catch you out here."

It was Kayla.

Kayla and I danced, not exactly together, but in close proximity, for a while. I couldn't believe that was her. Like the first time you realize Clark Kent is actually Superman, the '50s polka-dot girl turned toward me and her features melted into Kayla's. She was such a hippie, even in polka dots. She spun around and waved her arms in the air and shook her body like it was a maraca. Our eyes locked and our hands shimmied out and we danced across from each other.

I was shomer negiah, which meant that I wasn't supposed to have physical contact with girls. In D.C., everyone Orthodox was shomer negiah. It was one more law,

Shomer negiah. One of the guiding principles in the lives of young Orthodox Jews, both in keeping it and in breaking it. Shomer negiah strictly means guarding your touch. We're not supposed to touch people of the opposite sex that we aren't related to. Some Orthodox Jews will shake hands with people of the opposite sex (and nothing else), while some will not. A few will hug. Then there are those people who act hella strict while they're in mixed company and then sneak into the back room and get furiously sexual, but I guess there's always the rebels. Not like I'd ever *be* one of them.

like keeping kosher or resting on Shabbos.

We danced, and I tried not to be freaked out by it. Then Kayla had to pee and I went to find a drink of water. I ran into a bunch of dykes from Womyn's Issues Now, this student group I was a member of. I talked with the WIN girls for a while about this retreat or something we were supposed to go on, then I lost sight of Kayla for the encore. I wanted to wait for her after the show, but this big butch top named Carlotta offered me a ride to campus. Even if I'd wanted to do the same long walk again, I would have said yes. Hardly anyone at school had cars. Being offered a ride is the post–high school equivalent of getting the keys to the eraser closet. I squeezed into the back seat with four upperclassmen queer girls. Their slight bodies and bald heads poured over me, and their eyes swam with sexual tension between each other and absolutely none for me, and it didn't feel one bit like a violation of shomer negiah.

That Monday night, I was back at Rabbi Samborra's class. Posters all over the Jewish Student Center said, RABBI SAMBORRA MONDAYS! THIS WEEK'S TOPIC—ADAM & EVE: BEHIND THE FIG LEAVES.

There, sitting directly across from me, was Kayla.

Even looking at her felt like a violation of shomer negiah.

Kayla grinned at me jovially. I ignored it, because I am horrible at crushes and the mere fact of a girl's glancing my way can crush me out for weeks. At that moment, Rabbi Samborra walked in, and we all rose. He smiled, motioned for us to sit down, and started lecturing immediately. I whispered "hey" back to Kayla, digging through my knapsack, and drew out my pen and journal to take notes like all the Orthodox kids.

As class ended, Rabbi Samborra, swishing on his black

trench coat, held up a finger. "Listen," he said. "I think you all should visit me for Shabbos one week. You'll get a break from your campus, and we'll all be able to spend Shabbos in a real yiddishe atmosphere. Ester, can you coordinate that?"

Ester nodded solemnly.

"Good, good," nodded Rabbi Samborra. "I'll see you all next Monday."

Wednesday or Thursday, Kayla showed up at the kosher cafeteria. She stood in the doorway, made small talk with Ester and the frum girls for a few minutes, then came over to the boys' table and plopped herself into the seat next to mine. The tables weren't officially segregated, but most of us were newly religious and we were incredibly conservative about everything. Kayla looked at me expectantly. I tried not to look eager. "Hey," I said, "what are you doing in these parts?"

She shrugged. "I thought I'd check out the Jewish Center—you know, in the daylight."

"Are you hungry? Do you want something?"

Kayla looked uncomfortable. "I'm fine," she said, "I already ate."

I looked at the falafel sandwich in my hands. It had come out sounding like an accusation that she'd eaten at one of the nonkosher dining halls on campus. I felt ridiculously religious.

My cheeks flared blood red. Kayla was blushing too. She blushed as fast and furiously as I did. Our eyes locked.

Frum. Literally, Yiddish for devout or pious. Among contemporary Orthodox Jews, however, the word has come to acquire a more general vernacular meaning that self-referentially identifies the speaker as *frum*—basically, it's the Orthodox word for *Orthodox*. Frequently used as a basis for comparison or for representing: "How frum are you?" or "Damn, baby, you are so frum."

She rolled hers and reached over. She lifted the half-eaten pita straight out of my hands, transferred it to her own, and took a huge meaty bite.

She grinned at me toothily, invitingly.

I couldn't appreciate the flirtation. I was too jumpy. I felt her fingertips brush my palms, the sensation of her skin on mine. The guys down the table were watching out of the corners of their eyes, listening in the dead spaces of their own dialogues. Kayla devoured a third of my falafel, the part where all the falafel balls had landed. She pressed a pita filled mostly with diced tomatoes and cucumbers back into my hands. She told me how she was reading from the prayerbook every day, trying to teach herself more about Judaism. She didn't want to be Orthodox, but she wanted to know what it was all about.

"I want that kind of fluency," she told me.

She reached a hand out to my plate and plopped my last stray falafel ball into her mouth.

I wanted to say, *Yeah, that's what I said at first, but why learn to swim and never jump in the water?*

I didn't tell her that. I didn't say anything.

"Hey, you look nervous. You're running to class, aren't you?" Before I had a chance to answer, Kayla slid her books under her arm and her jean jacket onto her shoulders. "We should hang out. How's Friday morning for you?"

I flailed.

"Fridays are great," I said. Fridays, almost nobody at the university had classes. Except for first-year language labs, it was like an extra day of weekend.

"Cool!" Kayla chirped. She scuttled out the door, but before she did, she planted a big loud kiss on my cheek.

The guys at the table didn't even pretend to ignore it.

Ester loaned me a shiur tape. It was a recording of a lecture by some famous rabbi, probably in New York or Israel, lecturing on some aspect of biblical law and how following it will make us better people. The rabbis didn't even speak in English. Technically, it was English, weighted with a strong Brooklyn accent, and Yiddish expressions that reminded me of my grandmother and Jewish holiday dinners at home. The Yiddish lulled you into a false sense of security, even if you only understood about 40 percent of the words. I popped the tape into my Walkman and let it ride. The lecture was about sexual relationships.

The rabbi was speaking to a girls' class at a yeshiva. He started talking about a Jewish girl who was becoming more religious, only all her new friends were boys. They told her they wanted to help her out. When she asked them about being shomer negiah, they told her it was old-fashioned and nobody followed it anymore. Her best friend hugged her and cuddled when they hung out and held her hand. "But all this time," the rabbi said, his voice dripping with sarcasm like a waterfall of irony, "they were just friends."

Well, all that changed one night. She and her new best friend, let's call him Nimrod, were up late. They were studying and then they were talking, and laughing, and then they weren't talking anymore.

"You're all adults, and I don't need to tell you what

Shiur tape. Shiurs are lectures, usually about Torah or Talmud or Jewish holidays or just about Jews in general, usually given by a rabbi or a scholar of some repute. When you go to yeshiva, all the classes are called *shiurs.* Shiur tapes, though, are a totally different animal. Essentially, they're just recorded tapes of shiurs, but people collect these things like baseball cards. Like comic books. It starts when you're about thirteen years old and, for many people, it never ends. You try to collect every shiur tape by your favorite rabbis, and then you lend them out to all your friends, trying to proselytize to anyone who will listen about just how su*perb* this rabbi really is.

happened then," said the rabbi. "But after that night, he didn't want to be friends anymore. None of the boys did. You think, a boy is so in love, he'll never tell anyone. That's garbage! He'll tell everyone he knows! All those girls who want boyfriends, I ask them why. 'To hold my hand.' That's what they say, 'I want a boyfriend to hold my hand.' Let me let you in on a little secret: No boy just wants to hold a girl's hand. He's thinking about how to get her to the next step."

I walked around campus, listening to the tape all week.

It was an Indian summer. Girls were digging out their tank tops, everyone was coupling up, the quad swam in a sea of picnic blankets and casually steamy kisses. From my Walkman-insulated world, I looked at people, non-Orthodox people, and felt like I belonged to an entirely separate species.

"Boys are nothing but perverts and filthy animals!" screamed the rabbi on the tape. "We don't need the rules to keep us safe! We need them to keep us *human!*"

Friday morning, I met Kayla at the Jewish Student Center and we walked down Pennsylvania Avenue to the National Mall. The sky hung close to the ground. Clouds swept over the Washington Monument. We walked around the grove of flags behind the monument to a dusty outdoor stage, and then over to a grove of twisted oaks. Soft green and yellow leaves lay in piles on the ground. We dove into them and emerged, our bodies sprawled vacuously across the leaves, our heads a few inches apart. We blinked at the clouds, facing them head-on.

"What do you think?" said Kayla.

"What do I think?"

"What are you thinking about?"

I fumbled. I ran through the things that were actually on my mind: shiur tapes. How close we were to Shabbos and whether I would go to the generic dinner at the Jewish

Student Center or show up at the local Orthodox synagogue and hope that one of the progressive Orthodox couples with cushy government jobs would invite me home
for dinner. Wondering if these leaves were still a little bit
wet, and whether my jeans would be stained on the ass.
Whether or not Kayla wanted to hook up with me.

I swiveled my head to the side. She was already facing
me, her nose a pale and delicate fulcrum that pointed
straight at me. When she exhaled, I felt her breath on my
cheek.

"I'm thinking about praying," I said.

She nodded. Because we were on our sides, her head
went left and right.

"Rabbi Samborra said our relationship to God is like
a parent-child relationship," I said. "But I have the worst
relationship with my parents. They're bossy and nosy and
I never tell them anything. So lately, when I pray, I've
been thinking about other shit instead, and even when I
try to concentrate, I still wind up letting my mind drift
all over the place. That's what I'm thinking about. What
about you?"

"I'm thinking about how easy it would be if I had
rules to govern everything I did."

I moved an inch closer to her. "Meaning you're thinking about going Orthodox?"

She moved closer. "Want to convince me?"

"Sure," I whispered.

I held my breath. We lay there for the longest time.
The clouds kept drifting past us and vanished behind the
city skyline. Our legs touched each other just below the
calf. Her tendon thumped faintly, methodically, as blood
and air pumped through her, the uncanny cyclic movements of her body. Her pinprick breaths melted against
my cheek, quicker now.

And then it grew cold, suddenly, the way it does in

Washington. The wind slapped our faces and neither of us had jackets, so we ran back up 21st Street to campus. The sun teetered on the horizon. "It's almost Shabbos," I said. "I'm going to change for shul. What are you up to tonight?"

Kayla looked embarrassed, and coughed her way up to an answer. "Oh," she finally said, blushing hard, "I'm going to a club with this guy."

I think someone told me later that things didn't work out on Kayla's date, that he kept trying to make out with her and she wouldn't. Word gets around in the Jewish world, and nothing is private for long, no matter who you are or how infrequently you show your face at the Jewish Student Center.

But instead of boosting my ego—Kayla had thrown herself at me, hadn't she?—the news made me feel even more insecure. I hated the idea that a girl might hook up with me just because she was interested in becoming more Jewish. I didn't want to be a missionary. I didn't even know what I was doing.

I mean, I really didn't. That night I went to services at the Orthodox synagogue, waited outside for a dinner invitation, watching everyone leave. I went home alone and ate cold bagels and egg salad.

The week that followed was torture. Long, exhausting, and lonely. My roommates were never home, and I made pasta and red sauce three nights that week. Kayla never showed up anymore, but she was a freshman and I was a junior so we never had classes together and we never saw each other on the street.

I began questioning everything. The outbreak of make-out couples on the campus quad intensified. I played out the previous Friday in my mind until my head nearly exploded. Her, lying on her back. Me on my side. My left hand was so close to her hair. If I'd rolled over, onto her belly. If my hand had brushed her hair aside. When a kiss doesn't happen, there are a thousand ways that it could have.

Early Friday afternoon, I took the Metro to Wheaton, the bleak final station on the red line. The air was fresh with rain. I made a left, then two rights, hiking along the unfamiliar suburban roads. The houses became sparser. I could sense civilization slipping away.

I was spending Shabbos in Silver Spring.

I got to a housing development that sloped down into streets that were lined with grass, front lawns that were more like meadows. Little black-hat boys played in the streets with red rubber balls as big as their stomachs. Girls trailed after them, tripping on their skirts. A stirring theme song played in my head.

I half-jogged, half-slid down the hill.

Rabbi Samborra's wife met me at the door. She was a skinny, timid woman who looked only a few years older than me, her hair tucked into a sock that matched her wallpaper-patterned dress. She led me through bedrooms strewn with kid-sized clothes and Torah-shaped pillows and open picture books that lay on the ground, signs of a sudden abandonment. She plucked stuffed animals off the floor, one by one, stacking them under her arm, explaining to me how they didn't let the kids play with stuffed animals that weren't kosher.

"I'd never thought of that," I said, awed.

She was a photograph from a National Geographic special. It didn't feel like we were comparing our cultures. Especially since she never asked me. She just sort of assumed I had no Jewish background, or maybe an incorrect Jewish background. Either way, I was ripe for reprogramming.

Eventually the kids trotted in. There might have been six or seven of them, identical micro-Jews who smiled shyly at me from behind doorways and pieces of furniture, and called to their mother in high, gravelly voices.

Eventually the rabbi came home. "It's about to be Shabbos," he said. "Do you read Hebrew?"

"Sure," I said.

"Good," he said, without missing a beat. "I can teach you."

And, on the way to synagogue, he taught me how to sing "Shabbat Shalom."

In synagogue, I sat next to the rabbi's sons, five, seven, eight, and ten years old. They kept showing me my place in the prayerbook. Even when I showed them I could follow the Hebrew words with my finger. They made it into a race, who could help me the fastest. I didn't want to rain on their parade. Rabbi Samborra sat in the front row, on a special velvet-padded chair. I sat facing the back of his head, a few rows back. I murmured my prayers louder than I ever did, swaying with a clear and focused

"Shabbat Shalom." The full lyrics to this traditional Jewish folk song are "Shabbat Shalom—hey! / Shabbat Shalom—hey! / Shabbat, Shabbat, Shabbat Shaaaah-*baat* Sha-*looom*." Every Jew knows it. Seriously, my friend Mendy's two-year-old daughter Golda knows it, and she doesn't even know *words*. What happens among Jews, though, is that we have this other cultural consciousness on top of the regular American one, except it's so tremulous that it almost feels artificial. We don't know the "Shabbat Shalom" song the way we know the McDonald's jingle; we learn it in from our parents and in Hebrew School, and we don't get much additional reinforcement in the outside world. It's this lack that sends us crawling back to Judaism, pushing aside the detritus of our memories to find something real to validate our religious experience, even if it starts with taking something as insignificant as the "Shabbat Shalom—Hey!" song and building those memories into a real, complex, and culturally valid portrait of our religion.

spirituality. None of that abstract mumbling bullshit for me. Everyone else around me might finish faster, but dammit, I was going to fucking communicate with *God*. The synagogue windows shone a gleaming red. The men prayed fast and voluptuously, black hats undulating with their swaying postures like an ocean around me. The women's section was narrow and docile, pushed to the margin of the sanctuary like an old memory. I felt swallowed by the sea of Jewish families, surrounded by middle-aged men and their children, their voices blending in a single, sonorous drone, and when I murmured my prayers, they got absorbed by the greater drone.

Dinner, finally. I sat at the family's table, the only nonfamily member, facing a row of boys half my height. Everyone sat waiting for my stories, and I realized I couldn't give them any. I had nothing.

"So, Moishe Shimon. You said you needed to get away from the city?"

The entire family waited like one big ear, ready to sweep up my problems with the secular world.

It wasn't that I didn't know where to start. It was that they didn't want to hear my stories about girls who flirted with you during Torah class. And they already knew about Torah class. Sex or Torah, everything I could give these people they either already knew or didn't want to know.

By Shabbos's end, I was back to believing in zero, as though nothing was Jewish but my blood, that my Hebrew pronunciation and knowledge and radical lifestyle were as alien to tradition as sushi and Saturday morning cartoons.

Only, instead of feeling ashamed, I was eager. This was just the beginning. I wanted to make it up to them, become a full-time, no-holds-barred Jew. Five thousand years ago in the Carpathian Mountains, my ancestors had worn these very clothes, had eaten this very food, and this antagonistic family was my last connection with them.

And I loved them for it. Like God creating Adam, I could make myself over in their image.

I really could.

3

the most unsuitable suitable husband in the world, ever

I'd been out of college for a year and a half, working as a researcher. I had my own cubicle and my own semi-powerful computer terminal. I cut out articles from newspapers, fact-checked on the Internet, designed informative PowerPoint demonstrations for projects that my coworkers saved onto the hard drives of their more-powerful computers.

I wasn't complaining. There was nothing to complain about—my bosses treated me well, never raised their voices, and smelled nice. I was still sure that I was going to move to San Francisco and become a famous writer one day, but from the view in my cubicle, that day felt very far away. I lay in bed at night, wide awake, staring out the window, at the ceiling, into the well-worn holes of the furniture of this post-college efficiency apartment, and I wondered, *What happens to people when they grow up?*

That night, I felt a tingle in my stomach, as though one of the fairies who lived there had died.

Holy shit. Where was my punk-rock zinester independent-movie-watching self?

In the morning, I ran to Janelle's house. Janelle was my best friend. When something exciting happened to me, I called her immediately.

She looked startled to see me, as if we were in a low-rent horror movie or something. She plopped me on the couch and made tea and I realized it had been six months since I'd seen her. My God, I thought. My job has finally eaten my life.

I asked her where she thought my old self went. She shrugged and said she thought it was an Orthodox thing.

I tried to tell her how, no, it wasn't an Orthodox thing. There was no such thing as an Orthodox thing. Orthodox people had annoyed me my whole life, with their smarmy rules and ego-braising self-satisfaction and the sexism that I knew wasn't Godsent, but all of a sudden, I was defending them.

I was one of them.

At 3:00 A.M., Janelle's roommate Abel stumbled in. One of his poetry teachers had taken him to a reading and afterward they all went out drinking and one thing led to another and, somehow, he wound up on the dance floor of Hung Jury, the only lesbian bar in Washington, with a bunch of straight poetry professors.

Janelle and I stopped paying attention to our own conversation. Abel had a way of absorbing any conversation into his own. Abel was gay and obsessed with himself in the biggest way but he never made it boring. He was like a reality TV show that you couldn't stop watching.

"All those fucking professors. Those fucking professors

and their fucking books." Abel threw his hands madly as he talked, swatting imaginary flies. "What the fuck do they think, somebody Xeroxes twelve copies of their poems and staples it and they call it a fucking book? *I* could write a fucking book. Shit, Matt—that boring-ass old job you have, you could fucking write a fucking book every fucking day of the week."

Janelle and I exchanged glances. It was nice to know we could still catch each other's eye and know we were thinking the same things.

"Hey," I said to Abel. "Do you really want to make a book?"

The following night, Abel and I got together at his toilet seat–shaped Macintosh and threw together a book. Typed, printed, proofed, and Kinkoed it. Abel and I drew a few pencil sketches in the blank pages to make it look artsy. There were only, like, two hundred copies of our book—okay, call it a zine, we really weren't that professional about it. We had a stark cover with Communist block letters and the Washington stars-and-bars flag that symbolized D.C. civic pride, the latest crusade among the activist kids. We titled it *With Our Shirts Off,* which was supposed to hint at something sexual, but obliquely. I think it was a really late night.

And then we threw ourselves a release party. Abel tried to convince all the local independent bookstores to host it, but they were gruff and unsympathetic. They demanded to see the book, so we rustled out our little stapled zines. They sounded like babysitters when they

D.C. civic pride. Nobody likes America, but Washington has no Congressional representative—a real underdog, and we liked that. Our friends graffiti'd the D.C. city logo, three stars over two black lines, all over town, and someone started a campaign to change the city's license plates to read WASHINGTON D.C.—TAXATION WITHOUT REPRESENTATION.

explained to us that this was not a real book, real books did not have staples. We were going to try bars next, but there were too many under-twenty-ones among Abel's friends so we finally just convinced the property manager of his apartment complex to lend us the keys to the recreation room.

Abel was a total scenester. He had all his usual groups of friends: the English Department kids and the gay club kids and the kids from last year back when he was straight and whom he still hung out with on the slow nights. I had friends, too, only I never spoke to them because I was always at work.

I bought a couple of wicker baskets from the Salvation Army store and dropped cheez balls and pretzel twists in. Abel bought enough beer to pacify everyone in the apartment building. If you didn't like our book, you could at least get a free buzz.

Seven o'clock hit, we opened the doors, and Abel was spazzing about people showing up and people leaving early. "We need to start the reading at eight exactly," he said. "People will walk out if we don't. There are other parties on campus. Parties that don't make them listen to poetry."

I told him to relax. No parties started till eleven. People weren't going to leave without hearing us. We were the attraction.

"Eight o'clock," Abel repeated. He ran upstairs to change clothes. Abel has a three-piece suit that he wears anytime he gets the chance.

"Eight o'clock," I agreed.

I sank into the couch and started eating cheez balls.

Our audience crept in. People drizzled by ones and twos into the rec room and onto the adjoining patio. They munched on pretzel twists, nervously eyeing the table of unopened beers and mixers, wondering who would break down first. Some residents of the apartment building popped by to see what was going on and they saw free food and a sign Abel hung that said BOOK PARTY—COME IN! and they spied on all the indie-rock–looking kids who were camped out inside the rec room that their monthly maintenance fees paid for.

My partner from work came, too. He was a short, compact man in his midsixties who always had a knife and a compass hanging on a loop from his belt. He walked straight over, shook my hand heartily, and then sat on a couch with a bunch of Abel's sorority girl friends and they started talking to him at once.

And there were my friends from synagogue. All the Orthodox kids showed up, all eight or nine of them who were around that weekend. That was the best. They were like my new gang. They had my back. Edgar zoomed into the room on his scooter, people clearing out of his path. He screeched to a halt at my foot. I was in the middle of talking to Abel, getting our sets straight.

Edgar grabbed my arm. He had cerebral palsy, he got around on crutches or on his electric scooter. His forearms were inhumanly strong. He pulled me down to the level of his face.

"I brought the rest of the gang, too," Edgar told me.

"I know," I choked. "They're right over there, they're drinking my beer. I can see that."

"I told Clare to come, too," said Edgar.

Clare.

My brain froze. Clare was this girl that Edgar had been talking about forever.

I'd kind of given up on dating girls when I became Orthodox. I had crushes on imaginary people instead. When people asked, I told them I was waiting for an Orthodox punk-rock girl who was so religious that she only wore skirts, except for rave pants, because they were baggier than most skirts. When I cooked for Edgar at his house, on the stove he couldn't use because he couldn't get out of his scooter, he'd told me wild stories about Clare, this girl he'd met in Israel. He swore she was wild enough for me and had just turned Orthodox. I thought that was a good sign. Just turning Orthodox meant she still had traces of the secular world, and maybe she could handle my weirdness and my Buffy the Vampire Slayer obsession.

I surged back into reality.

"Clare is coming," said Edgar.

"Matt, curtain call," said Abel. "You're on."

"Hey look!" said Janelle, pointing to the door. "It's your parents."

My eyes shot to Janelle, then to the crowd, then to the door.

My mother and father were disrobing from their winter parkas, peeling off gloves and scarves and hats. Behind them I saw the signature white of my grandmother's frosted hair. Five feet to my left, I could see my set list for the reading, story titles scribbled in Sharpie black on white computer paper. Two of the first three stories had sex on the first page. One was a poem called "Orthodox Girls" where, at the climax, I fake an orgasm by yelling, "Yocheved Yocheved YOCHEVED."

Abel pushed me onto the makeshift stage. The seats were all taken. People hovered in the back. Somehow, we'd filled the rec room with a standing-room-only crowd. Toward the back, two girls in long skirts sat on the edge of one sofa. I spotted them as soon as I took that first deep breath before I started talking. Long skirts, pulled-back hair, sitting apart from everyone else like they didn't know anyone. One of them had to be Clare.

I read, nervous and frenzied. Then I introduced Abel for his section—we both gave each other cozy fake introductory remarks, saying that I'd toured Indonesia with Pearl Jam, that Abel's poems were adapted into a mini-series for *Masterpiece Theatre*—and then we both read again. By the end I was getting so into the stories that I was flinging spit and sweat at the people in the front row and jumping all over the place. I wasn't doing the characters' voices but I was telling the stories with a ferocity that built as I spoke. I'd never read like that before. I'd always hated slam poetry—I didn't even think I could write poetry—but I felt like a slam poet in front of the crowd that night. I read one story about kids who held jazz concerts inside the pyramids outside Cairo and a story about when my father was a DJ in the Amish country outside Philadelphia and one about fifteen-year-olds having sex. After we finished, everyone was coming up to Abel and me, asking, *How did you decide to put a book together?* and *What are you going to do next?* and stuff. I brushed out of the crowd to find my family.

My parents were helping my grandmother with her coat; they had to catch the last train back to Philadelphia. They just wanted to see the book and to see me read. I tried to think of the last time I called home. It was pretty pathetic, how tightly they pulled the umbilical cord, and how easily I could let it drop. I was still itching to meet Clare the Orthodox Seductress.

My dad pulled my mom away from Abel. She was trying to buy a handful of copies of the book without my knowing so she could give them out to the family back home. "There's sex inside," I cautioned her.

"It's okay," said Abel, pocketing the money with his left hand and autographing my mother's copies with his right. "They're adults."

During my set, I had kept apologizing to my grandmother. "Sorry, Grandmom, there's some curse words in this one and I don't know how to change them."

"That's okay," she'd said, in a stage voice. "You think I've never heard these words before?"

All Abel's indie-rock girlfriends in V-neck sweaters loved her.

I packed my family into a cab, their books tied in a plastic Safeway bag. My mind was racing.

I was tripping over my own skin. I ran inside and downed one of those monster 24-ounce beers. People were drifting out, saying their goodbyes or just hanging and chatting and popping cheez balls. The two girls in long skirts brushed past me, kissed Abel on the cheek, and thanked him for a great night. I drained a second beer and walked behind Abel, demanding, "Who the hell were they?"

Abel shrugged. "Why, do you like them? Jeannie and Karma are professional fag hags, they work in Dupont and they live there too," and I wanted to tell him, no, I'm looking for my dream-ass Orthodox girl to sweep me the fuck off my feet, but then I felt the telltale bump of Edgar's scooter riding over my toes. He yanked on my arm and dragged me over to meet Clare and her friend Ahuva.

Clare was cute in a dumplinglike sort of way. She had long straight black hair, golden olive skin—her family was from Guatemala—and clothes that said hippie, but clean. A scarf with African prints and a long flowy skirt. Her hair was pulled neatly back in a single ponytail and I remembered that there was some sort of code with Hasidic girls that one ponytail meant you were old enough to start dating, while two braided ponytails meant you hadn't started dating yet. Did Clare even know that secret-code stuff?

Ahuva, Clare's friend, had a badass nose ring and spiky hair and a scowl that never evaporated. God only knows what they thought of me, in my New York F-train baby T-shirt and jeans. No respectably stringent Ortho-dox man wore jeans; they were a sign of the depravity and lack of formality in the secular world.

Ahuva was wearing pants. She was definitely butch. I'd never been on an Orthodox date before, but I didn't need any more spelling out: She was the muscle.

We sat around. I offered Clare cheez puffs—and Ahuva, too, I guess. They declined. I grabbed a handful and began popping them into my mouth like Skee-Ball. I suspected my breath smelled like beer and I was abso-lutely sure my stomach was empty.

We tried to make conversation. We ended up talking mostly about Edgar.

We tried to make the conversation bigger—I asked Clare about her trip to Israel; she asked about my unof-ficial appointment as Edgar's cook—but we kept faltering. Everything we said ended with yes-or-no. It was a hard game to keep going. Clare talked about this restaurant she ate at and I didn't want to ask, is that place kosher?—be-cause obviously it wasn't. Ahuva chewed her cuticle. She rolled her eyes.

Eventually we had to give up the room, it was 10:00 and the people upstairs went to bed at 10:30, so I walked Clare and Ahuva out and I told Ahuva it was very nice talking with her and then I switched my gaze to Clare, and I said that I was thoroughly drunk but I still thought she was really cool and did she want to hang out next Monday? I said Monday because it rolled off my tongue. I was trying to sound like I knew what I was talking about.

Clare said, hell yeah. They asked directions to the sub-way stop and then left the building. My nerves were danc-ing on their ends, she'd said, *Hell yeah,* which meant that she at least partially cursed! That night, I was so money.

There were even leftover cheez balls.

Sunday night Clare called me and told me we had a problem. Monday was Tu B'Shevat, the New Year of the Trees, which wasn't a major holiday so it didn't have any actual rules but she wanted to celebrate anyway. I was like, so you don't want to go to a bar? She told me I should come out to the Maryland campus in the suburbs, where she lived. The Jewish Student Center there was putting on a Tu B'Shevat activity night.

"Activity night?" I repeated.

"Come on. Weren't you ever in third grade?"

"Sure I was. We got beat up for participating in things called Activity Night."

First we all sat on the floor in a circle. Clare's friend Ahuva conducted the Tu B'Shevat seder. It was supposed to be a festive meal, only, because it was the New Year of the Trees, we drank grape juice and ate foods that came from trees, starting with pomegranates and pouring through bananas and apples and figs, all different kinds of foods that were not filling and that only exacerbated our hunger and jolted our sugar count until we were jittering up and down, hopping on our asses in Indian-style sitting positions. Then we planted seeds in recycled glass jars and signed petitions about clean air and then we did some other art project, maybe dioramas of farms?

A full moon outside lit up the campus, making everything bright as day. Sprawling grass fields covered the place, oscillating up the hills. There are no hills in Washington, and no grass either. The air tasted funny, too, crisp like autumn. Maybe it's the way the air tastes whenever a season changes. I'd never lived in suburbia.

Ahuva pulled out a pail filled with colored chalk. Clare whispered in my ear that this was the condition for

Starting with pomegranates. The actual Tu B'Shevat seder has an order for eating fruit. You start with pomegranates and then proceed through figs, dates, grapes, and finally to olives.

Ahuva's leading the seder—that afterward, everyone would help her chalk the streets. Chalking was the process of sprawling subversive sayings on the sidewalks and pavements and public buildings on a college campus. Ahuva had just joined the campus feminist group, and it was Women's History Month. She had volunteered to flood the University of Maryland with feminist propaganda.

"You had to persuade her?" I asked, tagging along after Clare. "Why did she have to be persuaded?"

"Ahuva grew up really really Orthodox," Clare said. "Now she's kind of over it."

"I'm not over it," Ahuva explained, whipping out a fat piece of purple chalk. "I didn't stop being Orthodox. I just stopped hanging out around Silver Spring."

Ahuva traced a big circle around herself, stepped out, and wrote SEXISM-FREE ZONE along the edges.

Clare scuttled a few steps down the sidewalk and drew a picture of two women holding hands. "What is *that* supposed to be?" Ahuva demanded.

"It's two women being happy," Clare explained. "They live in a world without prejudice."

"That's dumb," said Ahuva.

"Maybe you could write something about lesbians as a caption?" I offered.

The heart of the University of Maryland was the Quad, a long, unctuous meadow at the center of campus, surrounded by the library and all the main buildings. For an hour we ran along the stone trails through the Quad, darting between buildings, scribbling pro-woman sayings and leaving pictures of flowers. (Ahuva looked positively pissed, but Clare insisted that flowers were feminist—"you can't be pro-woman and be against girly stuff, and besides, what about Georgia O'Keeffe?") The other girls, mostly clueless but nonetheless enthusiastic, copied Ahuva's mantras and embellished them with drawings of punk-girl smiley faces and fists. I wrote slogans from the Take Back the Night march and Bikini Kill albums, and I didn't realize how militant I was sounding till I wrote across the statue of an American Bald Eagle in front of the library, CUNT—IT'S NOT A DIRTY WORD. Clare, who was still allegedly my date for the night, read it and frowned. "Yes it is," she said to me.

"Really, it's not," I said. "We learned about it in women's issues group last week. 'Vagina' comes from a Greek word meaning 'sheath for a sword.' 'Cunt' used to be a term of respect for women rulers of countries."

"That's from the *Cunt* book!" said Ahuva.

"They let you read those books in Silver Spring?" I asked.

Ahuva looked at me with something in between flirtation and daring, I couldn't tell which.

"Those are the kind of books you have to leave Silver Spring to find," she said.

We finished chalking and went back to Ahuva's room for beers. Clare was edgy and tentative, and had to catch the last subway into the city, but she insisted that she'd drive me. Ahuva's room was a purple and black glowing pile of radiance. The walls beside her bed were covered in posters. There was one of Björk, naked and laughing, clutching a fig leaf, that I'd never seen but that felt, the way the best Björk songs did, like something out of my dreams. And then she had posters for Ani DiFranco and the Dismemberment Plan and the *Muppet Show,* a stuffed animal of Janice sitting on her bed, a copy of—wait for it—Michelle Tea's book *Valencia,* which my friend Erin had just sent me. I picked it up and started thumbing through it. Ahuva came back, two six-packs of some

The Cunt book. That would be the book called *Cunt,* by Inga Muscio, a kind of feminist manifesto published by Seal Press in 1998.

cheap beer dangling from her fingers, and stopped when she saw I was fingering her book. "Oh, *Valencia,*" she said. "That's—"

"The eye-opening story of a single, adventure-addled girl looking for friends and escapades in San Francisco's Mission District," I finished.

Our eyes were both gleaming.

Everyone else in the room went silent.

"Cree-*py,*" said Clare, giggling nervously.

Beers were passed around. I dug through Ahuva's stuff, her CDs and movies and books. It turned out, not only did Ahuva have the *Muppet Show* book, the mammoth illustrated anthology with all the best episodes written out in script form—which I was weaned on, raised on, until all the pages fell out and my parents threw it away and I haven't seen it since—but she knew all the songs by heart.

"Mahna mahna!" I yelped, enthralled, as I opened to that page in the book.

"Doo do do da doo da da doo do," sang Ahuva.

The space and aspiration, everything that people don't get exactly right when they sing old songs, she had right to the second. She bobbed and curled her short spiky hair and it bobbed the way the Mahna beard hair bobbed, back on television so many years ago. I wasn't sure if Ahuva was revisiting my childhood or remixing it.

Their friends were actually pretty cool, too. We got to talking about kosher food and how our nonobservant friends didn't understand how hard it was to never set foot in the cafeteria, and how, when you're hungry at 2 A.M., you can't just call Papa John's pizza delivery, and, holy shit, maybe we *were* all punk-rock outlaws in a different world. Maybe timidity and rage were just our different ways of dealing with the situation. That's what I said, aloud, and Clare said, "But who's raging?" and I told her, raging is the basic aesthetic of my life.

"Well, why?" she said, matter-of-factly, and it totally surprised me. It blew me away. If only because she was so calm and accepting of the basic fact.

I shrugged.

"Because it feels better than sitting quietly and letting the Republicans take over the world?" I suggested.

"I could see that," said Clare.

At the end of the night, Clare stuffed me into the back seat of her car, hopped onto the Beltway, and drove me back into Washington.

"So, umm, thanks. For tonight, I mean." I fumbled with the strap to my knapsack.

"Sure." She ground the steering wheel with her fingers.

"This was definitely better than a bar," I managed.

"Except I'm not," she sniffed. She almost said it to herself, into the window, head tilted away from me.

"What do you mean?"

Clare gulped.

And then the torrent came.

"I don't want to keep doing this to you. I didn't know how to spill it—I'm not Orthodox. I mean, I went on that program with Edgar, I learned all this Jewish stuff, but it's not *good* enough. No matter what I do, nothing feels good enough."

"That's okay," I whispered. "It doesn't have to be an all-or-nothing thing. First you take on the little things, then you take on more...."

"But you don't *understand!*" Clare cried, real tears rolling down her cute dark newly Orthodox cheekbones. "My favorite food is *bologna and cheese sandwiches!*"

There was silence. Between us, in the car, all around. Somewhere, a car honked, but that was blocks away. It could have been miles.

I wanted to rub her back, murmur to her that everything was going to be okay. But that would have meant touching her.

"I totally understand," I told her. "I once ate this granola bar without checking to see if it was kosher first."

I thanked her for the ride, leaped out of the car, and ran across the circle into my apartment building. That was my first Orthodox date. And, for the first time, I felt like there was someone faking it just as much as I was.

4

crash landing

San Francisco was fresh, a rush of movement and sun, like the first time you get a new favorite song stuck in your head. I was young, beautiful, and in love with the idea of being in love, and I had no one to give it to but the city of San Francisco.

Something about San Francisco changes you when you get here. It's like pouring yourself through a Brita filter, where tiny stones and chemicals siphon out certain parts of you. Suddenly you're standing at the corner of Market Street in clothes you never dreamed you would wear, writing the memoir of your wild childhood in your head, and singing your favorite song out loud, not giving a damn who hears.

And nobody cares, cause they're all singing at the top of their lungs too. That's why so many people here come out as gay, or as fetishists, or healers, or Buddhists. It's also why so much art gets made—because people don't shoot you down. Whatever your trip is, whatever you're doing, everyone else is doing something that's just as supremely ridiculous or outlandish.

In Washington, all my friends were political peons or consultants or consultants in training, working a twelve-hour day every day because that was what we went to school to do. Never mind that we had shit work, days that were literally spent alphabetizing files and scheduling package deliveries. We were on a quest. Even if that quest was a corporate ladder, we had been trained to climb it.

One day, I got bored. I stared at my computer screen and realized that it only had two dimensions. On my desk I had an inbox and an outbox, and in my year struggling to keep the piles down, the only thing that I'd accumulated was dust.

Then I read *Valencia*, by Michelle Tea. It was a true-life memoir. It was about staying up all night and running to the ocean and talking to strangers. It sounded like this Michelle Tea was having more fun with her life than I was.

So I told my job I was moving to San Francisco.

I'd heard about all the freaks and poets and performance artists who lived there. It seemed like the perfect anti-Washington: where nobody had real jobs, and when they did, they didn't actually *do* anything. I always had this vague idea about San Francisco in my head—my parents used to tape *Tales of the City*, God knows why, an innocently dirty PBS melodrama about twenty-somethings who smoked a lot of pot. I knew the Beat Poets, whom I tried to read in high school but didn't totally understand. And I knew C. D., who was ten years older than me, had majored in post–gender studies at a New England college, and lived in San Francisco with her girlfriend. I also sort of knew her girlfriend, and I knew these two gay guys whom my ex-girlfriend Shawna used to have crushes on. That was about it for my friend base.

For all practical purposes, I moved to San Francisco with a clean slate and an empty phone book.

I got to San Francisco a week before Passover began. I almost lost Passover that year. It's a battle, you know—your first Jewish holidays in a new place. Each time I caught the rhythm of life, like the worst basketball partner ever, God faked in a different direction.

Passover is the most fundamentalist holiday we have. Sure, we don't eat bread or rice or grains or anything that contains them, but we also can't own any wheat products, and we even try to avoid looking at loaves of bread in the supermarket. My first day in San Francisco I was zipping through Chinatown, thinking how this might be the only neighborhood in the entire city where the grocery store windows weren't lined with loaves of fresh sourdough. I spent all morning procrastinating at City Lights Bookstore, then walked to the edge of the Financial District, where the red-gold cereal prize of the Chinatown arch stretched across Grant Avenue like a big cartoon ambassador to the tourists of the world. If you looked through its belly, the first sign you saw was a big maroon awning in Hebrew. This was Sabra, the only kosher falafel place in San Francisco.

I went in and asked if anyone knew of an Orthodox family I could hook up with for Shabbos. The waiter, a jumpy kid with a yarmulke and long thin tzitzis that trailed to his knees, told me to take a seat. I got an Israeli fruit drink, which tasted less like juice than like a pulpy, cotton candy version of the actual fruit. I cracked the can open, pulled out my journal, and waited. Those days I was chronicling everything. I started to draw a picture of the Israeli fruit drink can, and somebody stuffing a bunch of fruit trees into the opening with a pitchfork. I was starting on the shading when the waiter returned with a scrap of paper on which he'd scrawled the name "Kaufmann, Kimmel and Elana" and a phone number.

I carried the piece of paper around for the rest of the day before I got up the nerve to call the number. A man answered.

"Hey," I said. "I'm Orthodox, I just moved here, and I don't know where to find kosher food or places for Shabbos or a synagogue."

He asked me a few questions to establish my Orthodox cred—he'd heard of Rabbi Samborra—and the next thing I knew he said, "Come for Shabbos, I'll see you Friday at sunset," and I was scribbling down his address and Muni directions to his house.

I was staying in C. D.'s walk-in closet in her wallet-size studio on Van Ness Avenue. She had a day job, paralegal in a major law firm on the 50th floor of a building downtown. I had the days alone to figure out the city and find a job so that I could afford to live here. C. D.'s landlords were insane. They had installed security cameras in the halls to check that overnight guests weren't staying more than the allowed fourteen days.

Mostly, I wandered around. Sometimes C. D.'s girl-friend, Henrietta, who'd lived in San Francisco for practically forever and was unemployed, would wake up with me and point me in a direction. Haight Street, or Japan-town with its stationery stores and Hello Kitty toasters. She knew all the undiscovered thrift stores, places that looked like they had thrift store clothes, and places that sold clothes that looked new but weren't.

For reference purposes, instead of a map, I used paperback books. I had my copy of *Valencia*, which was already starting to get dog-eared, and I tried to find Valencia Street, with the hot window-shopping mystery girls and inimitable hipster coffee dives that the *Valencia* book talked about. The first day, I walked around the Tenderloin, looping around blocks because I hadn't figured out that Market Street is on a diagonal, and when I finally found Valencia Street I walked down four blocks, past an abandoned church and a homeless tent city and these projects that looked exactly like the Algon Avenue projects near my grandmom's house from when I was a kid. But no cool, ambiguously gendered hipsters. No cafés. No Michelle Tea herself, whom I figured I'd automatically run into on Valencia Street, because if we were going to be best friends, it would happen naturally, right?

In despair, I made my way back to C. D.'s house. I curled up on the couch, coddled a yellow legal tablet between my legs and elbows, and wrote Ahuva a letter. My life looked so much better on paper. I could draw a picture of a cable car on the back and she would get so horribly jealous, she'd fall in love with me for sure.

C. D. had a doctorate in sex therapy and had lived in the city for almost a decade. She knew the craziest people, the most intricate, hard-to-track-down niches of society. On Tuesday night, Shawna's almost-boyfriends took me to a bunch of hole-in-the-wall clubs and grazing spots, each more select and esoteric than the last, culminating in Trannyshack, the drag show at the Stud Bar, where Heklina and Pippi Lovestocking ran through entire wardrobes of the briefest dresses, all sequins and sparkles, and we danced long after the city-mandated last call ended, until even the DJs yawned and one of the boyfriends was talking about going to work in three hours and maybe he should just stay up all night instead of going to sleep?

That kind of shit never worked for me. I had to sleep.

The next morning I had to wake up promptly at 8:00 A.M. to call and see if any temp jobs were available.

No jobs, I reasoned as I walked home from the club, meant fewer nights out, more time in C. D.'s closet, and closer to the precarious deadline of my return ticket. If I couldn't afford San Francisco in the first month, with no rent or utilities to pay, I was only going to sink deeper over the course of the rest of my natural life.

I crawled home to find C. D. curled up on the couch, watching TV alone in the dark. She had on a long T-shirt and was buried in blankets. Her girlfriend wasn't home, it was 3 A.M., and I didn't even notice. I crawled on top of the blankets in my club clothes and rolled up on her lap.

"Everything was so beautiful tonight," I said, ready to cry, all the hopelessness welling up in me like cigarette smoke exploding my lungs. "It was so big and I'm never gonna be able to do it."

I had a picture in my head of me climbing to the top of a mountain, then discovering it was a cliff and falling off.

C. D. took me into the Sunset District, near the beach, to Brigit Brat's house. We rode a bus from downtown, out near the ocean, and then another bus swept us through Golden Gate Park. We rode past trees as tall as cities, thick like rising loaves of bread. She briefed me on Brigit, dishing gossip like a teen movie.

C. D.'s girlfriend Henrietta used to date Brigit's current boyfriend. After the initial burst of hostility, they all started talking about music, and then they all became friends. In her pre–San Francisco life, Brigit Brat used to be a rocket scientist—no kidding—but then she went insane. That was back before her surgery, back when she was still a man. Brigit kept telling herself, if she could build advanced spacecraft for NASA, she could deal with having a male body, but in the end, her heart won out. Brigit became a woman, left her job, and started playing metal guitar full time.

Brigit's boyfriend Essex answered the door. It was actually Essex's apartment, which his swanky computer job paid for. Brigit just lived there. Essex was perky and upbeat and talked like a valley girl, only he used bigger words. Geek words. Hair spurted from his head in every direction, floppy like a palm tree, and he wore slick polyester shirts that looked like Star Trek uniforms.

Brigit, when we walked in, was huddled over a speaker, cranking wires. When she stood, her head scraped the doorway arches. She was skinny, too, waify like me. She had a guitar strapped around her shoulder, and I think its body was wider than she was. She looked like if she bent over again, she would snap in half.

Essex vanished into the kitchen, promising cookies and Danish.

"Danish?" I asked C. D.

"Pastry chef," she mouthed back.

"Don't worry about him," said Brigit, plugging her guitar into the newly wired amp, "let's just play."

That's why we were here. C. D. and I, we were forming a band with Brigit Brat.

C. D. strapped on another of Brigit's guitars, a wideneck model with a glittering checkerboard body. The guitar Brigit wore was neon purple, gleaming like the 1980s, plastic seahorses flanking the bridge on either side. I walked over to the microphone stand she'd set up and I pulled my harmonica out of my pocket.

Brigit started first. She ran a pick along her strings, one at a time. The sound turned into horrible, static-rimmed thuds on the speaker, shaking our stomachs and chins. The rhythmic strum got quicker, turned into a chord progression, leaped into a song. C. D. jumped in, tweaking notes, flooding a guitar solo through Brigit's wall of noise. I blasted my harmonica from the bass end where it was loudest, riding the mic on top, blowing straight in, listening to the fuzz come out. I caught C. D.'s eye. She caught Brigit's eye. Brigit swayed into the music, lunging forward as if she was shokeling.

We rode that song for ten minutes. Brigit and C. D. traded leads, one guitar falling back into the rhythm when the other broke it. I played a bass line on my harmonica, doing quick techno lines like a sequencer, pumping long single notes like a didgeridoo. By the end of the song, Brigit was sweating. I was shaking. C. D. fell back and sank into a beanbag couch, stunned.

"Hi," Brigit said to me. "It's good to meet you."

I smiled back.

C. D. vanished into the kitchen for a drink, and I faced Brigit while she sends stories through me. I felt like an amp, like she was pumping the air when she talked. Within five minutes of meeting her, Brigit told me how unstable she is, how she had been institutionalized and that she was bulimic.

Maybe that's why I felt so safe with her.

"Honey," Brigit said—when Brigit talks, she always whispers—"I'm one of the unhealthiest people you will ever meet."

"You're one of the healthiest people I've met in months," I said. "My friends back east won't even tell them*selves* what's wrong with them. You tell complete *strang*ers."

"Everybody has a freak flag," Brigit said calmly, that voice of pure conviction and truth. "Some of us wave it high. Then there are the people who act normal, and their problems stick out even more. We're all part metal, and we're all part easy listening."

I wanted to ask what part of her was easy listening.

As she talked, she walked over into the kitchen, pulled out a portable blender, and began to puree a protein shake in the living room. It was like she couldn't sit still. Her spindly legs were miles long under her brief skirt, flamingos against the brown shag carpeting. "What's your excuse?"

"My excuse? I don't have an excuse. I'm a freak, I'm pretty candid about it."

"Then why are you wearing that beanie?" she asked.

I liked Brigit a lot. She was wise, she'd been through more shit in a day than I had in my whole life. She looked at people and she could tell major things about them. My gashed silence was its own answer to her question. She shot out a hand and gave me a tour of her guitars.

There was the zebra-striped one, which she had pulled all the electrical wiring out of, and she was fixing it up to sell on eBay.

There was a guitar whose body was specially constructed for Brigit in Los Angeles. The engineer built it for her dexterity and distortion and for someone of Brigit's exact frame, six foot eight and 120 pounds. I knew about being underweight and thin—C. D. had given me a bodysuit top one week, and she said I looked better in it than she did. Except for the estrogen part, I had a really great body for a woman. For a man, I had an awful body. I was too skinny and my muscles were tight, not layered, and my face would never look hard and weathered enough. I was cursed with being cute.

Brigit, though. Brigit was beautiful. She had the longest, thinnest hair, suicide blonde, parted in a small triangle so that her face cut out timidly beneath it, like the Lady of the Lake in *The Lord of the Ring*. She cradled the last guitar in her pale thin arms, a modest-looking plain black model with a V-shaped chin. She handled it like a baby. "This belonged to Randy Rhoads," she said, sadly, almost reverently. "Do you know who he is?"

Around her, I felt strangely unafraid to say, no, I did not. "Was he—wasn't he a hard rock singer?" I ventured.

"He was Ozzy Osbourne's guitarist," Brigit said. "He died in a plane crash. Only, nobody really thinks he died—everyone's got a theory. He left a show in a huff, he and Ozzy had a fight. This was the last guitar he played," Brigit said, definitely reverent now, taking it back from my hands, sliding it into the closet between a furry, leopard-print guitar and one with orange and green swirls.

That last pattern looked familiar, strikingly familiar. I twisted around.

Under Brigit's bed, in rows like a platoon, were a dozen pairs of high heels, each with its own pattern and color scheme and stiletto length. Each matched one of her guitars perfectly.

Friday afternoon, I took the bus all the way down Geary Boulevard to the Kaufmann house. I bought a bottle of wine at the kosher store on the corner, then walked up to his house. The door was ajar. I walked in, dropped the bottle of wine on the front table, and followed the thin trails of conversation into the kitchen.

Two kids a few years younger than me, teenagers, were sitting at the table. Shira had spiky hair and glasses like an indie rock star. Yitzhak was wearing a Dismemberment

Randy Rhoads. Ozzy Osbourne's guitarist and collaborator in his post–Black Sabbath career. Rhoads allegedly died in a plane wreck in 1982. The circumstances were mysterious—Rhoads, who had a chronic fear of flight, requested to take a joyride on a plane. The only other passenger was the band's 58-year-old seamstress, who happened to be on tour with them at the time. Like Moses and Elijah, his body was never found.

Plan T-shirt. Both were rare as hell among the staid, conservative Chabad community that I grew up around. The first thing Yitzhak did when I walked into the room was ask what I was listening to. He unclipped the headphones from my neck and listened to my CD. His head bobbed up and down with the beat.

From the other end of the kitchen, Mrs. Kaufmann came in. Yitzhak didn't snatch off his headset and hide it the way every other Hasidic kid in Northeast Philadelphia would have. "Shira," said the mother, "have you shown our guest to his bedroom yet?"`

"No," I answered for her, "but that's okay. I mean, you don't have to put me up. I can just walk back to my friend's house. I live here now, in this city."

Mrs. Kaufmann kept talking as if I hadn't said anything. "There isn't any other Orthodox Jewish scene in San Francisco, except for here," she said.

"But it's not far—"

"Where are you?" asked Shira, from the table, where suddenly a map of the city was unfolding from between her fingers. I told her. She measured with her index finger. "Four point two miles," she announced. She wiggled her hands in the air. "Well, four miles and a knuckle. There's no way. It would take you hours."

Yitzhak showed me the basement. It was a stone room, lined with bookcases. There was a pull-out sofa with fresh sheets. I guess they were used to overnight visitors. The books, too, weren't standard Hasidic fare but included popular novels by authors like Stephen King and Tom Robbins.

For the next twenty-five hours, I shadowed Mr. Kaufmann. He was a professor at UC San Francisco in the Economics Department, and by the end of Shabbos dinner he'd told me to call him Kimmel. Saturday, he introduced me around at shul and when we walked back to the house after the service, he acted like we were old friends. I got the feeling he did this a lot.

I calculated the beginning of Passover in my head. Today was the eighth of Nissan.

Passover started on the fifteenth.

I started dropping hints. By the time I left the Kaufmanns' on Saturday night, I had an invitation.

I had a whole week until then, which I thought was a huge amount of time, until I used it all up. I told C. D. that I was looking for an apartment, but most of the time I just spent walking around the city. The night before Passover, Jews are supposed to search for crumbs of bread in the corners of their houses. I was living out of a suitcase. I took the ritual candle and feather and swept the corners of my suitcases. Since the search is a commandment, you're supposed to hide some bread crusts so that you definitely find something, and I took my stale bagel from C. D.'s refrigerator, carried it to the roof of her apartment building, and set it on fire. I watched it burn to ash with San Francisco Bay in the background. I was sending smoke signals to those faraway island towns—that's what it felt like.

Then I took my suitcase, grabbed a bus, and landed at the Kaufmanns' house.

There were something like twelve people there for Passover—yeshiva boys, random Israeli tourists, and even one whole family. Since Shabbos came right before Passover that year, we were there for three nights and three days in a row. The pull-out sofa in the basement was occupied, and several air mattresses and a pile of sleeping bags had been added for the overflow. I unrolled a sleeping bag. The spot next to mine was claimed by Yossi, a Chabad kid my age whose entire family was staying at the Kaufmann house. Yossi spent the whole week before Passover going to prisons and holding mock seders with inmates, part of an outreach project. He was Jewish, impressive in the classic mold of Cecil B. DeMille movies like *The Ten Commandments*, muscley, pear-shaped, with a stocky red beard and piercing blue eyes. He almost never took off his black hat, except to go to sleep. Even when we dozed in the basement in the afternoons, its walls made of cement and stone, the only cool spot in the overheating house, he kept his hat on, tilted over his recumbent body, touching his nose like Indiana Jones.

Chabadniks had all these customs for Passover that were different from Passovers with normal Jews, even Orthodox Jews. We all replace our normal silverware with special Passover silverware that's never touched bread, but Chabad was so strict that, if a fork fell to the floor, they kicked it into a corner and left it on the floor until the end of Passover. Also, they peeled everything, even fruits like apples and tomatoes, in case any bread had touched its skin in the store.

The Kaufmanns didn't eat any packaged food on Passover except for matzohs, but that was style, not law, and somebody smuggled a couple kosher-for-Passover cartons of orange juice from New York and kept them at the bottom of the refrigerator. Somebody else brought a basket of strawberries. Yossi's ten-year-old sister was addicted to strawberries. Her parents told her that, as Chabadniks, it was their custom not to eat strawberries on Passover because they were impossible to peel.

"Nothing's impossible to peel," she said. "You can even peel chicken."

Seder. The ritual meal of Passover. There are fourteen official steps to the seder, but the point of it, besides eating matzoh and about a zillion other ritual foods, is to take us symbolically through the Exodus from Egypt. There's a special book that everybody reads out loud from, and a special order to eating foods, and explaining each of those foods, plus a few silly songs at the end that are propelled by the drunkenness of consuming four cups of wine on an empty stomach.

Her parents shook their heads, but she dug out a peeling knife and pierced the strawberry vein. Delicately, slowly, she serrated a strawberry until it looked like a dreidel, a sharp pointed bottom and its sides as angular as dice. She placed the berries in a neat pile on a paper plate, and when she finished cutting an even dozen, she ran up to the roof and ate them all.

I'm not telling you about the seders because, well, they were boring. Another dozen guests showed up for the first seder, mostly religious orphans and students. Five hours, four cups of wine, a 100-page book that you're supposed to read aloud both nights—you can imagine how the night ran. I hadn't eaten all day—you weren't supposed to eat any bread products, in order to cleanse your body and make it ready for the incoming matzoh—and the wine took me, fast and hard. The high point of the night was that I sat next to this girl a few years older than me who had met Perry Farrell at a seder a few years ago, and they'd gone on a few dates. I was all curious but she ducked my questions. Kimmel Kaufmann heard us talking about it and told me that the local Chabad used to have giant carnivals for Purim and Chanukah where Perry DJ'd and hung out for days afterward, learning Torah with his kids Yitzhak and Deena and whoever was around, but now Jane's Addiction was back together and he wasn't coming by as much. "We gave up on the concerts, too," Kimmel said, wistfully. "All those boys and girls dancing together, it wasn't

Perry Farrell. In the early '90s, Farrell was the lead singer of Jane's Addiction, an alternative rock band, and one of the first really cerebral bands out there. His lyrics were all about alienation and teenage cynicism and otherworldly spiritual experiences and group sex. I started listening to them when I was fourteen and dropped out of my synagogue youth group. I didn't really know about the group sex lyrics, but I could tell it was something illicit. For a while, they were my favorite band in the world.

tznius." Later that night, when the meal was done and everyone was slowly collapsing on the living room sofas, he asked me what exactly I was doing in San Francisco. I told him I wanted to be a famous poet.

He nodded. He gave me that look that my parents gave me when I was ten and told them I wanted to be an X-Man.

"Do you have any backup plans?" he said.

I said I was playing harmonica in a metal band.

After that, Kimmel began to look at me with a newfound admiration. He was like me, I could tell, a musical hanger-on who never played music himself. For weeks after Passover, I came to his house every Shabbos, and every Shabbos he tried to convince me to stay on Saturday night for a music jam. Sometimes, there were travelers, Israeli teens who strapped guitars to their back and embarked on their Greyhound peregrinations across America. Professional Jewish musicians showed up, too, like Asi Spiegel and Shlomo Katz, who jammed on the Kaufmanns' old stand-up piano. I played harmonica, usually, or sometimes I hammered on Deena's old djembe. Deena was the Kaufmanns' oldest daughter. She lived in Israel. When people talked about her, it was always in a hushed tone, either reverent, as if she was superhuman, or as if they were weirded out by her.

Of everyone that I met at the Kaufmanns', the most distinctive was Jacob. He and Yitzhak were friends growing

Tznius. Literally, modesty. The way a Jew dresses, the way we behave, and the way we carry ourselves with other people.

Asi Spiegel. A Chabad rabbi who also plays guitar and records and tours professionally. Imagine a Hasidic version of Bob Dylan, only with a beard that looks like Dylan's hair.

Shlomo Katz. Leader of the Happy Minyan Band, a neo-Hasidic jam band influenced by the rock stylings of Rabbi Shlomo Carlebach and, of course, the Grateful Dead.

up, and he lived a few blocks away. His parents were Reform, but they hung out with Kimmel and Elana, and they always had Yitzhak come over after school. Now they were older, and Jacob occasionally came for Shabbos. He listened to the same music that I did, and we could trade band stories like old roadies, him with Bay Area punk bands and me with East Coast punk bands. A few times after I started coming to the Kaufmann house, Jacob began wearing a yarmulke nonstop, sleeping over in the basement and keeping Shabbos straight through until Saturday night. One week I came in and the entire family was sitting around Jacob like a bridal reception, clutching hands, beaming cheek-to-cheek. Kimmel waved me in. "Jacob has just told us," said the rabbi, "he's becoming baal teshuva. He's going to be Orthodox."

Dinner that night was celebratory. To the Kaufmanns, this was reason to rejoice, a major change in the climate of Shabbos. That meant Jacob would come to the Kaufmann house every week, go to shul with us, even sit with us through the weary Saturday afternoon service while the old men talked in the background and the rabbis sang wordless, tuneless songs that none of us could recognize.

Okay, I said it.

I was getting bored of Shabbos at the Kaufmanns'.

A few weeks later, I met Deena.

By then, Shabbos had gotten to be a pattern for me. I got on the Geary express bus Friday afternoon. I bought a bottle of wine or some Chinese vegetables from one of the stores where nobody spoke English. Once I brought the Kaufmanns a bunch of cactus leaves, but nobody knew how to cook them.

But Deena. One day I walked into the Kaufmann kitchen without ringing the doorbell, and there she was, wearing a sari and an Indian half-shirt that fell to her knees and chappals and a braided scarf around her waist. I was about to tell her that she shouldn't cook without Shira or Yitzhak or someone there because everything was kosher and nothing was marked and nobody ever knew if they were using a dairy spatula with a meat pot and a pareve lid. I saw the outline of pants beneath the half-shirt and assumed she wasn't Orthodox, because in Hasidic houses, that's the way we tell.

She turned and smiled at me piteously. "I promise you, it will be okay," she said. "I'm a Kaufmann."

That made her Deena. Shira looked rebellious, short punk-rock hair and a grin as if she was always hiding something. Yitzhak was charismatic. One day, he would be the working man's rabbi. But Deena was the third child, the mystery child. She was the one whom everyone called a misfit, independent-minded, and punky and spunky, over-the-top even for the Kaufmanns, who were over-the-top to begin with.

I sat on a countertop with my legs dangling into the drawers and watched Deena cook. I offered to help but she said no. "Talk to me instead," Deena said. "Tell me about the Torah portion this week."

Now here's where I'm going to confess something. I'm an awful Jewish learner. It's not just that I'm awful at learning the Hebrew language, but one integral part of Orthodox Judaism is to learn some part of Torah every day. I have a total blitzed fascination with stories. I try to learn, but I go so slowly, every word whispers in my ear to pull off to the side. When we read about Jacob wrestling an angel of God, I wonder if Jacob vented his frustration in a mosh pit, and if Jacob's wrestling felt like purging yourself of bad shit, the way I did when I slam-danced. We read about Joseph interpreting the Pharaoh's dreams, and I started thinking about my dreams last night, and what Joseph would say they meant, and then I started to think about hanging with Joseph. Would he be cool and approachable? Would he be traumatized from all his years working as a slave, the way my best friend Amy in high school was traumatized by being sexually assaulted? My mind was a rabid beast, wild and out of control. And because I couldn't focus on one thing, I was really bad at learning Torah.

I started anyway, telling Deena about this week's Torah portion. It was about the Red Heifer that Moses sacrificed in the Temple, which was also meant to cleanse dead people, or living people who hung around dead people, or something like that. But then I talked about how Chabad didn't allow women to sing, even though that was a minority opinion in the Talmud. "But hey," Deena said to me, "You know that part in Talmud Berachos where Shmuel says—"

"But that's a minority opinion," I said. "Nobody holds by that anymore."

"Well, *we* do."

"Oh my God," I said, "They're oppressing you."

"Strike two," Deena said, sipping fish sauce from a ladle. "If anyone's oppressing me, I'm oppressing myself. And I certainly don't feel oppressed."

"But," I struggled from my perch on the counter, "but, don't you ever want to look behind the curtains? You're Orthodox. Your Judaism doesn't have an on/off switch. Don't you feel like you need to know how all the laws got that way?"

Deena shrugged. "Don't you believe in anything that you don't know backward and forward?"

"Sure," I said at once. "I believe in God. That counts, doesn't it?"

Again, the sauce blowing. Again the indifference.

"That definitely counts," said Deena. "Me believing that I don't need to understand all the legal stuff, that's part of me believing in God."

I remembered how Hasidic Jews used to seem so alien. Back in Washington, Orthodox Jews dressed like everyone else. Hasidim were a cross between mystics and zombies. We had regular jobs and studied secular subjects in school. Everything Hasidim did was explicitly Jewish. Even the way they dressed, like wearing colors besides black and white would somehow piss off God. I was awestruck by the Hasidic rabbi at our synagogue. I wondered if I could ever be Hasidic. When I asked my friend Gavin, he told me that I could never be a good Hasid because I think too much.

Deena ladled again. She had cooked that sauce for three hours. I hadn't done one thing for three hours in a row since I was twelve years old and obsessed with Nintendo.

"Some days," I told Deena, "I wish I could just say yes and not have to question it all. I wish I could be crystal clear, like you are."

"You really think so?"

"I think so."

"Yeah," said Deena. "I think so sometimes, too."

I was totally crushed out on Deena. Saying this won't surprise anyone, I promise. Her sisters asked me questions about her, even though they saw her more than I did—how she was doing, where she hung out at night, how were her art projects and her drumming. They flashed covert smiles when we walked into the room at the same time. Deena, who was notoriously modest, usually shrank from contact with anyone who might be a Prospective Husband. She never shrank from me, though.

Right after Shabbos that week, I snuck up to the second-floor office to check my email. Deena saw me come up from the back stairs. She called me into her room.

Hers was the only bedroom in the house where the walls weren't stark white. Deena painted on the walls with gusto: anthropomorphic trees dancing, brilliant blue spheres exploding in every green and yellow streak across the sky of Creation as birds and fish and mammals crawled out from the horizon. Deena was the only person I knew who could fuse art and religion so seamlessly. As much as I tried with my poems, they always wound up sounding either cheesy or heretical. The cheesy ones I threw out. The ones that sounded like heresy, I read on stage and the Orthodox people who heard them said I was either mentally unbalanced or evil. But I really wasn't evil, I was just trying to get my priorities straight.

I kept opening my mouth, about to tell Deena. But she jumped topics so seamlessly, segueing our conversation like a choreographer, and I struggled to keep up. Eventually, I let it slide.

I became a cog in the Kaufmann system without realizing it. Every Shabbos for months, I showed up at the house, docked my bags in the basement, set the Shabbos tables with the kids, sat in synagogue for long hours, waiting for the old Russian men to appear so we could have a minyan. Life was such an efficient ecosystem. Miles from C. D.'s apartment, hanging out with people whom I never talked to during the other six days of the week, Kaufmannland really *was* Shabbos in a vortex.

Deena returned to Israel. The days got longer, and Shabboses dragged out. Waiting for the old Russians gave way to waiting for the sun to set, and we sat in the huge sanctuary for hours, counting the minutes till Shabbos ended. The rabbi and the men there looked like hollow logs, drooping eyes, singing dreary, drippy nigguns until Shabbos was finally out. I was sure they had been there forever, been old forever, doing Shabbos like this since the first time God decided to rest on the seventh day.

During the week, I explored. During Shabbos, I sat at lonely tables and wondered if I would turn old like this, singing nigguns till my cheeks sagged.

But one night at a poetry reading, I met a girl who was going to El Salvador for a month, and I stayed in her apartment, in a different neighborhood. The rabbi in that neighborhood was this chipper, upbeat, kind of goofy guy, Rabbi Mendy. He was only a year older than me, and he acted more like a friend than a rabbi. I started going to his house for Friday night prayers and dinner, walking home to sleep in my own bed, and by the time summer started, I had almost completely stopped going to the Kaufmanns'.

5

box

Box went on testosterone and, within two weeks, his breasts had shrunk from fists to knuckles. His voice got deeper and then cracked and got deeper again, as if God was playing cat's cradle with his larynx. He gave me all his old Bondage Fairies comic books, which I left out for my roommates. They were colorful stories about Japanese manga fairies who giggled a lot and watched each other get fucked by woodland creatures and sprigs of leaves. Up until the moment they started beating each other, the Bondage Fairies were cute, friendly, girl-next-door types in leather. When we lived together and Box showed the comics off to me, I always thought that, for comic book characters, the Bondage Fairies were hot. But in a really creepy way.

I was kind of disturbed by them, and kind of utterly fascinated. I tried to explain that to Box, but Box was officially too masculine for Bondage Fairies. He was becoming a boy for real.

We almost didn't meet in the first place. Box moved into the apartment I was subletting, and we had a week of overlap. The other housemate, Kathryn, was polite but avoided me. Kathryn was a sharp, tough-looking dyke with short spiky platinum-blonde hair. She hadn't wanted to rent to a boy, and especially not to a straight boy, but they needed to find somebody fast. She asked me questions during the interview that had no right answers, like, "Does it bother you to live with lesbians who are into recreational bondage, or would you enjoy it?" and she kept leaving little notes for me, like DOWN BOY DOWN! on the toilet seat.

I let my inner femme hang out, swilling every sentence as a question, wearing my baby T-shirts and getting all "honey, *please*" on the phone with my friends. I didn't know why it was happening—maybe it was like people who visit down south and end up with a southern accent?—but, for the first time in my life, I wasn't around people who would kick my ass if I talked that way. I think everyone in the entire city was used to boys talking that way.

By the end of my stay there, Kathryn had eased into me, let her guard down a little. It was the slow, easy progression of becoming friends with the people you live with, trusting them with all your little secrets and neuroses and the behaviors you try to cover up around people who don't know you intimately.

And then poor Kathryn had to deal with Box—who introduced herself the day she moved into the house, between loads of her heavy bookcases, as a fag-boi genderfuck non-op transsexual who specialized in having sex with other girl-born boys.

Fag-boi genderfuck non-op transsexual. Also called boi, as in "a boy by choice" or nonbiological boy.

This was my first month in the Mission.

Box moved in late in the day, during the first vestigial weeks of spring when the sunsets still came early and it got bitterly cold at night. Kathryn was out—any time she left the house, I couldn't help it, I automatically assumed that she was going to a bondage dungeon—and the only sounds in the entire old Victorian were the heavy moving-in thuds coming from Box's room. I didn't have any plans because I still didn't know anyone in San Francisco, and after spending the last few nights sitting in cafés, staring at girls and hoping one of them would have the guts to talk to me, I decided to stay home and make some serious mix tapes for my friends back in Philly.

I boiled water in a teapot and dug my jumbo bag of Chex Mix out of the kitchen pantry. For an hour, I sat with blank pieces of paper and the feeble stack of CDs that I brought from Washington scattered all around me. I told myself that I wasn't being reclusive. I told myself that the minute I seriously needed friends, I would go out and find them.

I knew that wasn't true.

I moved my blank mix tapes to the living room. Because Box's bedroom and mine shared a wall, I made as much noise as I could. After a few minutes, she crept through the living room, making apologies for disturbing me. I told her that she shouldn't be sorry because it was her house now.

Box smiled this pithy smile, half shy and half embar-

The Mission. The Mission District, the arts district, the hipster district, the district of poor white kids who lived side-by-side with working-class Latino families, who also lived side-by-side with rich-but-trying-not-to-look-like-it white kids. That book *Valencia* took place in the Mission, so naturally, I decided I needed to live there. It wasn't hard, either—cheap apartments abound, and the area itself is kind of a trapeze net for twentysomething kids without much financial mobility.

rassed. "What's all that?" she said.

I cleared some space on the couch. "What did you mean when you said that you were, you know, a fag-boi transsexual and all that stuff?" I asked, without making eye contact.

Box crawled up on the couch with me, tugged the last few inches of blanket to slide her feet into, and, smiling softly, said that she was actually mostly talking shit off the top of her head.

"Mostly?" I said.

"Don't worry," Box said, like she could see the rest of our lives from her end of the couch. "You'll see what I mean."

Those first days, Box made me feel so free. No matter where we were or what time of day it was, Box acted like we were in kindergarten and the recess bell just rang. She was the first person in San Francisco who actually listened to me instead of telling me about herself. I think it was a relief for both of us to just exist, and not have to constantly explain ourselves.

Box wore these kooky outfits every day that were more like costumes: androgynous rayon bodysuits in a brilliant blue, dark gray pinstripes and top hats, candystriped platform shoes that verged on being stilts. I was like her sidekick, not asking questions and still learning the lay of the land.

Box didn't have any job that I could identify, and I was temping, calling the agencies every morning at eight and staring furiously at the phone, trying to will it to ring, and so I didn't have much of a life either. I needed money and I needed friends, and in my head was this temp job where I would have a cubicle surrounded by cute secretaries, all of whom directed independent films and tended bar in their spare time, and they would invite me to concerts and premieres. A magical temp job, and I'd be hired to write silly captions for their catalogs.

This was never going to happen. I was going to remain friendless for life. All the great writers and independent filmmakers had friends already. They didn't need me clinging on.

Every day, I called the temp offices as soon as I was awake and, after my case workers told me there were no jobs, I walked onto the bucolically termite-eaten back porch. Our yard was half garden, half tenement, and it looked just like the apartment building in *Tales of the City* on TV. A rusted bathtub in the yard held a bed of roses and oregano plants. Two neighborhood cats sometimes crept through our yard and wrestled in the dandelion patch.

There I wrapped the thin leather straps of my tefillin around my head and arm, prayed, and then showered and toasted a bagel. By this time Box was usually up, stumbling onto the back porch with a fresh sex dream to tell or a story of last night's lasciviousness. Half punk, half slut, Box perpetually hung out with her friends at the Lexington, the only lesbian bar in the Mission, and complained about the boring suburban heterogeneity of queer culture in this city. I never told them how they *were* the local color, the weird paradigms that make the scene so varied and different, but why burst their bubble? They were so much more vibrant when they were angry.

Tefillin. Leather straps that you wrap around yourself when you pray in the morning. The English word is *phylacteries,* but I don't know anyone who's ever used that word aloud in a sentence.
The boring heterogeneity of queer culture in this city. I felt giddy to be a part of their conversation circles, as if I was the first explorer on an undiscovered planet. My Orthodox friends disapproved of homosexuality in theory—only, to them, homosexuality meant two men having anal sex. How to process boys who weren't born boys, girls kissing each other? The Torah never said anything about girls. The Torah *definitely* never said anything about this.

After a few beers, Box and her friends went out dancing, to the Café on Market Street, which held mostly raver boys, buffed-up WB-model guys who shrieked with girlish enthusiasm at the wild unruly mob of ambiguously gendered maybe-dykes. On Thursdays they hit Reform Skool, the industrial party at the Stud, and Saturdays they went to the all-night hip-hop party at the Endup.

Sometimes I tagged along. Those days I was being religiously diligent and trying not to touch girls. I was still having a long-distance flirtation with Ahuva. We were too afraid to name it anything official, but I was checking my Hotmail inbox often enough to call it love, or, at least, obsession. She could only email once a week, so it was a low-octane obsession, enough to keep me invested but not enough to make me neglect the rest of my life. Especially now that I had Box to tell me when I was spending too much time on the computer. She yanked me off with those little-boy hands of hers, threw me into the walk-in closet, and made me change out of my pajamas and into club clothes.

Those nights at the Café and Badlands and the Stud, Box and I cruised through the crowd easily, wide-eyed. Every disco ball amazed us and every crazy-haired raver girl was beautiful. We weren't looking to get picked up or laid or to have drinks bought for us—although, when one of the ripped middle-aged bodybuilders offered to buy us drinks, thinking I was gay or that Box was a boy, neither of us would say no. I wasn't out to find someone to have a relationship with. I could pour all my energy into making new friends and having adventures and dancing.

Partying all night with dykes seemed like just the right balance. I'd get incredibly drunk and do stupid-ass things that had nothing to do with girls or sex. I wrote haikus about people I didn't know and then I read them to the whole bar. I made props out of Box's weird fashion accessories, and played with them all night as if they were toys. One night, just as the Lex was closing, I saw Michelle Tea, the writer whose book had convinced me to move to San Francisco. I whispered to Box and pointed her out confidentially.

I figured that Box's friends, the dyke scenesters, had already noticed her, but instead, they noticed *me* noticing her. Within seconds, two big-shouldered butches grabbed me by the arms and dragged me over to Michelle and convinced me to talk to her. She had just flown in from some exotic reading somewhere and you could see she was trying to clock some quality time with her girlfriend, and also the bar was closing and they were trying to clear people out. I kept giving the "one second" sign until the bartender ran out of other people to hustle and started pushing me out as Box and her friends watched from the street and Michelle, obviously a friend of the bartender, sat at the bar and tried to ignore me in that developed, polite withdrawal that you cultivate when you're famous but you still hang out at regular-people places.

But with Box around, I never felt too embarrassed about anything. Box was always coming up with newer and bigger and more embarrassing things, stunts that made me feel so incredibly virginal in comparison. At night, Box was in performance mode, showing off for her girl gang. During the day, we were more tired and more introverted, but no less insane. We met at JaValencia and got supercaffeinated sodas and pretended we were millionaires and window-shopped. We went to the corner delis, and I showed Box all the strange markings on foods that meant they were kosher, small printed K's inside circles and triangles and heart-shaped outlines. Box met me at Dolores Park with her arms full of bagels and hummus and juices and ripe purple avocados. Dolores Park was where all the gay men suntanned. I hoped that

Box didn't want us to spend all afternoon watching the swiftly browning asses.

But Box rolled her eyes and motioned to a spot lower closer to street level. "Matthue, you *know* I loves the ladies," she said.

Maybe, but I knew that Box had a fascination for the boys, too. How else to explain the flamboyant wardrobe, Box's pronoun use for herself (which fluctuated daily between *she* and *he* and *it*), and even the spirit gum facial hair that appeared in different patterns each day? Not that I cared. Box's constant lady-lovin' problems gave me a rest from overanalyzing Ahuva's latest emails, and Box's genderfreaky nonchalance made me feel easy around her. I didn't have to keep my sentences short and manly, or worry about what people said about my tzitzis or my yarmulke. And Box was even down with my weird eating habits.

We spread out Box's picnic blanket and dug into the bagels. We sat on the edge of the grass, facing the oncoming hill of traffic, lined on both sides by palm trees. It was so California. The cars drove leisurely, wary of parkgoers, and it wasn't uninteresting—but why were we watching traffic when there was a whole park with grass and acrobatic dogs and hot dogwalkers?

"What time is it?" asked Box.

"A quarter to twelve," I said, reading the belfry clock on the old church across the street.

Box noted where I was looking. She loved secrets like this. She dished out surprises like a reality TV show host. "You see where you're looking?"

"At the clock tower?"

"Mm-hmm," said Box. "Now look about thirty feet lower."

There was a group of kids, arms crossed, smoking cigarettes. One of the girls wore an aquamarine minidress and black thigh-high go-go boots. Another was goth, but in a hot undead vampire way, not an emaciated Marilyn Manson way. A third had on a sexy cowboy suit. The boys all looked like Ricky from *My So-Called Life*, nelly and with great hair and over-mascara'ed eyes. I leaned back into the pillowy cotton bunches of our picnic blanket. Box narrated to me.

"They call it the Breakfast Club. They're all recovering alcoholics and drug addicts. And they're all fucking *hot*. Everyone says this meeting is the number one source of sober hookups in the Bay Area. They meet in that old church and everyone sits in the pews. Boys, girls, nobody cares what you are, they just want to get with you. I mean—kids wake up *early* to get here."

"Shit, and nobody even starts *work* that early around here."

"No. I mean—*really* seriously early. Check out that Ricky's makeup."

We gazed, unabashedly checking out the miniskirt girls and the Rickys. From our patch of grass, we were total voyeurs. They flaunted and flamed those paisley shirts and their toned post-teenage bodies, but there was no way we could ever make eye contact, not with that four-lane boulevard between us. It was almost ridiculously safe.

I am not so good at cruising. I'm checking out someone, and the minute she flashes a smile back, my eyes take a sharp Olympic dive into my coffee. When a girl I don't know starts talking to me, I flare up like an infection and I can never reply with more than a mumble.

Box ripped into her bagel with straight, sharp teeth. She ground sesame seeds between her molars, cocking her head to the left to see that go-go boot girl.

"I think I like the boys better," she said, quietly, lost in thought. I was still thinking about how I was too shy to talk to girls I didn't know. Now, I wondered what Box's excuse was.

One afternoon she got a package at the house and I happened to answer the door. The house was an old Mission Victorian and the old wooden doorway was about two and a half feet wide, paint flecking all over, catching in your hair and your clothes when you walked through. I stood between Box and the delivery guy, a squeezed-in third party. She got out her ID and handed it over for the guy to check. When he passed it back, I put out my hand. Box froze and shot me a look. A hostile, get-the-fuck-off kind of look. I pulled away, gave her my best *i-wub-you* shoulder-squeeze, and she rolled her eyes lovingly. We waved goodbye to the delivery guy, who must have thought we were the weirdest domestic partners he'd ever delivered to.

"You really want to see my ID?" Box said, leaning against the door inside.

"Yeah!"

"I never show it to *any*one."

"Ever?"

"Not even bouncers. I always know someone who knows someone. And you really want to see it?"

"I don't *really* want to see it. I mean, I don't *need* to see it or anything."

"I haven't shown it to anyone since Ohio."

Box left Ohio four years ago. She never talks about it.

"Whoa."

"Yeah." She flopped open the gatefold of her wallet, pulled out her ID, and thrust it at me.

The picture that stared back was of a blonde, long-haired hippie chick. One nose had a modest little piercing, not the bull-like septum ring that made Box's face so round and colorful. Her mouth was curled into a warm, naïve smile. The blonde hair looked real, not dyed.

I glanced at the name on the wallet. *Darla Joyce Persofsky.* Box saw my eyes flicker.

"Don't tell anyone," she said. "Ever." She went to grab her license back, but her fingers hesitated one minute, letting me hold onto it, letting the words linger.

Box's friends were all wispy girls with glam-rock hair, thriftstore outfits, and $300 leather steel-toe boots. The girls Box liked were tough-faced construction-worker types with stiff jeans and solid pecs. They weren't boy-dykes. Box was a boy-dyke, short hair and clothes that no one of any respectable gender would touch. These were *men.* They were tougher than biological men. They could kick the ass of an ordinary person just by looking at them wrong. They wore hard rubber dildos that they never took off, or so Box told me, and they made jokes about how bio-men were useless because their cocks weren't always hard.

These men-by-choice would fade in and out of Box's life, sometimes within hours, sometimes over weeks. They treated me either humorlessly, like they didn't get the point of my quiet, docile presence in Box's life, or like they thought I was cute.

At the Lexington Bar, though, Box and I both checked out the femmey girls. We both agreed they were more interesting to watch. Almost all the dykes in the San Francisco scene were butch—soft butch, hard butch, or transitioning. Femmes, anyone in a skirt or lipstick, were a rarity. Whenever a femme walked through the bar doors, the Lex lit up like Christmas. Box's eyes and mine met each other's, like, *it's showtime.* We could spend hours sitting inert, letting our eyes trail after them.

What brought an end to those nights was Box's new daddy.

Drake was a thin, wiry blonde with tight, skinny muscles and a chiseled face. He wore plain white tees and a belt you could just imagine him doing unspeakable things with. A lot of leather daddies wore facial hair stuck on with spirit gum or packed their packages obviously, sometimes cartoonishly.

Drake didn't need to do any of that. He was butch as shit. Even his *eyes* were butch. James Cagney once refused to grow three days' stubble for a movie role. The character was supposed to be low-down trailer trash, and Cagney wanted to be clean-shaven, so he told the director, "I'll *act* the beard." That was how Drake saw life. Sitting at his solitary table at the Lex, watching us fumble for chairs and oversize stools, I could imagine Drake growling at a movie director: "I'll *act* the testosterone."

Things between them developed fast. The pasta and sautéed zucchini that I would cook for dinner sat in serving bowls, uneaten, and I spent more nights at home alone, writing. I talked to Box more on her cell phone than in person. Most of the conversations were about Drake. "I'm not sure if I like him. But I want him so bad." "Does he make you feel good about being with him?" "Yes. I mean, no, he makes me feel *bad*. But I love it when he makes me feel bad." "Then that's *good*, right?" Sometimes, Box or one of her friends would call and tell me what club they were at, and I'd go track them down. Often, Box's posse of dykes were in the middle of the dance floor, and I spotted them first, Boxless. They all looked like freaky punk fifteen-year-olds in their Adidas blue-and-red sweat suits and army camouflage shirts. I danced with them for a while. My tzitzis pogoed up and down as I danced and my girly clothes meshed incognito with the dykes in their flamboyantly gay-man outfits. I always bought girl clothes these days. They were the only shirts that didn't look horribly oversized on my skeletal frame. The dance floor was like a middle ground where their girl-becoming-boy style met my boy-hiding-in-girl style. And then, on the far side of the bar, I spotted Box and Drake.

Neither of them drank. Box usually ordered Virgin Marys and faggy-looking sodas with a cherry floating in the ice. Drake got soda water, but they always served it to him in a beer mug. On the dance floor, you could draw a straight line between the butch dykes and the femme dykes, everything easy and recognizable. Box and Drake made it more complicated, splitting the simple idea of *butch* into fresh-faced boy and dark, ferocious man.

I slid into the empty seat at their table—tonight there was an empty seat—and Box and I grinned at each other. Drake reached over and patted me amiably on the head. It felt a lot kinder than it sounds, almost natural. I felt a shiver of goodwill, like that was Drake's way of saying hi, and, like, I *liked* it. I froze up. What did it mean that I liked to be treated that way? I wondered if I was exuding some docility pheromone and Drake could smell it. Or if he'd been with people like me, and something about me signified to him that I was submissive. Was I submissive? What did that *mean?* Why was I obsessed with every-thing meaning something? I checked the way I was sit-ting, the position of my wrists. Was I talking wrong? Had I lisped or something?

Drake receded into his chair. I looked at Box, con-cerned. She smiled back. I realized she had a black leather collar around her neck, with no unclasping mechanism I could see.

The music was blaring, but the silence at our table was deadly.

"Oh, honey," Drake said, after a minute. "You can talk to Matt. You can always talk to Matt."

"Geez," Box said to me, suddenly animated. "What have *you* been up to tonight? It's fucking good to see you."

Later, in a secret private moment, Drake was on the dance floor, doing his version of a hot dance, which involved holding a long-neck nonalcoholic beer bottle in one hand and grinding between two girls. His posture slumped like a gangster pimp. His free hand rested on one girl's stomach, and his ass jutted into the other's pubic region.

Box, meanwhile, was gushing in my ear.

"Drake *loves* you," she announced. "I told him how close we are and he thinks it's good for me to have someone on the outside to talk to."

"Someone on the outside?" I shouted back.

"You know. Who's not part of our game. Isn't he great?" she yelled above the music.

"Sure," I said, "if Eminem turns you on."

"What did you say?"

"He's great," I mouthed, nodding my head to the music.

Box waited, dancing in her seat. We watched Drake on the floor with the two girls, heating up. The girl in front was leaning back into him, her eyes closed, rubbing against his breasts. Box's eyes gleamed. She watched them intently.

I felt this weird combination of disgusted and turned on, and being turned on confused me. "Box," I asked, "doesn't it bother you that Drake is grinding with other girls?"

"No," Box replied brightly. "Drake is going to take me home and make me fuck his ass with all the sexual energy that we build up."

I thought of Ahuva, only checking her emails once a week, of our sporadic phone calls that, when we managed to find each other at home, lasted hours, all our accumulated stories pouring out. Rabbi Shmuley Boteach says in *Kosher Sex* that it's not forbidden to notice hot girls on the street, as long as you know your wife is the hottest of all and it makes you look forward to coming home to her.

I didn't totally understand the mechanics of it yet—like, would seeing another woman's breasts make me impatient to touch my wife's breasts?—but I figured I still had time to work it out.

"So you're happy?"

"I'm happy," Box said.

"I'm glad," I said.

I didn't see Box at all for the next few weeks. I moved out of my sublet and found a permanent place a few blocks away, on the other side of the Mission. I emailed Box my new address and stuff, and asked how things were. Box wrote back a two-line reply that said, "Daddy is treating me well and i am happy he lets me be his favorite play toy slaveboi." I winced.

That email marked every inch of the distance between us.

I was about to delete Box's email right off the screen when I saw that there was a second page. I scrolled way, way down to find the single line, printed in the smallest font ever: "Congratulate me! I started T."

T meant testosterone, and in Box's world, getting the go-ahead for hormonal treatment was like getting the Legion of Honor. You had to see a doctor for months before you could even get considered for approval to go on testosterone. Besides the intense regimen of routine physicals, you also had to see a psychiatrist. The psychiatrist had questioned Box and Drake's relationship as much as I had, maybe more—but she said that, theoretically, it had the capacity to be a mentally healthy relationship. It seemed like the extreme-sports version of role-playing, but, you know, Dungeons and Dragons helped me get assertive when I was a kid in summer camp.

Seeing Box in the actual flesh was totally another matter. His phone was always off, and I could never hear the house phone ring. He never went to the Lex anymore, since he didn't drink and didn't need to pick up girls. I walked by the old house, where I could see Box's bedroom window. Like most of us back then, Box never really slept. When he was in there alone, dark blue and white Christmas lights illuminated his room. When he had company, he swathed the room in red Christmas lights.

Tonight it was black.

He finally called me, early one evening, four weeks to the day after that last night at the Lex. His voice had the fuzziness of a cell phone in an office building, but even with that, he sounded low and husky. It wasn't like his voice had changed; more, it sounded like the same voice with bass added. It had the same treble and tone plus a new low end. He asked me how I was doing and if I'd gotten any new temp jobs, and about Ahuva. I quickly changed the subject.

"What have you been doing?" I asked, and that was all Box needed. His voice hit the high end as it spilled out, what he'd been working on. He burbled and burbled about some intangible thing, how great it felt and how exhilarating, and something about getting dirty. At first I thought he was talking about Drake. Then he said something about uniforms, and I said, what about Drake's uniforms?

"Not Drake," he said. "My tranny wrestling league."

The first competition took place on one of the first Sunday afternoons in spring, at 2:30 in the afternoon, which was early for most of us. Even people without day jobs felt the exhilaration and slow burn of Saturday nights, and on Sundays, our mornings started even later than usual. I told Box we should say 1:00 and people could bring brunch, but Box vetoed it. He said people would be getting up early enough as is.

"Early?" I asked.

"Yeah," Box said. "Like, Breakfast Club early."

We started going out again, promoting at the Lexington and Badlands and the Café. Box, given a task to do, embellished it vigorously, handing out cards and flirting with strangers like nobody's business. Tranny wrestling, at first a way to get Box's crowd of friends involved in his new passion, grew to include this new extended family of whoever wanted in. Sunday afternoon was the new Saturday night in the Mission, or you'd think so from the way people talked about it: Who was going. Who they were bringing. What they were going to wear.

I stood in front of the altar that was my closet, actually a column of dark gray plastic milk crates containing my T-shirts, jeans, and Shabbos clothes folded and stacked in little compartments. Bright neon yellows and oranges and blues shone, beckoning me the way blank paper calls to an artist, whispering *Mold me. Mix me. Make me your slate, and draw yourself into the shape you want to be.*

And I whispered back: All I wear is T-shirts and jeans. How is that going to make me a creature unlike any other?

My wardrobe answered me, *Well, shit, Matthue. I guess that means your personality will have to do the trick.*

I woke up at noon that day, showered and prayed, then spent an hour making hash browns for breakfast. Left the house at 2:00, realized that everyone would be fashionably late, and so I went back inside and checked my email for another thirty minutes.

Mission Park was the kind of place that law enforcement ignored. Vagrants, homeless teenagers, and winos slept in there, even though the rusty old sign outside said it closed at dusk. Common cop wisdom was, the trouble that happened inside Mission Park would stay inside

Mission Park as long as you didn't rattle the cradle. They were mostly right. The gates to the park, always locked, had rusted over. To enter, you had to crawl in through a sheath of gate that had been peeled aside like a six-foot-tall can of sardines.

When I got there, though, things were already jumping. I crawled through the gate and emerged in the middle of a basketball game. Box's friend Stash was playing. She had the ball. Three other girls hustled on her back. I didn't recognize any of them.

When they spied me, Stash clasped the ball in her arms and whistled to the sidelines. A sweaty, athletic-looking girl with a curly afro and '80s-style fuzzy wristbands jogged up. "Yeah?"

"This is Matt. He's on your team. Matt, that's Ames and Corrina. They're on your team. Now look alive."

She checked me the ball. It thudded on the dull black concrete. I checked it back.

I could feel the hustle of people jogging into position behind me.

Stash tried to pass around me. I pitched my body left, into her path. I made a play for the ball.

Stash's head twisted, following me. I got her confused, and her dribble got sloppy and out of control, but she managed to knock the basketball to the right. I lunged for it, but it was out of my reach. Halfway down the court, the girl with the afro snatched it. Nobody was even close to her.

She moved fast. The afro girl ripped the ball into the box of her personal space, dribbled it up, and jumped for the net. Her body dangled there, frozen in midair in a perfect vertical layup pose.

Then, from nowhere, this girl with a foot-high beehive in a yellow-and-purple Lakers minidress appeared.

She vaulted through the air, hand outstretched, the

basketball hovering at ground zero. Her hand hooked neatly over the ball. She caught it, brought it down to the Earth as she fell, pulled it close to her body, and transitioned into an easy dribble.

She spun around, did a quick rebound, and made an easy, clean three-point shot.

Beehive Girl was fabulous.

I'd been on top of Stash through the whole round. We were both sweating through our shirts. The ball, having swished, rolled away to a quiet concrete corner of the basketball court.

"Smoke break," announced Stash. The cigarette already dangled from her mouth.

We sat against the gate in a ring, me, Stash, Ames, and Beehive Girl. She snapped a pair of sunglasses onto her face, big and tacky and retro, with a leopard-print pattern around the edges. At first I thought she was a cross-dresser. As Stash grumbled about the play, Beehive Girl fished through a new blue sports bag until she produced a shiny green bottle. She tilted her head back and downed a deep shot. It was a fifth of whiskey. "You want some?" she asked me. Dazed, I looked from the bottle to her glasses to her breasts. You could see her squashed-up cleavage. She was real.

"Sure," I said, dazedly, hitting the bottle.

"That's Corrina," Stash explained, taking the fifth from my hand as soon as I'd downed a swallow. "She plays in heels. It makes it fair for the other kids."

I nodded. Another few shots of whiskey and I'd understand perfectly.

So there we sat, swilling whiskey and smoking cigarettes. This was our first-quarter break from basketball. Less than ten points into the game, and we were already distorting our vision and filling our lungs with heavy, dead air.

"Have you seen the rest of the park?" asked Stash. I hadn't. I mean, there was one time I went with this friend-slash-poetry idol to buy coke around the corner, but I hadn't actually ever seen the park.

"Not in daylight," I murmured.

"What?" Stash wasn't really paying attention to me. Instead, her eyes were taking in Corrina and the slow toke of her inhalation. Her cheeks caved in and her lips pursed out. You could hear the air being sucked out of everybody's lungs in pining sighs.

"Nothing," I said, and got up to wander around.

There were actually children in the sandbox, a few stray women standing around watching over them. The entire children's area smelled like pee, but welcome to American public parks, and anyway, it could have been a lot worse than just the smell.

The rest of the park was the confusing part. Aside from a few drunks (the middle-aged, homeless kind), the park was dotted with fluorescent Day-Glo dykes. Evie wore a pair of Salvation Army–colored '70s coveralls with the number 69 emblazoned innocently across her chest. Pony wore a bikini and water wings. Box wore a sport jacket, a thin black tie, a neon pink shirt, black shorts, and pink striped tights with his platform shoes. They were all crowded in a semicircle on the plush, overgrown green grass. I ran up to Pony and some other kids and dove into the grass beside them.

"Matt!" Pony squealed. "It's so great you came. Did you get a number yet?"

I looked up. The sun blinded me. Pony took a step to the left, blocking out the radiance, and her face against the bright blue sky looked imperial, like this day. In the background was a big chart, matches and winners, and another big cardboard diagram labeled RULES FOR WRES-TLERS.

"I, uh," I stammered, "I think I'm just gonna be a cheerleader today."

Pony looked half confused, half determined to persuade me to change my mind. As a sign of my determination, I hugged her. Hugs were the easiest, most direct way to remind all Box's queer friends that I was safe. It reminded them of my scrawny frame and that, if I ever started acting assholically boyish, they could tip me over without much effort.

A shadow cast over both our heads.

"No wrestling for you, big boy?" said a low and even voice.

I stood slowly, drunkenly. It was Kathryn.

But Kathryn as I'd never seen her before. When we lived together (Kathryn, the intimidator—did we ever *live* together? I felt like history must be lying), she always said she was into bondage, but I never believed her. The way she talked about being a member of a bondage group, I thought it was like a yoga team.

But today she wore leather boots that strapped up to her thighs, four-inch heels that glowed black in the daylight. She had on a blood-red bustier that swelled her breasts into monstrous, formidable mountains and matched her lipstick eerily. And—and this is the stuff that sticks in your head forever, the too-crazy-to-lie-about-it details—she wore a pale-blue tutu.

She leaned over—the edge of her round tutu created a rim to lean over—and gave me a firm, careful hug. I squeezed back with my encroached neck and chin.

"Good to see you," said Kathryn. She seemed to mean it. "I've got to go. I'm the ring girl today, I made cards and everything. But I'll see you in the ring—you're wrestling, right?"

Before I could answer, she was off.

We settled down to watch the first round. It was Pony

versus Stash. Stash was a wiry boy in a sleeveless army shirt, and she was nimble. But Pony was just an asshole about competition. When Stash threw her to the ground, Pony let out a squeal, started biting and kicking, and even kicked Stash between the legs. Stash had trouble walking for a few days after that. Pony thrashed out with her water wings and breasts until Stash sat down to rub her eyes. Box, the referee, slammed the ground and did the count. Stash was down for ten. She was out.

The next two wrestlers were getting warmed up, Box psyching up the crowd. Kathryn pulled Pony's arm in the air and pumped a fist of victory beside a big yellow sign that said ROUND 2. I got to my feet. The quarter break had to be over by now. My alcohol-dazed mind didn't connect that I was sitting with all my former game mates. I gave a little wave to Box, turned around, and tried to figure out where the basketball court was.

"Hey, Matt. Where are you going?"

I spun around. Slowly, slowly. It was Drake.

"Hey," I grinned weakly.

He walked up, laid an arm across my shoulder, and walked with me. "I want to hit the basketball game," I told him, very honest and eager.

Drake looked over my shoulder. "Bad news, Matt," he said. "I think you missed the game."

I felt my stomach fall. I'd been gunning myself up for the game. The fresh-shaved grass smell was like the first day of spring, steeping my bones in that jumpy, adrenalized feeling of wanting to get my groove back on the court. And also, queer pickup basketball was my only guaranteed escape from getting slammed to the ground by dykes twice my size.

"That's okay," I mumbled.

"No, it's not. Come on." Drake wrapped his arm into a headlock and pulled me over to the court.

This gang of neighborhood kids—"neighborhood" meaning they weren't white and they were all probably born here—had half the court. They were wearing actual basketball jerseys and headbands and sneakers that they could probably move in. I had on my $20 Chuck Taylors, which were made out of canvas and flat as a board. Drake wore tall lace-up Doc Martens boots, which were perfect for hiking and hunting but probably did him no favors on the basketball court.

Drake whisked the ball from Corrina's sports bag. I stood near the half-court line and he checked it to me. The ball flew in a perfect V. Drake's hands. Ground. My hands.

I started a slow jog across the court, keeping the ball tight. Drake jogged along, hunched over, his arms flitting around me easy, ready to take the ball if I let it loose.

I pulled back, feinted left, ran right, and tried an easy shot off the backboard. It bounced off. I could feel my arm wiggle. I wondered if it was nervousness or drunkenness.

Drake was on the ball, ready to catch it, but I squeezed in. I was smaller and more agile. I seized the ball, did a quick revision layup, and swished it.

"Nice job," Drake grinned, clapping, as he ran to half-court and opened his palms to receive the ball. I tossed it to him. He spun it around his waist, it lingered for a second in his hand, and then he ran.

Drake was good. He wasn't a showoff, and I could tell he was taking it easy on me. He never took the easy shots, always went for the confrontation, didn't push me out of the way or feint around me even though I would have been no match for him sober. Certainly in this condition, I was less of an obstacle than his boots, even. But Drake played well, following that good sportsmanship code you always hear about. He was like the top athlete in junior high school. While all the nearly best kids were slamming you against the bleachers and taking the easy points, the number one kid always gave compliments freely, and gave the assists to the under-dogs.

Drake cheered for me when I got shots, and never gloated at his victories. He told me when I threw like a girl, and we both laughed. "Doesn't that count as sexist?" I asked. He grinned guiltily but didn't say anything like that again. Some of the biggest sexists can be natural-born women. But they know when to push it and when to leave it alone.

"Hold your hand like this," he said, pantomiming shooting a basket.

"Isn't that what I was doing?" I mimicked him, throwing the ball a foot in the air, then catching it on the way down.

"Nah, you were going like *this*." Drake's wrist flipped weaker. "You're not giving it direction."

"I'm not giving it direction?"

"Flick your wrist to the left or to the right. Push more on one side of your fingers. Try it."

"Push more on my fingers." I repeated Drake's words, puzzling the meaning out of them.

"What are you, drunk?" Drake said. "Come on. Try that shot again."

Sporadically he would stop the game, make me retake a shot, and each time my mind learned something new about basketball. I could feel my brain changing shape. I could feel myself getting good at basketball.

Some other kids, the first-round losers from the wres-tling match, along with some other dykes who just didn't care about wrestling, came over to the court. Drake del-egated teams, appointing each new person to one team or the other. As it fell, we both were the team captains.

We also covered each other, blocking and dodging when one of us had the ball, hovering over each other in case of a pass.

The game went spectacularly. I don't know when we started keeping score and when we stopped, but soon the game evolved into a frenzy. We yelled out directions at the other team. We yelled at our own team. Box started playing in his platforms. Stash, who was utterly drunk by this time, ran into the game, took on both teams, made her own plays, and after sinking two layups with no problem, tripped over her own shoelaces, the ball fell down, and she began kicking it like a soccer ball. "That's *shit!*" yelled Corrina, who couldn't decide whether to cheer or be on a team. She grabbed the arm of Pony, still in her bikini, who was next in line to wrestle, and she charged Stash. Corrina and Pony took her on. Stash aimed the ball, kicked it into a wide arc in the air, and it landed squarely in the center of the basketball hoop.

From across the court, the burly Latino guys whistled.

"Go!" yelled Drake, and a bunch of dykes who actually had teams leaped on the ball and fought for it ferociously.

Then, for no particular reason, Pony and her wrestling partner started wrestling. In the middle of the basketball game. I chased after the ball, too. I suddenly remembered I was supposed to make this a valiant fight. I was a basketball player now.

"Attaboy," said Drake, tousling my hair as we ran across the court.

Hours later, Box and Drake and I sat around a table at the Lexington with a couple of other kids from the game. We drank cold beer. Rather, we didn't drink it, we held it up to our foreheads, pressed our palms against the glasses, lowered our chins near the surface, and felt the icy glow. Our combined sweat pierced the bar and made everything smell like stale cheese. Drake tilted his bottle toward me.

"You're not bad, you know," he said. "You got those Iverson genes. Keep working them, and you could have yourself a decent game."

"My game's already decent," I protested. "I'll take you any motherfucking day of the week, Drake."

Drake didn't laugh, although I kind of wanted him to. He stuck one firm hand across the table for me to shake. "You're on."

"You're on."

Corrina came over, her Lakers minidress stained with sweat, but she still looked like a million dollars. Her heels were unwobbling, her posture was immaculate, and her breasts were still like two police sirens, perfect and bright and inevitable. She picked up Drake's beer bottle, drained it, and flung herself into a chair.

"How do you get your hair to stay up like that, Corrina?" I asked.

"Willpower," she said. "Pure fucking willpower."

She pulled off the beehive and it gave easily. Strands of hair stuck out of place, but the whole mound, twisted in its intricate pattern, stayed in one congealed clump. She put it on the floor next to Drake's motorcycle helmet.

We drank. We didn't talk much. When we did, conversation came in small, abstract bits. We'd just sweated so many calories in a few hours of basketball and wrestling and sexual tension that now our brains had basically shut down. It was as if we were asleep, but instead of snoring, we drank beer.

Corrina and Pony were giving each other the eye, and you could tell there was footplay involved. Drake was over at the bar picking up another round, and he'd gotten into a conversation about motorcycles with a burly, moustached biker. Box was sitting there, staring at me, totally dead to the world. Exactly the way I felt. He leaned over, put one hand on my chest, and asked if I was feeling okay. I was feeling so much more than okay.

"Hey, Box," I said, "will you give me boy lessons?"

"Boy lessons?"

"Yeah. I think I like this being-a-boy thing. Will you show me how to do this shit, playing sports and all?"

Box grinned. "I think I can do that."

6

how to be a boy

The first friends I made in San Francisco were all dykes. Then they all started becoming boys.

Part of that change was the normal ebb and flow of the waves of friendship, meeting people and then meeting their friends and dumping the people you started out with, but that's not what I mean.

Short hair, dumpy combat slacks—all that was standard dress code for a Mission dyke without a desk job. Then a funny thing happened. Their voices started changing and their mannerisms became brusque. They went from butch to butcher-than-butch and then, before you knew it, they were getting testosterone injections and their chests were more hairy than mine.

I was a natural-born boy, and I'd spent most of my childhood hiding from people who looked like that. I'd moved three thousand miles to get away from muscley men and football season and dates where I was expected to pay and put the moves on girls who didn't like me but feared growing old alone. I was happy to be in a place where I could be quiet and timid and not have to know who was running for the Eagles every week.

And here I was on a crisp Tuesday afternoon in San Francisco, facing off against Drake and a bunch of his clones on a half-size hilltop basketball court in the heart of Corona Heights.

Drake and I patted each other on the back, running across the court between plays. We called each other names during the game, *bitch* and *cocksucker* and *dillweed,* and it felt like bonding. I missed an easy pass—"Put in the contacts, Roth, and tie your fuckin' shoes!"—and Drake's three-pointer fell short. I told him to stop playing like a girl.

In Northeast Philly, when we played basketball, it had taken me till I was twelve to convince the other kids to pass to me. I couldn't shoot worth a damn, but I was a great runner, and I could duck out of anybody's way. That was my special skill, developed from being beat up so constantly. It was like a mutant power.

In this game, they made passes to me, low and sly, and no matter how tight Drake or Ken or one of the others was on me, I could always skit through and grab the ball. I was like a mole, or a ferret, or one of those fast skinny hole-digging animals in the zoo. But Drake never let me be *that man,* the safe one who always scores the assists. He wanted me to grow a backbone.

"Shoot, asswipe!" he yelled. Corrina, her wig off, hair in a crew cut with an Elvis cowlick, was on me. Her hands shot all over the place, thudded the ball. I had to re-grab the ball to not drop it. I grasped at the bottom. The rubber tore the skin off my fingertips.

"Get open!" I yelled back. Vy and Ken were tight on his ass.

"Fuck yourself!" Suddenly, Drake was on the other side of the court. He tried to duck them, but he was surrounded. There was no way he was getting anywhere near this basket.

I twisted around. I took a long step, bounced under Corrina's arm and threw her off my back, looped the ball up with my right arm—my bad arm—and watched it loop around the net, roll off the backboard, and clunk on its lackadaisical descent into the hoop.

"Nice one," said Corrina, shoving me on her way to the sidelines. She wiped sweat off her face with one hand, and swiped a beer bottle off the ground with the other. She watched Drake and Ken towel themselves off on the other side, and drained the bottle.

"Too bad you can't make it next week," she said to me as we pulled sweaters on, watching dark fog clouds swoop over the mountains to the west. "Box said it's some Jewish holiday?"

"What?" It was early summer. It was only, like, three weeks after Passover. There wasn't another Jewish holiday scheduled for months.

"That's what Box said. He was using your old calendar at the house and he said next Tuesday, there's a Jewish holiday and we have to make sure someone else comes to basketball."

Observant Jews always pay attention to fast days and biblical holidays, the ones where we can't use electricity or spend money or drive cars. But the minor holidays, like Chanukah and Purim and Tu B'Shvat, can pass by without a blip on the radar if we aren't paying attention.

So I instantly got worried, scammed someone's cell phone, and called the Kaufmanns to find out if I was not supposed to be using electricity or something. If the answering machine picked up, I would get paranoia of the worst kind.

Shira answered. She laughed when I asked her. "It's Lag b'Omer, Moshe Shimon," she told me. "You're allowed to drive, I promise. My father is planning a celebration in the park. Are you going to come?"

I stammered an explanation and got off the phone quickly. Corrina noticed the look on my face. She asked me what was up.

"False alarm," I said, passing the phone back. "Is break over?"

"We're through, Matt," she said. "Have you seen the fog? It's freezing. Drake and Ken and me are grabbing cocktails at the Lex. Are you in?"

"Not today, thanks," I said. "I have to write."

I hadn't seen Box in weeks. He was busy trying to organize tranny wrestling into a citywide activity with a comprehensive website and message board. I'd been going to open mic nights constantly. I'd come home every night sweating from yelling my heart out.

It wasn't that Box and I drifted. It was what happened when slackers stopped slacking—they had life to carry them along. And our lives, while not in different places, weren't headed in parallel directions.

And that was how Drake became our umbilical cord.

I passed through the doors of my building, climbed three stories to my apartment, pulled the bathroom door shut, and ripped off my clothes. In the distance, I could hear the phone ringing. It stopped abruptly as the jet of hot water shot on.

Twenty minutes later, I slipped out of the shower, pulled the towel over my head, and from the dead silence of my apartment the phone rang again. I scrambled into enough of my clothes and ran to grab the phone.

"Roth."

"Box."

"Good to fucking hear your voice."

"Get a last name."

"It's a one-name deal. Like Prince and Dubya and Zsa Zsa. Do you miss me as much as I miss you?"

"More. Zsa Zsa's name isn't one word, it's two. How did you know how long I take to shower?"

"I used to *live* with you, dipstick."

"Oh yeah, you did, didn't you."

"Neither of us ever left the house so we saw each other all the time. Now, neither of us ever leaves the house and we never see each other. Is that ironic?"

"I don't think that counts as ironic, Box."

"Whatever. Can I celebrate your Jewish holiday with you next week?"

"What?"

"Lag b'Omer."

"What?" I said.

"The Feast of the Thirty-Third. It's the traditional Jewish day of going out into the woods and playing music and constructing bonfires and frolicking in areas of forestation and meadows and groves outside major urban areas. One popular custom includes eating fresh fruit, especially pomegranates and figs and dates."

That was Box, not me. Confused as to how exactly Box had become such an authoritative voice on Lag b'Omer, I held my breath. I waited.

"It's also the birthday of this dude. Simon ben something."

"Rabbi Shimon bar Yochai?"

"Him!" Box squeaked decisively, and I pulled the phone away from my ear.

"Should I ask?" I said into the receiver.

"I *had* twenty-three minutes to do research," Box

Shimon bar Yochai's birthday. Actually, it was the anniversary of his death. We still celebrate it. Go fig.

murmured defensively.

"Box, you're the best. You are the absolute best and I miss you like fuck."

"That's a yes?"

"Yes *please.*"

"Cool!" Box exclaimed. "Now I have to go, I'm preparing the message board. You should log in and post something. WWW dot Boxology slash wrestle."

I tried to explain how my computer wasn't hooked up and I usually had bad luck with message boards, but Box had to run, anyway. And I could always practice my performance poems more.

I was spending an inordinate amount of time alone. And I guess this is a common phenomenon among castaways and hostages, but people who spend most of their time alone start talking to themselves. I don't know if it was coincidence that this is when I really started writing poems in earnest, putting gallons of thought into finding the most effective way to talk to myself. Internal rhymes. Rhythms like an '80s hip-hop song. Finding topics that were not clichés—if I was going to write a love poem, it was not allowed to be about love. I wrote about wanting a girlfriend who would let me fall asleep while she was talking and not get mad. I wrote poems about my favorite food, olives. I wrote a poem called "Good Thing I Don't Touch Girls (or I'd Touch You)."

I learned the streets of the Mission, practicing these poems. At first I walked around with sheets of computer paper I'd printed out and stolen from temp jobs. As I started memorizing the poems, I left the papers at home, and walked down Mission Street like an institutionalized homeless person, reciting panegyrics off the top of my head. I started leaving the Mission, crossing over into other neighborhoods as side streets wound into circles and flat bayside Mission streets turned into Castro hills.

I still had a little money saved from my year and a half at a day job in Washington. Temping was keeping me afloat for a while, and working all day on poems felt like an investment. Only, I knew it would never pay off. Even if I became the open mic king of the city, there was only so far that could go.

Box and I walked to the M streetcar, the one that went to Stern Grove. We walked there the long way because then we crossed through Church Street in the Castro, where all the platinum blond waiters hung outside Sparky's Diner, smoking and vogueing and looking like a bunch of beautiful androids. I had Box's roommate's African drum strapped to my back with two itchy straw ropes. We got to the station, slid our passes through, and climbed on the train as I warned Box about Jewish events. "They're weird and socially awkward and there's a bunch of people, like stockbrokers and shit, who you have nothing in common with except being Jewish. And there'll be kids."

Box was grinning like an alligator. "Except I'm not Jewish."

"I said, there will be kids."

Box feigned shock. "I *am* a kid."

"Box!"

"I'm fine! I'll be good, I swear."

Now, the minute Box said *I'll be good* is the minute I started to worry in earnest. Before that, taking Box seemed like a good idea. Box was my best friend.

But this was Box. And Box was unpredictable.

Today Box was dressed curiously toned-down, in three-quarter-length army pants and a baggy beige polo shirt. I guess it was another kind of drag for him: regular prep boy. When Box was a girl, he could never dress like a girl, even though girls have so much more freedom in what they're allowed to wear. I always bitched him out over that. I grew up on the East Coast. I always wanted that freedom. Growing up, I had a drawer with a bunch of T-shirts and a drawer with fancy slacks, and that was about it.

That day was warm in the Mission, but as soon as we were past the Castro hills, the ocean winds started freezing the world around us. I had on baggy raver jeans and a baby T-shirt, with only my wool tzitzis as an undershirt between me and the elements.

It was midafternoon when we got off the train. Stern Grove was way out near the Pacific, stuck between rows and rows of identical near-the-beach homes that reminded me of the Jersey shore. All of them had awnings, and their stucco walls were all painted the mint green or pale pink of a box of salt-water taffy.

Across the street, huge redwood trees rose from the ground and sloped down below the level of the road. Stern Grove wasn't like a hill or a valley. From street level, the forest looked like it was sinking into the ground.

Near the ocean, it was always about to rain. The sky hung low and foggy over the redwoods, and the branches drooped, leaves turned toward the ground as if they were frowning at us dully. A walking ramp wound around the trees, progressing downward into the grove. We traipsed down, half walking, half running, the way kids do when the slope gets too narrow and vertical to navigate by ordinary strides. The path kept splitting onto nature trails.

We followed the concrete. We could smell hot dogs roasting, could see the inverse cone of smoke rising up on the other side of the clearing. There were cars parked haphazardly on the grove floor, trampling grass into flat patches like crop circles. I stifled a groan. The people who rode cars through the park like the grass was disposable—yeah, those were my people.

There was already a small crowd. Yuppies—men with

corporate-logo baseball caps and plastic shoelace-tied safe-
ty glasses, women in smart pumps and polo shirts—stood
wistfully around the fire. Lag b'Omer is one of the few happy Jewish holidays, when you go into the forest and roast
marshmallows and celebrate being free. The name literally
means the thirty-third day of the Omer, which is a seven-
week daily count that starts during Passover, and symbol-
izes the seven weeks of sacrifices made during the times of
the Holy Temple. Lag b'Omer is also the day—okay, so I
lied about its being singularly joyous—when the students
of Rabbi Akiva stopped dying out from the plague. Lag
b'Omer is a traditional day for weddings. Two-year-old
boys have their first haircut on Lag b'Omer.

The rabbi in charge was leading me around and introducing me to people whose names all seemed to be Thad.
I was thinking of introducing him to Box, although Hasidic rabbis are not generally known for their enthusiasm
for transgender people. I was still having trouble keeping
Box's gender pronoun straight. I doubted the rabbi could
handle it.

Box shot me a worried look. I tried to look all confident. I thought of my friend Mike's crazy dog when we
were growing up who would roar his head off whenever I
came over. His mother said, *Dogs can smell fear*. You had
to project confidence.

Nonchalant. Steady. I remembered, I am an Orthodox Jew. There is nobody here who knows the rules
better than I do. I walked as if I owned the park. "Hey,
Rabbi!" I called out.

"Moshe Shimon!" the rabbi shot back. "Can you un-
roll the volleyball net?"

I had my mouth open to introduce Box.

"*Now,* Moshe Shimon," he prodded.

I looked at the rabbi. I looked at the people facing me.
I was going to protest, but there was no good reason for

me to stick around and shmooze with yuppies.

So I trotted off obediently to the meadow. Box followed in my footsteps, flashing the rabbi a quick salute.

We found Jacob, a stone's throw away from the pile of iron beams and patchwork netting, lying in the grass with two girls. Their hands were folded over their stomachs and they all stared up at the sky. I walked into Jacob's field of vision, looked down at him, and blinked. "Don't you have a job to do?"

"Fuck that shit," Jacob said. "Have you checked out the sky?"

Jacob had the vestigial tracings of a beard—tweezed curlicues of hair that sprouted from his fifteen-year-old face like roots springing from a potato. It looked like a Hasidic beard. Hasidim aren't allowed to shave, and from about fourteen till twenty, they have baby beards that never quite fill in. Jacob wasn't a Hasid, but he'd just started becoming observant. He hung out at the Kaufmanns' house on Shabbos, dressed like a rude boy, in two-tone checkerboard ties and sport coats that made you wonder whether he was dressing up or making fun of people who dressed up.

Today he wore a sky-blue and orange gas station shirt that said *Earl* on a sewn patch, jeans cut off at the calf, bright purple Chuck Taylor shoes. He stuck his hand out for me to shake. "This is Box," I said. Jacob transferred his hand without otherwise moving. "A pleasure," he said.

He introduced us to Darcy and Stella. Darcy was lanky and tall, six inches taller than Jacob, with big eyes that took in everything. Stella was shorter, packed in layers of hoodie, flaming red-and-gold-streaked hair.

We made a circle in the grass next to the volleyball net, still inert, although nobody seemed to mind. We lazily tossed a blue and yellow beach ball. Darcy and Stella watched us. I think they were still trying to decide whether we were cool older people or just weird.

"So," Jacob said, "Matthue tells me your name is Box."

"Uh, yeah." Box swallowed. He shot a sideways glance at me.

"Cool name."

"Thanks. I made it myself."

"You know, that's cool," said Jacob. "I want to change my name. At first I was just going to take the Hebrew name, but my Hebrew name is Jacob too, only you pronounce it weird. If I'm going to change my name, why not change it to something new, like Hamburger or Flash? Hamburger is ironic. Because I'm a vegetarian. Hey Matthue, did you see if they were cooking yet?"

That was how Jacob talked, like a roller coaster. You had to hang on or else you could get flung overboard.

Like a sixth sense, Darcy's head perked up, then swiveled toward the bushes at the far end of the park. We followed her gaze to see a skinny black figure emerging. He walked with a swagger, his body whisper-thin, tight black jeans, a plaid tartan skirt, and a black leather jacket spiked and studded with band pins. His hair was a thin mohawk, dyed in alternating shades of fuchsia and green. Darcy and Stella ran to hug him, and then he sauntered over and hugged Jacob.

The kid had one of those faces that never grows old, an acne-traced, five o'clock–shadowed baby face. Jacob told me his name was Nail.

"Yeah," said Nail, gripping my hand. "That's me."

He pumped my hand vigorously, a strength that I couldn't match. Darcy and Stella watched him the way girls watch movie characters. But Nail was back to Jacob. "Show me around," he said, and Jacob led him off toward the grill, which had just started smelling like carbon-crispy veggie burgers.

I turned back to the field. Box slid down from his

perch on the ladder. He pulled the final knot taut. "There. Volleyball is officially in the house."

The kids cheered. The rabbi, who had just walked over, folded his arms and, under his Hasidic layers of beard, nodded fondly.

They were selling burgers and hot dogs, but because we'd helped out, we got ours for free. The rabbi made Box's hot dog personally, dumping extra handfuls of potato chips onto the plate like a reward. "Praise God, all the *goyim* should be this helpful and friendly," the rabbi announced to everyone around, and Box struck a muscleman pose.

My cheeks turned a bright ketchup red.

Then the rabbi fixed Nail a plate of food, because Nail never showed up at these things and he wanted Jacob's friends to feel at home. He made Nail put on a yarmulke to say a blessing over the food, though. As they negotiated, I snuck around and helped myself to a veggie burger from the one corner of the grill that wasn't dripping with meat juice. Nail was arguing that he couldn't wear a yarmulke with his mohawk. Eventually they compromised. Nail wore a white polyester yarmulke impaled on his hair, floating like a ghost a foot above his head, hovering and disembodied in the early evening light.

Somehow, the bonfire got lit. Its massive light drew us there. The crowd had swelled. Families huddled together in the chill night, watching embers shoot out from the fire. The teepee of firewood was six feet tall, dangerous and impressive, like a house of fire. Faces were silhouetted in the darkness.

"Nail, back up," said Jacob. "That shit could set your hair on fire like Michael Jackson."

Nail, curious, leaned toward the fire even farther.

Box rolled his eyes, but kept his attention on Nail.

I stepped closer to Box, apprehensive. Jacob and Darcy sat on a log, arms wrapped around each other, and I kept thinking about what would happen later that night when one of their parents would pick them up and they had to go home. How long had it been since I had to be anywhere? I was farther from having someone to go home with than I'd ever been.

Box looked at me.

"Matt," he said, "are you thinking too much again?"

I nodded dumbly.

He pushed me toward the fire. "Go at it," he told me. "Where's your drum?"

I stumbled forward. People were singing Jewish folk songs and the wordless harmonies of Hasidic nigguns. Some of the Modern Orthodox women were joining in, and the Hasidic boys looked nervous. Rabbi Mendy called me over. He was a Hasidic rabbi in the Castro, but he was my age, and we were kind of friends. He was sitting by the fire, right up in front, banging on my drum in a rhythm that was one beat behind the rest of the crowd, trying to catch up. He told me it was his first night ever playing the drums. His two-year-old daughter Golda sat on his lap, tapping out beats on the rim. The two of them together, teaching themselves to play, was the coolest, wildest thing in the universe. I didn't want to take back my drum and break that perfection. But Mendy insisted. He raised Golda in his arms and swirled her around the bonfire and I wished that I was

We were kind of friends. I mean, except for the rabbi thing, we were totally friends. It was just weird to have a friend who was also a rabbi. I imagine it must be like having your father be a senator. You can't just call up and ask them for girl advice or say "fuck" in front of them without also saying "fuck" in front of God—except, I'd be more willing to say "fuck" to God, who would know what I was talking about, than to a respectable (and legit) member of society.

that young, that I could have memories as good and pure and simple as this.

I sat with my drum and listened to the other drummers and the singers and I tried to blend into the song. My palms flapped against the leather drumskin, my eyes half closed, singing the yodelly niggun loops of the Shimon bar Yochai song with everyone else. I listened until I couldn't hear my own drum beat at all.

Jacob's father drove down the hill and swept himself and Darcy away in a red sports car, and they waved goodbye. Nail and Stella had disappeared into the night. Box and I hiked back up to street level in a crowd of Hasidim kids in their black hats. We crossed Sloat Boulevard, blazing with the light of a million suburban commuter cars momentarily frozen by the red light at the intersection.

"Is this what civilization is like?" I asked Box.

"It's okay, dude," he reassured me. "Now we have a backup plan."

We waited on the side of the road for the Muni streetcar as cars swept by us. The streetcar rolled up and we collapsed into our seats. I rested my chin on the drum.

At the last stop before the streetcar dipped underground, this teenage gang boarded. Eight or nine guys, big guys, all in matching clothes, bandannas around their wrists. Box had just taught me about flagging, where different-colored handkerchiefs symbolize different sexual deviancies. I was pretty sure that wasn't what these meant.

Two of them stuck by each set of doors on the car. The others hung out in the center of the aisles, walking

Handkerchiefs symbolize different sexual deviancies. "What, like Boy Scout merit badges?" I had asked Box. He replied, in a single breath: "Blue is bondage, red is fisting, yellow is for golden showers and pee play, black is domination. If it's in your left pocket, it means you want to be on top; right is bottoming."

back and forth, just looking hardass. One of them slid into a seat across from Box and me.

We made uneasy, tenuous eye contact.

He nodded.

Box nodded back at him.

"That your drum?" he asked me.

I nodded.

"Let me try?" His knuckles clenched and unclenched, clung to the knees of his baggy corduroys.

I swung it over to him.

He ran his palms over the surface of the drum, feeling it out, wax on, wax off. His knuckles clenched. Slowly, he started etching out a rhythm. He played with his fingertips, glossing the surface of the drum, barely touching the skin. His head moved imperceptibly with the beat. The other kids in the aisle stood still, then sat, watching him, like they were remembering bonfires of their own.

"This is a Ghana drum," the kid told me. "She come from a village near the Bushmen lands. You play her when the moon is full and you help the moon to not be ashamed, it will let everything hang out. You know?"

"I know," I said.

He looked me in the eye. "You know?"

"I know," I said, meeting his eyes without blinking.

"Yeah. Yeah, you do know."

The train swelled to a halt. The tunnel lights outside froze in place. We all jerked forward, like God had italicized the world, and then we sat straight again.

The kid rapped his knuckles on the head of the drum as if he was nibbling with his fingers. One palm scraped the leather hide and then he dove into a beat, something wild and feral. His rhythm peaked and the train swung into motion. I made eye contact with the kid. He nodded like he expected that all along.

They left at the next stop. Our new friend spun the

drum back into my grip, jumped up, and scampered off the train at the next stop. I glanced at the seat where he'd been squatting.

Sitting there was a little fist-sized stuffed animal.

"Go on," said Box. "He left it for you."

I was about to ask how he left it for me. I could have sworn the seat was empty when he jumped off.

Box pinched my ass. I leaped up, and, suddenly standing, I leaned over and picked it up. It was a porcupine. It really wasn't any bigger than my palm. Soft, hairlike pieces of felt rose up for its spikes.

"You think so?" I asked Box. He was a boy now, but he still had that girl's sense of magic.

"Sure," he said. "Name it Log."

"Log?"

"Like Log b'Omer." He said it the way my family in Philadelphia did, like *log* in English.

The train stopped again, our stop. The doors slid open, and a drowsy, lamplit world stared at us.

I slipped the drum straps back over my shoulders and followed Box the long way home.

7

hit reset

On September 10, 2001, C. D. made a picnic lunch for two. We sat in a garden on the roof of the tallest building in San Francisco. I worked at an office job down the street. C. D. had just quit her job as a paralegal to follow her true passion—astrological predictions. Today she had something to tell me.

"My mentor was doing a reading about me and Henrietta," she said. "She looked at my life and she said she couldn't see anything past this week. She said everything was black, like my future was on fire."

"Shit," I breathed out. My spine shuddered, like all these things I didn't believe in were crawling up my back.

"Yeah, for real. Anyway, I just wanted to tell you. In case anything weird happens to me." She stole a rippled pickle slice from my salad and plopped it into her mouth.

Then she changed the subject.

"So how about you?" C. D. asked. "Is the new apartment going okay? Are your roommates as cool as me?"

I told her they were doing the best they could.

That day, before we left the roof, I told C. D. that Rosh HaShana was coming, that I was asking mechila from everyone. I asked if she forgave me for anything I'd done to her, knowingly or unknowingly. It was a simple ritual. Usually it was just a way of getting on my friends' good sides—they said yes, I was absolved, I came off being sensitive, and I got God points for being extra religious.

"I'll think about it," she said.

Then I went back to work, late, but nobody noticed. My job was so boring. Office jobs all are. People expect you to take an hour to type up a letter, and it took me ten minutes, maybe, and for the rest of that hour, I surfed online and wrote tons of emails to my friends. I typed these fabulous stories, somewhere between exaggerations and outright lies, about the bands I saw in concert and the glamorous writer friends whom I met and didn't exactly hang out with, always with one finger on the minimize-screen key.

Frederick, my boss, knocked on my cubicle wall. I made my email screen vanish. I think he knew, but he didn't say anything. Frederick was a mostly good guy. He talked in short sentences and gruff syllables and always squeezed my shoulder when he criticized me, as if he was apologizing. Today he squeezed my shoulder right off. "Matt," he said, "will you come into the conference room with me?"

Asking mechila. Literally, forgiveness, but we use it in a bigger, more meaningful way. The actual phrase from the prayer book, which, in fifth grade, we used to run around asking each other, was "Do you forgive me for everything I've done, intentionally and unintentionally, with or without aforethought, over the past year?"

From anybody else, it would sound like a creepy come-on. From Frederick, it sounded like a bonding experience, which could be even creepier.

It didn't take long. We sat at the end of the long conference table, me at the head, Frederick to my left. He told me I was getting laid off.

That night it got worse. Ahuva had sent me this email a few days earlier, intense the way we always were, and at the end she wrote about getting a tattoo. It was probably a joke. Ahuva liked pushing my buttons. I was learning how to be Orthodox and she was trying to forget how. But one thing was pretty clear, Orthodox people did not get tattoos.

That afternoon, I wrote back. I said, if I got a tattoo, it would be her name. In Hebrew, with Talmudic Rashi letters wrapping around each other like vines.

After work when I checked my email, there was already a reply. Ahuva only checked email once or twice a week, never multiple times on the same day. I clicked it open.

Even if that was a joke, she wrote.

I knew the rest of it.

I scanned the words quick. I closed the email and deleted it before I let it rip my stomach open the way I knew it would.

You know I'm not good at trusting other people. Don't put my name on you. Don't even joke about permanence.

If I ever talk to you again, it's not going to be for years.

I'd just always thought we had each other's backs. I never thought, of all the ex-Orthodox people I knew, she would be so...*parochial.*

I went to bed early that night, thinking, if I was on East Coast time, it would already be the middle of the night.

I'm not going to talk about everything that happened on September 11—planes crashing into the World Trade Center and the Pentagon, the world exploding on daytime TV. The phone lines didn't work. The TVs were only broadcasting from remote transmitters outside the city. I spent all morning on AOL, watching the screen names of my New York friends pop up, and that was how I found out they were alive. Jonas had an internship with a law firm in the World Trade Center that he'd quit the week before. Gavin worked there, but that morning he had a meeting across the street. He was staring out the window behind the CEO's head when the building erupted. My friend Rivkie's sister, eight months pregnant, was working on the thirty-eighth floor. She ran down the stairs like nothing—she was Hasidic, and this was her seventh time being pregnant, so having a twenty-pound stomach was as easy as carrying an extra bag of groceries—she leaped down the stairs, two at a time, and took off toward home without a second thought.

I called Ahuva. I spent an hour with the phone in my hand, dialing the first digits of her number, hanging up, hitting redial. I wanted to see if she was okay. If she wasn't okay, there was nothing I could do about it. America was burning, but the only thing that mattered was this girl who didn't even want to talk to me. I couldn't remember where Silver Spring was or where the University of Maryland was or how far they were from the Pentagon. I hit the last number, heard her answering machine click on, and hung up.

A month before, the host of the open mic at Paradise Lounge had asked me to perform there, and at the time it seemed like the biggest thing in the world. I'd been doing open mics for months. I was always working up to some goal. I don't know what it was but I knew I could get there.

After I hung up on Ahuva's answering machine that night, I thought maybe Paradise Lounge was the goal. When Sean Penn broke up with Madonna, after all, he got onstage at the Paradise and read poems and got booed offstage. More importantly, all my underground poetry heroes went there. Not getting booed off was a goal, but I wanted more. I wanted to show everyone what I was capable of.

I had five days to get ready.

On Tuesday night, worn out from watching the World Trade Center on TV, getting in touch with my family and so much crying, I went to the Notes from Underground open mic. On Wednesday, I went to Brainwash. Thursday was Dalva, in the smoky back room of a Valencia Street bar that was inhabited by yuppie dot-com types on every night except for Thursdays. That was the plan.

Only, on Tuesday night, I met Anastasia, and things kind of changed.

Anastasia was a pixie-girl lesbian with Peter Pan hair and leopard-print cat ears. She only wore clothes that she made herself, most of them with a needle, scissors, and a single sheet of secondhand fabric. Her shirts hung on her shoulders, delicate and carefree, always about to fall off. She played guitar. She sounded like Jewel, only less fake, but with the yodeling. Her voice was high and airy, and in the space of a note, it dropped to a tiger growl. I started the night off doing poems about food, and then my poetry friends came up and read poems about love and stuff. I empathized tremendously.

Then Anastasia came up, and everybody groaned because she had a guitar and we just *knew* she was going to sing awful songs about unrequited straight-girl crushes. Instead she did these fast, acoustic-rocker songs about driving across America and living on the edge of town, plus she was gay, so that scored points with the crowd too.

Anastasia closed with a song called "Tomato Soup." We bonded at once. At the end of the night I was packing up my journals—I always brought, like, twenty journals to readings, I don't know why—and she came up to me and asked what I was doing and I said, whatever you are.

We went to Safeway, the big 24-hour Safeway in the Castro where gay men pick each other up. It's a known fact, there was even an article about it. It was eerily empty, as though everyone in the city was taking a few days off from picking up hot boys to mourn. That seemed logical, but were people not eating food either? We ran through the empty aisles, giddy and ethereal, like time had stopped around us. Empty supermarkets might be the most fun you can have under one roof. I mean, they have everything—weird cooking tools, oddly mis-shapen stuffed animals in bargain bins, sleazy romance novels that we took turns reading aloud to each other from. Safeway already had Thanksgiving stuff, so for five or six aisles, Anastasia carried around a squeezable turkey that would say things like *God bless us, every one!* and *It's TURRRRkey time!* The floors were freshly waxed and we slid down the aisles. Eventually we bought orange juice and a bottle of vodka and went back to my place, talked about writing a song together, but then we talked about talking instead. I told her about my mission to go to an open mic every night until Sunday, except for Shabbos of course, so I could become as sharp and exact as possible. She told me she'd come with, she always needed to keep herself sharp.

I don't remember who fell asleep first—I'm lying, of course I do, it was her—and, drunk and woozy, I rested my head on top of hers, feeling her so soft and fragile in the crook of my shoulder bones.

In the morning, when I woke, her hand was tangled between strands of my hair as though she'd been stroking it in her sleep.

Not that it mattered, I thought. She was gay, and besides, I was a poet. I read too much into everything. Years of unrequited crushes on girls had taught me that no girl wants you to be the girl in the relationship. They want you to act cool and confident.

"Where are we going tonight?" she asked when she woke in the morning.

Wednesday night Anastasia and I went to the singer/songwriter showcase at Brainwash, a trendy café with an adjacent laundromat, just in case you thought that was a good idea—you know, to go to a café and do your laundry and listen to some live music while you sip your coffee. The machines charged something ridiculous, like what, $5 for a load of laundry. Twice what you'd pay anyplace else in town. They didn't charge a cover, though, so you got your entertainment for free.

Or not. Some nights, there were so many soulful dreadlocked boys singing about girls and Jah and smoking pot that you wanted to fuck art, fuck yourself, fuck the idea that maybe one day you'd become a famous poet and sell the rights to your "Orthodox Girls" poem to some Hollywood studio for a million dollars.

And then some days, I really believed in it all.

Only, until I made it, everything was practice. Honing my skills. Learning how to manipulate a microphone. Learning which poems worked best fast, and which ones needed to be slowed down. Which needed breathing room to let the words rub softly up against each other. Which should be given space and air and allowed to blossom. Performing poetry, you could do a million wrong things, and not many right ones. The slightest misstep, and not only would you lose the audience's trust, but you'd sound like a whiny fourteen-year-old. Mentioning the words *soul, rain,* or *bosom.* Doing a love poem that wasn't clever or ironic. Rhyming. Anastasia made me feel so comfortable, like I could say anything to her, but more than anything I didn't want to look like a poetry dork in front of her.

Yeah, she followed me home the next night too. And we stayed up till five o'clock in the morning, talking, although I couldn't tell you what about. Music. Books. Being on the road. Anastasia was from Pittsburgh, and she'd moved here straight from there, although, from the distant, removed way she talked about moving, it seemed like she'd taken her time getting across the country. Months? Years? The less I asked her about her past, the safer it felt. Otherwise, she might start asking me questions about my own background. She knew I was Orthodox. I don't know if she knew what it meant. In terms of touching girls. In terms of sleeping with them. *Her.* She was gay. I kept coming back to that refrain, even though, at night, I was thinking more and more that it wasn't true, or, at least, not entirely.

That first night, the sign-up list had been short, plenty of time for everyone to take as long as we wanted onstage. Not at Brainwash. The list was twenty people long, and even though the friendly, lackadaisical hippie host allowed you to ramble on as long as you wanted, the crowd would kick your ass. Anastasia and I whispered requests in each other's ears. We were already familiar with each other's oeuvres. This was good.

It was a week before Rosh HaShana. All week, Jews around the world were saying Selichos, an extra prayer in the morning, where you tell God that Rosh HaShana is coming up and how sorry you are for all the shit you've done that year. Sometimes I had issues with praying, like I was reciting the words without believing in them enough. (Other times I liked that—being mechanical, using the prayerbook as a script when I didn't know what to say on my own.) My mattress still smelled like Anastasia, that adorably feral combination of sweaty armpitness and honeysuckle-and-vanilla that she wore instead of showering in the mornings, and I don't know if I was supposed to feel sorry about that.

For Shabbos, I stayed at the house of a friend of a friend in Berkeley, a Modern Orthodox group house, kind of a legend, where we held giant potluck dinners that were not only vegetarian but, even better, kosher. Meat had never been cooked inside those pots and plates. The house had started when everyone had been in college. The inhabitants were long graduated, but they still held services and dinners and potlucks. I rolled up on the living room couch and fell asleep as people were starting to freestyle over Shabbos nigguns. Saturday I stayed in Berkeley, went to synagogue and had lunch at a stranger's house, and smiled politely as I took third helpings of their food and answered all their questions about how I was making it living in a city where there were no Jewish girls and where my full-time job was trying to get a job. I did what I did best—I smiled—and I replied that, if God wanted me to date, God would send me a girl, and until I got hired I would pay the rent by performing poetry.

And, on Sunday night, I took all the anxiety that was twisting my stomach into pretzel knots and blasted it out on the Paradise stage.

There was a brick wall behind me. A black and battered microphone sat on a stand, way too tall to be at lip-level. I grabbed the mic with both my hands and coughed into it.

"Next Tuesday is the Day of Repentance," I said.

"This week we say prayers to apologize for all the shit we've done this year."

I swallowed. I ripped out my journal.

"This is all the shit I've done this year," I said.

I started into a poem.

Anastasia didn't come. It was a bar and you had to be twenty-one to get in, and although I was still trying to pretend I didn't know how old she was, last night we did that flirty can-I-see-your-ID-picture thing because in driver's license pictures, everybody looks drunk and uncaffeinated and somehow really horny. I saw her birth-date and did the math in my head. She was nineteen. But Box came. So did my gay frat-boy friend Jerrica, who hated poetry but thought I was cute. And there were my poetry friends, who would be at the Paradise no matter who was performing. I closed with that poem "Good Thing I Don't Touch Girls (or I'd Touch You)," which was the closest thing to a love poem I'd ever written about Ahuva. I read it and let the paper flutter pathetically to the ground when I walked offstage. I swallowed the last words of the poem. It felt like saying goodbye.

And that was that. Fame in, fame out. There was a ten-minute break, and then they started on the list of readers for the open mic.

Bambi Lake, one of the regulars at the Paradise poetry shows, once said, "You can't be a star in your hometown because everyone sees you doing your laundry." Once I stepped out of the bar where people were screaming my name, and onto the street where nobody knew my name, I felt like a vortex for all the silence and empty stares that people threw when they walked by. I got on a bus going up Market Street.

I showed up at Notes from Underground, where the drunks were nursing paper coffee cups and the bar kids were eating after-hours hamburgers from the street vendor. Anastasia and her friends were scarfing espresso shots that our friend Kim, the bartender, passed them from behind the counter. There was some guy sitting on Anastasia's lap, and when I saw him from the door, I thought about turning around and going home. But Anastasia caught my eye and I had to stay. Nonchalantly, she tossed him off her knee and ran over to hug me.

I tried to talk to everyone, but after being onstage for an hour just talking, I realized that I had forgotten how to hold a conversation. So I sat there, listening to everyone, resisting the half-asleep and drunken instinct to applaud whenever someone finished a sentence. Anastasia ground her knuckles on my knee. This guy named Tree who *looked* like a tree—he was skinny, with octagonal glasses and big burgundy dreadlocks that always had shit caught inside them—was talking about this Haight Street dance club they'd snuck into earlier that night, how they got busted for being underage (he giggled that last part as if it was the punchline to a dumb joke). *Underage, heh heh.* He sounded like a skeezy old man talking about himself. I tried to listen. From the way he told the story it seemed like everyone sitting at the table was there. This kind-of-pretty girl at the next table was rocking her head in her arms, so sick and clogged with alcohol. I thought about what it would be like to get her a glass of water but I didn't want to, I was there with Anastasia. Eventually Anastasia climbed off my lap and got the girl a glass of water. I looked at her, startled. Had we been thinking the same thing? Were the hooks of a long-term relationship settling into my brain? I know, I was thinking paranoid, but I *was* paranoid. When I had called my last relationship a rumor, I was speaking optimistically.

When the drunks finished their hamburgers and the bums stopped paying for coffees, and when the night air turned brisk and the Notes crowd thinned, Kim started packing up coffee mugs and turning up stools. After a while, we were the only ones left, and eventually she kicked us out too. She had to go to sleep and we should go to sleep too.

Outside, the wind sweeping down Haight Street and hitting our faces, I asked Anastasia if she was coming home with me. She said, "Why don't you come home with me instead?" We went to her place—which she told me was a sublet but was really her and a friend crashing on some people's sofas. They'd had a bedroom but got kicked out when the occupant came back from Europe early. I was learning to take things as they came and so I didn't say anything, just rolled into the meniscus of the sofa with her, and in the middle of the night Anastasia woke me up by kissing me like a monster, like she had just discovered she was straight and all the accumulated lust was pouring out.

I woke up the next day, Monday, in a dark room I didn't recognize, and no obligations, nowhere I needed to be. Anastasia shook herself out of bed before me. She'd just gotten a one-day job at a coffee stand, giving out free Dixie-cup samples of decaf latte. She bent down and kissed me on the forehead and disappeared out the door. I was wide awake but I didn't want to show it.

As soon as she was gone, I shrugged out of bed, grabbed my knapsack and the leftover chapbooks from the previous night. I dug my hand into my pocket and found $20 in crumpled-up bills that I didn't remember having until I remembered, *my show*, oh yeah, I'd gotten paid to do poetry. This was the stuff they don't teach you about in high-school English Lit. And then I remembered: If my show had been last night, that meant that tonight was Rosh HaShana, and I had about six hours of forgiveness before things turned ugly.

I walked to Urban Forage, the raw-foods café on the corner, and got some drink that tasted more bitter and syrupy than coffee and woke me up faster. I walked home down Market Street, got home at 9:00 A.M. like it was an office. My room felt like an industrial freezer, the first traces of sunlight on the edge of shadows. I tiptoed through to the kitchen. My roommate Veronica was asleep in the living room. She was a stripper, and her days started in early afternoon but went till four or five in the morning on work nights. The phone rang. It made me jump. Nobody called this early in the morning except for bill collectors and bad news back east. It was C. D., just getting into work. She apologized for not making my reading. Shit, I was still thinking about her vision of the apocalypse. I was just happy she was alive.

"That's okay," I said. "But how are you and Henrietta?"

"Henrietta?" she repeated, like she didn't know what I could be talking about. "Oh, you mean the premonition?"

"Yes, of *course* that," I said, impatiently.

"It didn't count," said C. D. "The pain in New York blacked out everything else."

Somehow, we had all forgotten how Rabbi Mendy's wife Tali was pregnant. Hugely pregnant. Nobody at the synagogue noticed, or realized, because pregnancy was a normal state for Hasidim, but when New York broke, so did she.

Mendy called me from the hospital. "Tali's in the E.R.," he said. "Everything's fine, thank God, but Golda is here and she's not used to hospitals and I was wondering if you were maybe free for the day?"

I told him I was on it.

We met at his house, a few blocks from the hospital.

Golda was in her crib, snoring peacefully. Her little lungs shot out huge noisy breaths that filled the small room. Trickles of sunlight poked through the border of the curtains. Mendy left me with another apology—"I'm sorry we called you out of the house so close to Rosh HaShana"—and I was, like, *Rabbi, don't apologize, you do not choose when a baby is going to fall out,* and I showed him to the door.

I heard a scuttle of footsteps, and walked through the kitchen to find Golda in her pajamas. She looked up at me, confused.

"Where Mommy?" she said.

I kneeled down to the level of her eyes. "She's at the hospital with the baby, remember?"

"Baby?" she repeated

"Baby," I said.

"Where Mommy?"

The second time Golda asked, she didn't wait for an answer. Her jaw dropped open and she started to scream.

One day I am going to make the worst father. Children crying make me crumble into helplessness. This feeling of utter sadness wells up and makes me all depressed and I want to concentrate on my own depressed state, not how to make them feel better.

I talked to her in that soft bedroom voice. I pleaded with her, showed her Mommy's coat and the door. I dug through her toybox to find an ambulance or a hospital or something, but Golda was ultra-protective about her toys and when I touched them, she started screaming about that instead.

I shrugged. I got up, walked into the next room, which was Mendy's office, and took out some computer paper and a set of Magic Markers. I threw them in a pile on the floor and started to draw.

Eventually Golda stopped hiding her toys under the

sofa and waddled over to me. With her index finger in her mouth, she said, "What you doing?"

"I dunno," I said, shading in the side of a woman's dress.

"Who that?"

"That's Mommy."

She plopped down, grabbed a marker, and started to draw on the other half of the paper. She drew another woman holding a baby. "Is that Mommy too?" I asked.

Golda shook her head. "This is Golda," she said. "I going to have a baby too."

Mendy and Tali came home later that night, swinging a baby carrier by the handle. Tali was quiet and stoned-looking, eyes focused on some other world. Mendy was all about the understanding manservant, rushing out a chair with lots of pillows, fluffing the baby's crib and getting glasses of water all around. Golda stood there with her arms outstretched, waiting for somebody to pick her up. I tried to be the consolation prize while Mendy scurried around, but she turned around so her back faced me and she flung her arms Mendy-ward.

When he returned to the room, Mendy scooped Golda up in his arms and jiggled her little body, face level with her eyes. "So, maideleh," he said. "What did you do today?"

"What you bring me?" she asked, eyes wide.

"Ah, gutte maideleh," Mendy swooned. "I can never keep a secret from you. You know, we have a new baby now."

"Baby for me?" said Golda hopefully.

Mendy reached into the hem of his coat and pulled out a pink box wrapped in cellophane and ribbon, a generic Barbie doll in an ankle-length dress.

"Baby for me," Golda said, wondrously, cradling the box in her arms.

"Happy new year," Mendy whispered, kissing her on the forehead, so gently that it didn't even ruffle the hairs over her forehead.

C. D. called once more, right before the holiday. It was late in the afternoon, there were, like, twenty seconds left before Rosh HaShana. I was braising a focaccia and sautéing olives and chard. My roommate Veronica held out the phone, "It's C. D., do you want to talk?" and I was, like, "I *can't.*" I heard C. D.'s electronic voice ring out. "Hey, I know I'm cutting it close," she said into Veronica's ear, and the tinny words buzzed out on the phone receiver so I could hear them, even if I tried not to. "But I wanted to tell him, I accept his mechila. His apology, I mean. I'll always accept it."

8

repentance

Right now I'm in my bedroom, unwrapping condoms, I don't know why. I only planned on unwrapping one, which is what Jews are supposed to do on Friday afternoons because, once Shabbos starts, you're not allowed to rip open wrappers. But it's been the shittiest day in the world, and it feels so good, like ripping the gift wrapping off a delicate and valuable toy on your birthday. Only, today, there's a whole shitload of condoms sitting in my bedroom, spread out, Go Fish–style, on my duvet. First I peel open one, and then another, and before I know it, there are enough gauzy latex Frisbees lying open to protect a cow from being milked. Standing alone, my feet surrounded by empty wrappers, I don't realize just how heavy I'm breathing. I feel exhilarated and ashamed. I'm hyperventilating.

This is me getting ready for Yom Kippur.

The hours leading up to sunset are always frenzied before a Jewish holiday. Once the sun goes down, we stop using electricity, answering the phone, writing, watering the garden, carrying anything outside our house—even keys—and doing anything that relates to our business or to the outside world. If you trace the world's religious evolution before Avraham, the first Jew, everyone at the time was worshipping idols—physical statues of humans and humanoids and animals that they revered as deities. And then Avraham came along, smashing all the idols in his father's shop, declaring that God wasn't something you could smell or taste or hear.

Actually, he said the idols fought each other and smashed each other up.

He even put a hammer in the hand of one idol, insisting to his father that his story was the truth. When his father said, that's impossible, it's just a clay statue, Avraham said, then why do you worship them?

That was how Judaism started.

Avraham left town, married Sarah, the mother of our people, and, instead of a physical representation of God, Avraham kept Sabbath, an idea as intangible as God itself, as a symbol of the covenant between God and people: because, unlike idols, Shabbos isn't a one-time deal. It comes around every week, and there's no amount of stored points like tear-off tickets in Skee Ball, you start from ground zero every Friday. Like everything else in Judaism, it's not what you did in the past that counts, it's what you're doing now. We keep God's commandments and we do the best we can.

But everybody fucks up, and that's why we have Yom Kippur. The Day of Atonement, when you apologize to God for all your sins of the past year and for the ones that you're going to inevitably commit next year. You spend the evening before the holiday and all that day praying that God doesn't hold your sins against you.

I do one final sweep of the house. Bathroom light on, refrigerator light off, tissues in the bathroom, my microphones and amp and CDs all packed away. I turn on the Christmas lights in my room, a single string of maroon lights that are dim enough to sleep with, but light enough to maneuver around my room in. I tie my keys on a string around my waist, tuck them behind my belt, and I'm out.

Usually just about everyone arrives at synagogue late, smelling vaguely of burnt vegetables. We all pray loud, at first a scattered humming, building into a frenzy of voices as more people arrive and the seats fill in. Because it's an Orthodox synagogue, everyone sings at different speeds, and the cacophony of a hundred cocksure voices, echoed in the high ceilings, turns into a symphony.

But tonight is Yom Kippur.

We don't smell like anything but soap tonight. Nobody has been cooking anything. Tonight, we're fasting.

We stand around, not talking to each other. I look into the faces of men I've seen every Saturday morning for a year, their heads capped with a small black phylactery box, hidden behind palm fronds, and in every kind of clothes from suits to T-shirts. We've been through so much. They barely know my last name.

We're all nervous, but we don't know what to be nervous about. This abstract idea of some dude who knows every thought you've ever had. You want to think good thoughts. You want to stop thinking totally. The hugeness of it—every single thing you've done over the past year—it paralyzes you. Even if you stand absolutely still, do utterly nothing but breathe, until the end of Yom Kippur, there aren't enough seconds to correct the entire past year of your life. Right about now, God should be starting to judge us.

Tonight is Yom Kippur.

Tonight, all I can do is pray.

Once a Jewish holiday starts, we're locked into it. There's nothing we can do about anything. No more roommates you can short-change or jobs to cut out early from. The last few days we tried to do things better, more honestly, staying at work those last few minutes. Now, at synagogue, we feel powerless, nothing we can do but ride the clock. Most Shabboses, we pray out loud, shout out giant dancing songs, but tonight everybody whispers to themselves. I want to feel the familiar voices around me, everyone out of tune, Tzvi singing all operatic and diva-like, Daniel clapping his hands off-beat and nudging my arm to make me clap with him. The cacophony that usually makes me wince, tonight I want to feel it, I want to lose myself. But everyone is like prey in the jungle, quiet, fearful.

Tonight it feels like I'm alone.

Tzvi whispers to himself. I can hear his singing voice drift higher, slowly and carefully, but at the end of each paragraph he reduces it to a whisper again. Rabbi Mendy holds his prayerbook up high, directly between his shoulders, burying his face in the pages. I whisper the prayers to myself and I can hear my *s*'s hiss too long, the guttural scrape of my *ch*'s. I'm embarrassed by the sound of my own voice. I wonder why everyone isn't staring at me. I know why. It's Yom Kippur. They're afraid too. I'm usually so good at being friendly, breaking the ice and putting my friends at ease. Tonight I can't. I want to scream. I finish praying faster than everyone else. I don't know how to fill the silence. I finish praying and I'm just standing there, my eyes reading the last words on the page over and over, because the rabbi's giving everyone time to finish and me, jumpy and nervous, I finished too early.

On my way out of synagogue, I usually wait for Tirtza, who lives down the street from me. We don't know each other at all outside the synagogue, but on Saturdays, if we're both around, we almost always walk home together. We have built our ignorance of each other's lives into a science, talking about everything innocuous there is: television, music, clothes, weeding our way down to irrelevant minutiae of Jewish law, like how to milk a cow on Sabbath and which side of a scythe is most proper to harvest wheat stalks. Tonight there's a minimum of conversation at the synagogue, almost no one in groups. I'm the first one outside. Tirtza, head parallel to the sidewalk, paces straight by me.

I get home, peel my shirt off, and crawl directly into bed. The red Christmas night lights shine dully, too dark to read and too distracting for me to sleep.

I close my eyes anyway. I feel like I've been running on a script all day, work then laundry then a brief meal, then getting dressed for synagogue. I'm tired. All I want is a long, silent close-up on myself, my face so big you can see the pores in my skin. I barely remember what I look like.

When Anastasia comes home after work, I don't notice. I'm gone and I'm weary and I'm so into myself. The prayers are stuck in my head like a pop song. The dull red shining through my eyelids flickers. It's not really flickering, it's me blinking. I open my eyes. She's practically on top of me, the sequins on her shirt glittering purple and red, dripping liquid mascara that started melting in the cab. She nuzzles my cheeks with teeth and then I lick her face. Her mascara tastes salty. All the academic books that I've read say that after work, strippers just want to cuddle. Not my girlfriend. She's always horny.

In Jewish law a man is required to keep his wife sexually satisfied. Anastasia isn't my wife but we act like she is.

The hidden, wild animal kisses come naturally to us, but the everyday kisses—in the morning, on the street, every driver watching us as I touch my lips to her cheek—are the most difficult. Together we are intimate but reserved, so hygienic with our feelings. We are like condoms, I think: She is that dark closet of emotions that I thought I would never rip open.

She keeps a drawer of clothes at my house. We share toothbrushes. The last time I got invited to someone's house for Shabbos dinner, the couple asked, *Is there anyone special you want to bring?* I was so close to saying, *Anastasia.*

At first she's quiet, peeling the blanket up and sliding herself under it, clothes still on, her bustier cold against my chest. Her hands are small and pudgy and they clamp onto my body, feeling bare skin on my pectorals, realizing that I'm naked. She squeals like she's glad, like it's her birthday and this is my present to her.

Her face is so close to mine, two curved bangs dangling by my eyes. She breathes out once, long and deep, letting out all the tension. Anastasia takes breaths with her whole body. I feel her ankles and her stomach and her pelvic muscles all untensing, breathing out against me. Her hips dig into my hips as her breath washes out over my face, the air picking up treble, creeping out as a moan. Her legs creep around my torso and she pulls herself tighter into my body. Her sequins dig into my chest and I can feel the sudden hotness of the top of her breasts sliding out of the bustier and rubbing my collarbone. Her hips buckle. Before I realize that she is, she's dry-humping me. I gulp. I am so not ready for this. In this agreement of kissing, she is changing all the rules, and suddenly I no longer know where my boundaries are. I wrap my arms around her and keep my hands as fists, clinging around her waist.

"Oh baby," she says. "Oh baby. Work was such shit.

Five hours of doing this to myself and all I really wanted was you." She whispers in my ear. Her breath is hot and leaves trickles of moistness in the inner curve of my ear. She gnaws on the bottom of my earlobe with her incisors and sucks with her gums.

I'm skinny and tall. She's skinny and short. I weigh 120 pounds, she weighs even less, but her knees are strong and she's pressing on top of my body and she has me pinned with her hips and her legs. Her hands hold me down, stop me from moving.

We're a boy and a girl in this mess of blankets together, fumbling to make a connection. We are trying to make each other feel a little bit better, a little more comfortable with the precarious balance of life. And then the voice in the back of my head asks, how much better do you need to feel?

I remember the rabbi's son back in Philadelphia saying, *Shiksehs are for practice* and then laughing. Nobody took him seriously, but, in our own way, we did.

She's grinding into me hard with her hips, suffocating me, her teeth ripping my lips open, diving her tongue down my throat like she's stabbing my mouth to death. She likes to use her tongue to look feral and ferocious, it hangs out like a tiger's, she licks my neck so predatorily, testing me out.

She pushes into me harder. I thought dry-humping was only what ten-year-olds did. She's screaming out in agony. Her torso is making a kind of figure-eight grind against me and I don't know if she's actually getting wet or getting off or just faking it really good or what. But she's so frenzied that I don't want to ask.

Now she's riding me, legs straddling my body as if there's not her clothes between us, like there's no gravity anywhere else in the room, rocking like a yeshiva boy in the middle of morning prayers. She thrusts my body into the wall. My shoulder hits. It makes a resounding thud. It echoes. She howls. Her breasts are popping out of her bustier and she clamps one of my hands on, tight, my nail against her nipple, which is erect as a spear. She thrusts against me again, and my head flies back, almost against the wall, into the pile of condoms.

I am not going to do this. I am not going to do this. There is a border between bending the rules and breaking them, and I want to stay on the safe side. I want a protective shield against them. Maybe that's what I thought, getting all those condoms, unrolling them—that I could somehow be both sexual and hidden.

I keep doing what I'm doing—which isn't a lot, I'm pretty much only a spectator—but Anastasia sees a condom sail off the bed and onto the floor, and lowers herself onto my chest, reaching over my head and digging into the pile.

"What the hell is this?" she asks, holding one up to the Christmas lights. The shadowy corners of her mouth twist up in a sly grin, and a trickle of laughing rocks in my ear. "Matt," she says, "what is this all about?"

"It's Yom Kippur," I tell her, as though it explains everything. "It's like Shabbos, only it's different."

I move to kiss her. Kissing is the way we break conversations when we don't know what to say, swallowing each other's words by way of tongues. Our lips meet.

She pulls away. She lowers her head onto me, then onto the pillow. Suddenly she's tired.

Her head clunks onto the bed, straight into the pile of condoms. She rolls her head to the side, brushes them away, and then falls back into place. She's asleep at once.

My heart is pounding too fast. Even if my pulse wasn't racing, the sound of my heart would keep me up. It's so loud, I'm surprised I can hear myself think.

I close my eyes and try forcing myself to dream. I start

thinking about Rabbi Samborra's Monday night Talmud classes in Washington, right after I became religious, how every week, no matter what happened during that week, I'd end up right back there. It had the complete certainty of sunrise, a certainty I don't think I have about anything anymore. I wonder if Rabbi Samborra would be happy to know I was thinking about him, even if I'd fallen this far down. Most yeshiva boys I grew up with breathed Talmud and fantasized about strippers. I think this made it official: I had become their exact opposite.

An hour or two later, Anastasia stirs. I have the back of her head cupped in my palm, her stringy black hair swims like water. She mumbles my name and I nod, softly, so she can barely feel the muscles in my chest move.

"This man tonight wanted forgiveness," she whispers. "I started to whisper the Lord's Prayer and tell him stories about when I went to confession. Some men are really into that." She moves her head a little. "We even have a wood ruler in the toy chest to fuck ourselves with. I started telling him about my *naughtiest* confession and he said, *No, baby, if you want to pray I'll tell you the words to use, but don't say that yet. Just listen to everything I did wrong. I've got a list a year long.* And then he started to tell me—"

"Jesus, don't tell me what the poor guy said to you!" I say. My lip brushes her earlobe. Are strippers not supposed to talk about their clients outside the office, the way psychologists don't? No, they need to. Strippers are like the opposite of psychologists: They need to talk about their clients so they can keep themselves sane.

"No, baby," she murmurs. "It's not that. He didn't tell me any secrets. He didn't really tell me anything. All he did was, he put his hand up against the glass, staring into my eyes. His eyes were tearing. They looked heavy like bricks. He said—wait, let me see if I can remember the exact words—it was like a mantra. *For the sin we committed before you by...*he said that. He said that maybe fifty times, over and over again. *For the sin we committed before you by lying. For the sin we committed before you by cheating.* Again and again. It was so weird. It made me think of you, Matthue, that day last week when you asked for forgiveness."

"Mechila?"

"Does that mean forgiveness?"

"Yeah."

"Well, say *forgiveness,* then. I don't speak Hebrew. I told you before, you're allowed to act like you know more than I do, but you have to teach me."

I close my eyes, feeling her body. We were in the kitchen the other day. We were marinating mushrooms together. I was slicing scallions to use for the garnish, first in thin slices, then dicing them until they were unrecognizable pieces of white-green. Anastasia was combining sauces in a bowl. The mixture started out the dark red of balsamic vinegar, but now it was a muddy brown. She'd come home from work late and started right on it. She was still in her work clothes, thin red fishnets and a black leather bustier. We were on opposite counters. When I looked over my head, I saw her raw, almost-naked back, perched unnaturally on her high heels. She hadn't even taken her shoes off. She looked delicious and random. From behind, she could be anyone. *Do you forgive me?* I said low, in a voice I didn't think she would hear. Of course she could. She turned around, surprised. *For what?* she asked innocently. *For anything.* When she heard that, she burst out laughing. *Of course I do,* she said, *I always do. I'm in love with you, don't you remember?* Later that night, when dinner was done and we were at a rock show, I'd held her in a mutual armlock, told her what I'd meant, how every year we ask for mechila, or forgiveness, for all the sins we've committed, intentional or unintentional, against all other human beings.

"Anyway," Anastasia murmurs, and her voice snaps me back into her. "This guy—he was a normal-looking guy, late twenties, thin scraggly beard and a starched white shirt, the kind that I always say looks good on you—he has his hand against the glass, and he wants me to put mine opposite it. So I do. And as he's telling me this list of sins, I know—he doesn't say it outright but he shows me to put my hand in a fist, to hit my breast every time he says a sin. Not hard—this part, he tells me—but just enough to make them jiggle the tiniest bit. And he's standing straight up in a kind of upside-down *V*, one arm against the wall, the other down his pants. And as he lists sins, he sounds more desperate every time. Every time he says a sin, I knock on my boob. And every time I do, he squeezes himself."

"You mean, he gives his dick a jerk?" I say. Anastasia, for everything she does, is notoriously bashful about talking explicitly.

"Hedonist." She spoons her smooth legs against me, one hand on my shoulder, rolling me over so my body scoops her up. She's staring at me. I'm staring at nothing. "That's all. Creepy, but they all are. Anyway, that spooky guy left a tip that was more like a *sal*ary. He paid for your next three birthday presents, I'll tell you that much."

"Mm," I agree. She feels so good tonight, like serenity. I don't want to do anything to change the mood.

"So he must have been Jewish, right?" she asks. "Otherwise, why would he say all that stuff?"

"Probably," I agree, more out of fogginess than cognition. This time I'm almost asleep.

"Weird," she says, closes her eyes again, and sinks down to my shoulder.

September in San Francisco is the warmest month of

the year. My windows are all open, and the soft, salty bay breeze sails from one window of the room to another, making the air smell like Atlantic City and summer vacation. I don't know how I got here. I don't know what I'm doing here. But I'm settling, I think. I'm figuring my shit out.

"Hey, Anastasia," I whisper to her right before we fall asleep for real. "Why do you like me, when you only like girls?"

"Silly," she yawns, almost asleep already. "You're not a girl. You're something else entirely."

9

bottom rock

It was the Folsom Street Fair, a Sunday morning bristling with insanity, the sky blue like an ad, the sun blazing hard and warm, close to the Earth. Ammi and her girlfriend Angela and I pushed through one of the tightest crowds in San Francisco history, half a million people squeezed into six long city blocks. Ammi had me on a chain and I was wearing this little collar that had dog spikes and a baby T-shirt that said ROAR on it, and no hat because my leather pants were too hot, so my black felt yarmulke lay bare on my head, gleaming dully in the shade.

I was drowning in anthropological giddiness. I wasn't into sex laced with pain, blood made me vomit, and

ROAR. Actually, Ahuva had made it for me. Several months ago, before she stopped talking to me. She was going through an obsession with iron-on letters. I kept trying to get her to make me a shirt that said TZNIUS IS TSEXY, but she never did.

leather just made me sweat and smell bad. But when my college girlfriend pinned me down as we fooled around, rendering me immobile as her feet shackled my legs, one hand pinning down my wrists, I felt weirdly comfortable. I'd never done all that making-out stuff in high school. I still wasn't sure if I knew how to kiss right. I felt way more comfortable being told what to do. I wondered, was I a masochist?

We were trying to push through to the drink stand, allegedly to get water, but Ammi, a computer programmer in the old-school San Francisco style—fix bugs all day and go wild in the gay clubs at night—got us Red Bull mixers. Since we were already dehydrated, why not go all the way?

We paraded down Folsom Street, squishing ourselves through clusters of the fat, hairy gay men people called bears. They thought I was adorable, and Ammi and Angela looked like such misanthropic dykes. They brushed the tourists away with big meaty hands and cleared a path for us. But the young models and the bodybuilder boys never let us pass. An Abercrombie steroid boy, biceps bigger than a girl's breasts, slammed into my face as he pushed by. I recoiled.

Ammi yanked on my chain. She rolled her eyes at my gross-out. So much of that day was like watching TV, me with my mouth hanging wide open, eyes scanning everyone. I didn't even have to choose whom to watch, or what to turn my face away from: Today, Ammi was in the pilot's seat. "Matthue, *look*," she'd cry, and I would, the chain would pull and my head would twist and I'd be face to face with whatever alien sex display had piqued Ammi's interest. The bears were the most absorbing to watch, their forearms were thicker than my head. I imagined what it would be like to have your bones crushed by that much weight.

Ammi and I never got split up. At the Fourth of July parades in Philadelphia, my mother lost me every five seconds. Any time Ammi didn't see me, all she had to do was yank on that leash.

You'd think it would be embarrassing, the way that six-year-old kids on dog leashes are, but I kind of liked being chained. There was none of the usual indecision about crowds—which way to go, how to push through, should I stop and talk to strangers. All day, people came up to us and stared at my yarmulke and my weird Jewish sidecurls and asked me, was I actually a Jew or was it just a really weird fetish? Most of them were placid straight couples out to see the spectacle. So much of the Folsom Street Fair was about exhibitionism.

Ammi just tugged and I followed along. People stood clear of the chain compliantly. It was almost like being in Hebrew School. Hell, it was like Orthodox Judaism. In this crowd, as strange and alien as anything in the world outside my bedroom, I had something to cling to. Every few steps, we ran into Ammi's friends. They stopped and compared notes about the crowd, where the best booths were, where to get the coolest free stuff. They oohed and aahed over me. I felt like a new bike.

We stopped at the AIDS Awareness booth. A muscley guy with tan, oiled-down skin was minding the booth. Ammi flirted with him. The flirtation between gay men and gay women is a subtle art. Ammi turned all the things he said into double entendres. He flexed muscles at her and pretended not to notice. Neither of them wanted anything to happen, but there was a comfortable space in their being able to push it. They had a stack of plastic black paddles to give away. Giveaways are my favorite thing in the universe. The muscley dude flashed questioning eyebrows at Ammi. Ammi shrugged. "Give me the test," she said. She giggled. He gave her a puzzled look—"What do you *mean,* honey?" and he rubbed her arm with his palm—then opened his trivia book and asked Ammi trivia questions about AIDS. She answered the first two, no problem. "You're good," said the guy. "You'll never know how good," said Ammi. He asked the third question. I called out the answer. The guy looked at Ammi. "Go ahead," she said. He gave me a paddle from the pile. It was cold plastic, the grip like a breeze in my hand. So cool. We forged our way back into the crowd, pushing our way down the street. More people took pictures of us than ever, and we were the sight for it: the girl in leather police gear, with her yarmulked boy-on-a-leash fanning himself with a paddle.

Of course, Ammi snatched it from my hand the instant we saw somebody we knew.

That someone turned out to be Tseitel.

We didn't actually know Tseitel. She looked familiar, but how many girls don't? San Francisco has a ghostly way of making everyone look almost-familiar, like your third-grade best friend twenty years later.

Ammi and I pushed our way through a throng of people watching a lashing demonstration, a skinny, naked capitalist-looking guy with a crew cut who lay crucified on an *X*-shaped cross. The lasher, a svelte, burly dude in a leather hood and gloves, was making a ring of the crowd, pushing people back so they wouldn't get caught by his whip. We just wanted to pass by. But it was sort of like driving by a car accident. There was no way to pass without staring intently. Tseitel pushed through the crowd from the other direction, carving her own path. She had shiny cheeks, little-boy hair, and a big body that she moved like she was showing it off, all breasts and shoulders. She threw her palms up and swatted aside those fraternity boys and their tanning oil. Ammi and I stepped out of her way instinctively. When she saw me, she stopped in her tracks and jumped across the crowd to me. "You!" she squealed, grabbing my forearms, squeezing my shoulders. "Are you really a Yid?"

I nodded, struck dumb.

Tseitel snapped her fingers, like, *eureka.* "We need to talk," she said—crisp, like a gangster—and then vanished into the crowd.

A few weeks later, I was at the Lex with C. D. and Henrietta. One of their friends was doing a poetry reading with a bunch of other women, a whole book release-slash-spoken word performance. C. D. and Henrietta were doing their best to not look ten years older than everyone else. I was doing my best to try to not look like a single straight guy at a lesbian bar.

The reading swept through five or six featured readers, then degraded to an open mic, then degraded further into a party, which faded into regular bar night. Girls came in from off the street, the ones who'd been smoking through the reading. The dyke-poetry groupies stopped hanging out on the pool table, and transboy hustlers in leather vests stood around it, fondling pool cues like crotches, watching the femmes sway across the room in slinky, hip-hugging jeans. Henrietta and C. D. and I retreated to

Single straight guy. I don't even know if I count as straight anymore. I'd always learned that the technical term for a guy who slept in a bed with lesbians and didn't try to get some hot three-way action going was *gay.* Was it just that I was scared? Was it that I was afraid to cross the borders of Jewish law? Maybe it was everything. Those days, I felt like the only way to avoid double-crossing God was to not move at all.

Transboy. They were born women, their faces swept with the hairless smoothness that only women have, but they wore their hair slicked back, their army vests tucked out, as they gripped their pool cues with the steady, confident air of men.

a table. C. D. got a fluffy green drink for herself, a Coke for Henrietta, and a beer for me. People were still reading, but the same woman had been on the mic for twenty minutes. She faded into the background like an old jazz song. C. D. and Henrietta sat in chairs. I had the booth to myself. They both wanted to leave, and they were talking about where to go, and suddenly Tseitel slid into the booth.

She smiled at me as if we'd known each other forever. She wrapped one arm around my shoulder, and said something to me in Yiddish.

On some days, when my ears are wax-free and I'm thinking clearly, I can understand the tiniest bit of Yiddish. That evening I was obsessed with C. D. and her girlfriend and the subtle ways of communication that transpired between people who'd known each other that long. Couples who'd been together longer than I'd had pubes. But suddenly, Tseitel was sitting at the table with us, shaking both their hands, asking how it felt to hang out with an Orthodox Jew, were we all just friends or something more? When she found out that C. D. and I had grown up in the same town, the floodgates opened.

I sipped my beer delicately, feeling like a spectator observing the whole conversation. "The first time I saw you," Tseitel explained, turning to me at last, "it was across the room at Rabbi Mendy's house one Friday night at Shabbos dinner. I saw you and I could just *tell* that you had something else going on. I mean—are you Hasidic?"

"No," I told her. "But I'm Orthodox. Being Hasidic means that you—"

"I know," she said. "I grew up Hasidic."

I opened my mouth and then closed it.

C. D. and her girlfriend left eventually, and the bar cleared down to a few remaining poetry junkies at one end and Tseitel and me in our booth. She told me she kept up the laws for months after she came out, breaking Shabbos only in public when she absolutely had to. Eventually, she said, she just gave up. She still believed in God and Torah and stuff, but she didn't feel so bad about not following the laws. She still went to dinner at the Kaufmanns' house occasionally, because her parents had been friends with Kimmel and Elana Kaufmann for decades, but she didn't feel guilty or awful about not keeping Shabbos or kosher or anything.

"My God," she finished. "You look like a zombie right now."

I felt my skin turning pale. I was thinking about Anastasia. I told Tseitel of that unreal first night, when I was wearing my hat and Anastasia hadn't known I was Jewish till I actually said it, the word *Orthodox* falling from my lips in three choppy, weighted syllables. I wondered if being around her meant giving things up, trading my own lifestyle for hers.

"That's ridiculous," said Tseitel at once. "I mean—she knows what being Orthodox means, right?"

"Right," I said.

"Well, babe. With that hair"—she yanked on my sidecurl—"you're never going to be in the closet. So you've got nothing to worry about."

I wanted to argue. Just this once, I let it slide.

After meeting Tseitel, I felt great about my life. I felt so great that when I got home, way after last call at the Lex, I called up Anastasia and asked what was up with us.

"I don't know," said Anastasia, as truthful and candid as she could be. She didn't know what machinations were happening inside my head. "Can I call you back later?"

"Sure," I said. From the corner of my eye I checked my clock; it read 3:10 A.M. "Are you busy?"

Pause. "Not exactly," she said.

I said, "Are you alone?"

"Umm," she said.

"Oh."

I wasn't trying to put a booty call through. I didn't even want to have a deep, meaningful conversation. It was just one of those times when I really wanted to pick up a telephone, dial a number, and know that the person on the other end really, unexpectedly, actually wanted to talk to me. In the background, a girl's sleepy voice pleaded with Anastasia—"Baby, who's on the phone? Come to bed"— and I made a flimsy attempt to hang up.

"Hold on," Anastasia said.

"Yes?"

"That way you're talking. The way your voice drops like that. You're mad."

"I'm not mad," I told her weakly.

"I want you to listen to me for just one second," said Anastasia. I heard her whisper something to the girl in her room, take a few steps, and then the sound of a door closing.

She came back on the phone. "I like you a lot," she said. "I think you're smart and funny and you're a capital person. I really love spending time with you. But I'm not monogamous. And if you're going to be my friend, I need you to understand that."

"Oh," I said.

"Really?" Anastasia didn't wait for an answer. Her voice was suddenly perky, warm and fulfilled and close. "You are the absolute best. Thanks for understanding. See you tomorrow?"

"You know it," I murmured, sliding the phone from my cheek silently down to the receiver.

I cook. When I'm upset I cook. When I was a kid, I played with Legos, and when I was thirteen, that developed into writing stories, and now that writing is what I do all the time. It counts as an escape, about as much as checking email counts as an escape. Cooking is my last refuge. I splash oil in a pan, throw shit in, and I don't stop till everything is fried hard and crispy.

Sometimes I don't even know what I'm doing. I chop vegetables automatically, subconsciously—carrots into wheels, peppers into nail-sized rectangles, spinach into strips. Eggplants, I roast over an oven grill till they liquefy. Lately I have started baking, and I beat the dough with my hands—no beater or spoon—until it congeals into a single squelchy blob.

But I'm getting ahead of myself. Mostly I roast vegetables. They're easy, they're already edible, and you can't mess up vegetables too badly. I mean, there's sour milk and salmonella and mad cow disease, but nobody ever got seriously poisoned by carrots. No matter what you do to them, they'll still be fat and orange and round. Vegetables are God's way of saying to humanity, *If you fuck this up, it's your own fault.* Whatever happened in my kitchen, it was my own fault: That was the stuff I could live by. That was my freakout zone. When my bed is not safe territory and even my dreams are about Anastasia putting me through a blender to turn me into a girl, the kitchen becomes my fortress of solace.

"Is it me?" I ask, that night, when all the lights are off except the single, sporadic light of cars on the freeway outside my window. Every five minutes, they wash the room, my duvet and my hair, in a thin coat of blue light. "Am I doing something wrong?"

"No, baby," says Anastasia. She hugs me closer. "Not at all."

"I don't want to have sex. You don't want to have sex with me. Right?" I said. "Right," she said. "And I like what we do," I volunteered. "I like what we do too," she said, "I mean—I *love* you," she told me.

I asked her: "So why can't we just be us?"

"Because I miss getting pussy," she said.

Do people actually talk like that? I live in San Francisco. Of *course* people actually talk like that. In a scratchless metal pot in my kitchen, rice inflates. In a pan, onions sizzle till a deep translucent yellow, and I stir them slowly, hypnotically, to stop them from browning. To make onions sweet, you can't stop paying attention to them. You have to mix in liquids, or liquidy vegetables like tomatoes, or you have to stir them constantly, never leaving them alone. I wondered what would happen if I left Anastasia alone by the fire, even for a minute. She would find someone else to—O Hashem I Am Sorry, I Can't Help Thinking This Way—to stir her onions.

Now that my house was within microscopic distance of being kosher, I started hosting Shabbos dinners. Not many Orthodox Jews came—not many Orthodox Jews lived in San Francisco—but people showed up, kids who started talking to me at bars because I had a yarmulke on, and some of my friends who weren't observant but just happened to be Jewish, and then my non-Jewish friends. Phred told all his friends he was going to become shomer Shabbos and call in sick to work every Saturday, even though he drove a car back home to Sausalito from my house.

My friend Janelle, who'd just moved to San Francisco, told all her friends about it, and then they kept asking if they could get invited. And it also added another dimension to our Shabbos dinners: everybody's skills got assimilated into the greater pool of culinary talent. We were like the Borg. Phred even posted it on Friendster: "Shabbos is better at Matt's."

The first-name possessive: I had achieved restaurant status.

Anastasia usually stayed away, not for any reason except that she worked nights. She'd come over after dinner, as everybody was burrowing into their other plans for the night, making arrangements to carpool to clubs. I felt like I had a secret identity, only instead of me dropping out of sight, the world dropped out of sight.

10

gay shabbos

My friend Aryeh was the secretary for Rabbi Rasnikov, one of the most important Orthodox rabbis in California. He made calls, organized special events, and reminded the rabbi when the sun was going down so he wouldn't forget to pray. Aryeh himself was a baal teshuva, twenty-six years old and just learning how to keep kosher and do Shabbos and walk the yiddishe walk.

When Aryeh decided to become observant, the first thing he did was grow a beard. When he told me that, I wanted to laugh, but shit, the first thing I did was stop cutting the sides of my hair so it would grow and twirl into the sidelocks that our ancestors used to wear, payos. I knew that 90 percent of playing the part was looking the part.

Generally speaking, Aryeh was more conservative than me, taking every word that every rabbi told him as gospel. He became observant through Chabad, a group of Hasidic Jewish missionaries, and he took on their beliefs like a new wardrobe. When I became observant, I did it on my own, and I had about a dozen different rebbes—some ultra-modern, some Hasidic, some harsh and stringent and biley. I threw their words at each other and I argued with them all. Most of my rabbis were from Modern Orthodox schools, where women wore loose-fitting pants and were allowed to sing aloud.

Even Aryeh had a bunch of rebbes, but his were all basically the same. No matter what Chabad rabbi you asked, they'd look the answers up in the same book—the *Likutei Sichos* of the Rebbe, the Chief Rabbi of Chabad, who died in 1994. Aryeh used to talk about how women were supposed to not wear pants and then he'd check out a girl in a miniskirt at the café across the street. I kept wanting to confide in him about dating Anastasia, or not dating her—our weird manic sleepovers where neither of us would sleep and we'd stroke each other's cheeks for hours in the dark. Her eyes sadly sang *I'm gay,* and my eyes got fearful when they replied back *I'm Orthodox.* Aryeh and I talked about being shomer negiah constantly, how much it sucked and how stressful it was. I still wasn't sure that I *wasn't* shomer negiah. Outside my bedroom, I was. I just came home every night to fall asleep with a girl in my bed.

Aryeh would say how hard it was to be shomer, and I'd say how hard it used to be when I was. We commiserated and wondered when our perfect Orthodox wives would find us, and I'd be about to say, "But there's also this girl Anastasia," and he'd open his mouth and say something

Rebbes. A rebbe is like a rabbi, but they're not the same thing. Every Orthodox Jew has her or his own rebbe, half teacher and half police officer, who answers your questions about Jewish law and tells you— or helps you to figure out—the dilemmas struck between Jewish law and your own life.

like "It's really not love I'm missing. I just miss pussy."

And I would swallow my words and change the subject.

One Saturday night, we were watching *The Maltese Falcon* for maybe the fifth week in a row. Aryeh had given up bars, and there were no cafés open this late, so when we hung out, the evening usually ended with our playing hand drums under the avocado tree in his backyard. This movie *Trembling Before G-d* had just come out, about gay Orthodox Jews, and everyone at our synagogue was whispering about it. So during the part where Sam Spade gets tied up and interrogated by the Moroccan double agent, I asked Aryeh about it. "Have you heard of this movie, *Trembling Before G-d?*"

"Sure, sure," Aryeh nodded, hung across his bed like a discarded coat. "That man, Simcha. He's good people."

"Simcha? You mean Sandi?" My eyes lit up. *Simcha* was the Hebrew name of Sandi Dubowski, who directed the movie. Chabadniks had this weird familiarity with and detachment from famous people in the secular world; they never watched television or listened to secular music, but they read *Rolling Stone* religiously, and the nationally televised Chabad Telethon fundraiser had Hollywood guests like Madonna and Vince Vaughn and Whoopi Goldberg speaking about how Chabad rabbis help all Jews, no matter who they are. Chabad kids always referred to Whoopi and Madonna by their first names, like old friends. Not like you had a choice with Madonna, but still.

"Sure. Sandi Dubowski, the—you know—the faygeleh. You know he's staying by Rabbi Mendy in a few weeks for Shabbos?"

"No way!" I said. "To start a rebel gay Orthodox minyan?"

"No, no way," Aryeh said. "He's staying at Mendy's

house, up Castro Street. It's a special event. It's gonna last all Shabbos long. I'm surprised you didn't know about it. Here, have some promotional postcards."

He stopped the movie and wouldn't hit PLAY until I'd taken a ream of *Trembling Before G-d* postcards and slipped them inside my bag, swearing up and down to Aryeh that I'd put them in all the hippest bars and cafés throughout the city.

"I can't believe this. Chabad is actually missionizing to gay people?"

Aryeh's face got that robotic look of reverence that all Chabadniks do when they talk about Chabad. "Chabad cares about everyone," he said. "No matter what they want in bed."

"I can't believe it," I said, tracing a postcard with my finger. "Chabad is having Gay Shabbos."

That made Aryeh's face turn as red as Christmas. "It's not a gay Shabbos," he said. "We're still Hasidim."

"Gay fucking Shabbos," I echoed, lost in awe and wonder.

"Just hand out the postcards," said Aryeh, unpausing the movie.

I handed them out, you know. I felt a little bit guilty doing it, since Rabbi Mendy was doing just fine as the straight rabbi of a mostly gay synagogue and I was afraid Rabbi Rasnikov was going to, I don't know, try to convert the keeping-Shabbos-and-kosher gay people to not being gay or something. But I still distributed the postcards. They actually advertised the film, not Gay Shabbos—a picture of two men in yarmulkes smiling solemnly at each other, *Now showing at the Castro Theater daily, with Saturday afternoon matinees.* The people in the rabbi's office had stuck computer-printed stickers over the show times with details that gave the address for services and information about paying in advance for the dinner that followed.

I left a postcard on the night table by my bed. Those days I was sleeping on a futon on the floor, and my night table was an inverted cardboard box that held my prayer-book, a lite-up clock, and two or three candles that I used in lieu of a nightlight. I showed Anastasia. "It's like both of our cultures together," I told her. "I mean, Jewish and gay. It's like a big melting pot. It's like America."

Her face clouded. "I'd love to, Matthue," she said, "I really would. But I have a show that night. I need to play."

"How come you didn't tell me you had a show?" I asked. I always came to her shows.

"It's on a Friday...."

"Oh yeah." It was all I could manage, distant and hollow.

That night she fell asleep at once and I lay there for an hour after I said my nighttime prayers, eyes trailing the outlines of car lights on my ceiling, thinking about Gay Shabbos, and whether our little synagogue was really ready for the big time.

Our local synagogue was not actually a synagogue. We held services in the modest basement of Rabbi Mendy's house, a dozen fold-up bridge chairs surrounding a modest wooden ark. Inside sat the smallest Torah you ever saw. There was no way they could use it for Gay Shabbos. Rabbi Rasnikov rented out the multipurpose room of an old-age nursing home down the street, which served as their church, synagogue, and the meeting hall for the nursing home bridge team. On the wall was a crucifix, a wooden copy of the Lord's Prayer, a Jewish star, and a blackboard with the bridge team stats.

Thursday afternoon before that Shabbos, I walked

around the multipurpose room, setting up rows of chairs. Aryeh ran in every half hour or so, dropping off food, fielding calls on Rabbi Rasnikov's cell phone. The rabbi directed me in my chair layout, pointing to areas where the chairs were uneven or tilted or something.

"So how many people are we expecting for Gay Shabbos, anyway?" I asked. The room was big and, except for the rabbi and me, it was completely empty. The rabbi stopped walking, froze in place. His hand hovered over the chair he was about to touch.

My voice bounced off the walls and rang in our ears.

"You mean, Shabbos Without Borders," the rabbi said to me evenly. "Could you please not call it that? We're trying to keep a mode of decorum about this. Have you figured out anyone who can be shaliach tzibur for the Friday night service?"

The day before, the rabbi had called me, as no-nonsense as usual. I said hi and he asked if I could think of anyone to be shaliach tzibur. You didn't need official qualifications to be shaliach, but he was the person who led the service; the shaliach stood at the podium and started all the songs and read all the parts that said *reader*. The shaliach was supposed to have a good voice, but in most Orthodox synagogues, it was usually the person with the loudest voice, atonal and discordant. He said he wanted somebody young and hip, someone who all the new people coming—he meant the gay people—could relate to. I think he

Shaliach tzibur. When we were growing up, shaliach tzibur used to be the most coveted position. For a full thirty minutes, you were in charge of the *whole entire class*—I mean, you had to read from a script and not deviate one iota, or else God would hear it and get mad—but, still, you were in an actual classroom, only you were in the driver's seat. I forget when exactly leading the prayer service switched to a position of horror, but it did—probably about the time our voices started changing.

was covertly asking if I could be shaliach, but obviously, Rabbi Rasnikov had never heard me try to sing.

"How about Tzvi or Avraham?" I suggested.

He asked who they were. I told him they were regular members from the neighborhood shul, and—I took a deep breath—they were also gay, which made them perfect for this unique bonding opportunity between two ordinarily disparate communities.

I thought I sounded like a perfect politician, a rabbi-in-training, almost. On the other line there was a dead, fuzzy silence. I could sense Rabbi Rasnikov's face turning red.

"Think of someone else, Moshe Shimon," he told me. "We'll talk about this tomorrow."

Now it was tomorrow.

I told Rabbi Rasnikov that I knew pretty much every member of the San Francisco Jewish community under the age of fifty, and there was absolutely nobody with a good voice. "Honestly," I said, "I probably sound better than any of them, and you don't want to hear me sing."

"Please, Moshe Shimon," he said. "Sing 'Mizmor L'Dovid.' "

I sang. He looked ready to cry. "You haven't thought of anybody else?" he said, almost pleading.

"I think Tzvi or Avraham would work," I shrugged. I unfolded another pair of chairs and threw them onto the back row.

"They're the homosexuals you mentioned yesterday?" asked the rabbi.

"They're them," I said. "But except for that, they're completely Orthodox."

He turned around as though he didn't know how to process that information. "They keep kosher?" he asked.

"They keep everything. They probably speak more Hebrew than either of us."

"Huh," said the rabbi.

"And they can *sing*. I mean, they know tunes for the prayers that would blow you away. Let me tell you. Last Shabbos, they were singing around the table after lunch for, like, three hours, doing Shabbos nigguns to the tune of Broadway musicals…." I stopped myself. This was not information that would persuade the rabbi in their favor. "Three hours. Of Shabbos songs. They're good."

The rabbi stroked his beard thoughtfully.

"I'll think about it," he said. His brain was already spinning; at least I'd got him thinking.

On Friday afternoon, the chairs were laid out, the stained-glass crucifix artfully concealed by a clean white cloth. At the front of the multipurpose room sat Rabbi Mendy's humble ark. Rabbi Rasnikov and Aryeh were arranging its curtain. Aryeh was edgy and restless. He kept running his eye along the details of the room. People drifted in and Aryeh checked out every person as they passed through the doors.

There were a few lesbians, voyeuristic-looking straight people, and oddly placed Orthodox Jews who were regulars at other synagogues and had come here to check out the spectacle. Some of the mainstream press were running stories about it, although the local Jewish paper didn't; they said they couldn't find anything newsworthy about it. That's the Jewish community for you: The Second Coming could happen, and if they hadn't reported the First Coming, they'd pass it up to talk about the latest charity dinner.

But most of the people there were gay men. Avraham and Tzvi and Sammy and Ramon stood at the back, in the makeshift lobby behind the alignment of chairs, kibitzing until the prayers started. At first it was just Tzvi and Sammy and a few of their friends, looking away from each other to throw glances around the room.

Then people started asides, and one conversation circle became one and a half, then two, then three. Before we knew it, the room was packed, people were milling around the front seats waiting for the service to start, speculating about what tonight was going to be like, talking like they usually did, about who looked good and who was sick and who was sleeping with whom.

Box had been taking me to gay male clubs since the month I moved here, but I had never seen the variety, size, and shape of gay men that I saw that night in that room of the nursing home. Tzvi was hanging out with a bunch of bears, big hairy gay men with beards or handlebar moustaches, stomachs that had their own equators. Ramon was wearing the black hat that he always wore, but he had a leather jacket on too. Avraham, who was pudgy and looked like a parrot, was surrounded by a bunch of Abercrombie boys with muscles that strained the hems of their Friday-white polo shirts. In another corner was a group of raver boys with outer-space pocketbooks, not even making a show of dressing up for Shabbos. With their striped rave pants and reflective sunglasses, I didn't know how to file them. I wanted to be angry because they didn't dress up for synagogue, and that was what people at synagogue always did. I mean, *I* went through all this shit to iron my slacks for shul, why do you get to dress like it's Sunday afternoon at the dive bar?

But then I saw the rabbis on the other side of the room, and the possessed-looking teenagers from Brooklyn in black suits and Hasidic hats, the ones who had flown in from New York for the weekend. Rabbi Rasnikov had asked a bunch of rabbis-in-training to come and mesh with the unaffiliated people here. I looked back at the rave boys with their crew cuts. Maybe I was okay with them.

And then I heard a wolf whistle from the doorway, right behind me. I spun around. Leaning against the frame, hands tucked in the pockets of his paisley tuxedo jacket like he was Sammy Davis, Jr., was Jacob, slouching, top hat pulled low over his eyes, casting his nose in five separate shadows. He looked less teenage and more teenage than ever before. His riff on the traditional Hasidic outfit was more swanky—and more subversive—than anyone could understand.

"Hey, Roth," Jacob said, cocking a finger-gun at me. "What's up? When are we gonna dav?"

Dav was short for *daven,* which was Yiddish slang for praying. I had picked up the short forms from the Silver Spring kids, who I guess had invented them. And now Jacob. This is how our religion spreads.

I looked startled. So did all the bears, who were hitting new levels of pre-synagogue flirtation.

Rabbi Rasnikov turned to one of the rabbis-in-training. "Yosef Yitzchak, a niggun," he ordered.

A rabbi-in-training, already sitting attentively in the praying area, started to sing. He swayed back and forth in his seat. Rabbi Rasnikov harmonized in and so did Rabbi Mendy. Jacob and I pushed our way through people, down the aisles to some seats near the front. Everyone else started clamoring for seats too. Jacob began swaying and, with one eye on the ravers in the back, so did I.

A niggun always follows a simple tune, one you don't always get when you start singing, but a niggun is supposed to be hypnotic. Even the idea of a niggun is. This very simple set of notes, all dissolving into a monotonous pattern of *yai dai's* in the toneless rabbi-in-training's voice, we got the rhythm at once, we started singing *yai*

Yiddish slang for praying. It was Jewish slang in that too-cool-for-school way. It came from the same place as those ironic hipster kids who say *phat.*

dai dai ba bum bai with him, even the people who didn't know Hebrew, everyone fell into the song. It was easy, simple, brain numbing, and everyone could do it.

The niggun finished and this clean-shaven blond guy in a bright sewn yarmulke and a sweater vest stepped to the front. His voice trembled a little at first.

So did mine. So did Jacob's, and Tzvi's and Avraham's too, the few of us who knew the words. We all felt kind of embarrassed to sing, like a joke we were afraid to show we actually understood.

We faded into the part of the prayer that everyone reads to themselves. Then the dude who was leading the service got to the first chorus, and when he opened his mouth, it was like someone turned on the surround sound. His voice hit the front wall, bounced back, and glistened through the chapel. The notes floated, held on the air. Each word was a power chord, searing through this guy's lungs. Sometimes I really like a show-off shaliach tzibbur and sometimes, more often, it bugs the hell out of me. Tonight I was just confused. If Rabbi Rasnikov hadn't wanted a gay guy to lead services, why did he ask such a gay-looking straight guy to be shaliach?

We finished praying, and there was the usual huge delay for tables to be set up and for Rabbi Mendy to keep announcing that everyone was welcome to stay for dinner but could people who hadn't made reservations please pay after Shabbos.

Jacob walked over to one of the rabbis-in-training. In a town like San Francisco, meeting someone Orthodox

The front wall. In Conservative and Reform synagogues, the prayer leader faces the rest of the congregation as if he or she is about to bust out in a lecture. In Orthodox synagogues, the shaliach faces the same direction as everyone else. It's a humbling experience. The shaliach isn't in charge of praying, he's just there to keep everyone going at roughly the same pace.

under the age of thirty was like finding buried trea-sure—even if he was brought in from the yeshiva for the occasion. "Hi, my name is Jacob," said Jacob. "What's your deal?"

The boy, taken aback, studied Jacob for a while, one hand stroking his beard. At last, he replied: "It's good to meet you, Jacob." He spoke quietly, swilling words like whiskey before they left his mouth. He had a baby beard like Jacob's, and pin-thin glasses that surrounded his eyes in perfect circles. "My name is Gabriel."

"Gabriel, that's cool," said Jacob. "Are you named for the angel?"

Beat.

"I suppose so," Gabriel said after a moment, sounding bored, like he'd done the research between Jacob's ques-tion and his answer. "Tell me," he said, "Were you raised in the Orthodox tradition?"

" 'In the Orthodox tradition'?" Jacob repeated. "What are you, a game show host?"

"At what age did you decide to become religious, then?" Gabriel ignored the Jakeishness of Jacob. He was just after answers.

We didn't ask if Gabriel was raised Chabad or not, but we could tell he wasn't. He didn't speak with enough of a Brooklyn accent. Even Rabbi Mendy, who was raised Chabad in New Zealand, spoke with a Brooklyn accent. He did everything right—he took a plastic wine goblet and made his own kiddish, he washed hands before we broke bread, and didn't talk until all the blessings were said—but there was a rigidity to the way he started kiddish, a fully thought-out consciousness about it, that was too choreo-graphed to be natural. Gay people have gaydar, the ability to spot other gay people in the room before any words are spoken or glances exchanged. We have Orthodar.

The tables for dinner were wide, they could hold

twelve people. The bears and the Abercrombie models were already involving each other in conversation. On one side of our table were me, Jacob, Aryeh, Gabriel, and another rabbi-in-training, who spaced out the first time Jacob starting talking about the concert that his band played last Saturday at Gilman Street. Jacob was in an acoustic punk band called Up With Hope, Down With Mayonnaise. They sang songs about robbing banks and chasing girls and breakfast cereal. The second rabbi-in-training asked if Gilman Street was a dance club and Jacob told him that mostly people moshed.

"That's the one where people jump on each other?"

"Yeah," said Jacob.

"Boys and girls together?"

"When we're lucky," said Jacob.

The two rabbis-in-training kept quiet for the rest of the meal, breaking only to ask Aryeh to pass the salt or where the men's room was.

The other half of the table was its own affair, a group of middle-aged lesbians, slicing their chicken with catholic docility. Halfway through the meal, Jacob's friends Darcy and Stella came in, looking around as if they were in the wrong place. Darcy had on a frayed denim skirt and Stella had on gothy magenta makeup. I waved them over to our table, Jacob ran to find extra chairs, and they poked around plates of green beans and chicken-tasting rice pilaf for the rest of the meal.

After we finished eating I invited a whole coalition of people to walk back to my house. Jacob and one of the rabbis-in-training were supposed to crash with me.

We were exhausted. Deeply, profoundly exhausted. The rabbi-in-training headed straight to his Shabbos bag and went to change into pajamas. Jacob pulled me aside in the hallway and asked, was it okay if Stella and Darcy stayed over tonight?

I asked him, where?

He shrugged. "We could all share your bed," he offered.

"Okay," I said wearily. "If my teenage lesbian girlfriend comes in and wakes you guys, just tell her I'm sleeping on the kitchen floor."

"Sure," Jacob said.

I woke the next morning in a nest of pillows. Group houses have a way of making all the necessary shit you need for a house vanish, but you wind up with piles of semiuseless stuff for all occasions. One way or another, we'd acquired maybe fifty pillows, a mix of Ikea, lacy Victorian drawing-room pillows, throw pillows from abandoned couches and loveseats, and book-size vanity pillows that Christian grandmothers exchange for Easter. I woke up with sunlight warming my face, the rabbi-in-training on my sofa, rocking his body as he read a book in Hebrew with his lips moving. I frowned. Had Anastasia come? She hadn't. I was alone. That was good.

I fished my yarmulke out of the pillows, slapped it on, and said Modeh Ani. I was still wearing my clothes from last night. "What time is it?" I asked, remembering then that I was the only one who knew where the clock was. The rabbi-in-training looked up, shrugged, went back to recitations.

Ten fifteen. Services had just started, and by the time we were out of the house it would be another half hour.

I knocked on my bedroom door. Jacob moaned. I creaked it open.

"Hey, we're leaving for synagogue," I said. "You don't have to come but there's gonna be lunch."

"Come on in," said Jacob.

He was lying on my bed, shirt off, Darcy and Stella each fading out of sleep on one of his shoulders. Darcy's hand fell across his chest, lingering innocently on his nipple. Not like she was playing with it, not even like she knew it was there. God, I remembered being that young, back when everything was sexual but before you became so aware of it all.

We got to synagogue just as the Torah reading started. I stood in the back and prayed, and I finished just as they were finishing reading. Rabbi Rasnikov stood to the side, presiding over the reading, while Rabbi Mendy buzzed straight through the Torah portion. The weirdly normal-looking shaliach tzibur from last night stood beside him, correcting Mendy when he got a note or a vowel cantillation wrong. It was okay, though. That was what you did for the Torah reading.

When the reading was done, Rabbi Rasnikov stepped to the front of the congregation to deliver the sermon. But instead he opened his mouth and said, "Today, we have a special guest sermon from a very heilege rabbi who's traveled from New York to be here." Rabbi Rasnikov cleared his throat. "Please welcome Rabbi Steve Greenberg."

Flashback. In Washington, when I was becoming observant, a visiting rabbi lectured at a Lunch-and-Learn on the laws about gay people. He said, you can't look at laws about gay *people*, because people are inherently kosher. But there are two popular ways of seeing male-on-male homosexual sex in Jewish law. Some people, he said, classify it as something we're told not to do—the Torah says that men should not fuck other men—while gay people's brains and bodies tell them it is permissible. The other major view, which my rebbe proffered, is that being gay isn't against Jewish law, but gay sex is.

Vowel cantillation. The annotations to Hebrew sacred books, called trup, swirls and dots that tell you how a particular word should be sung.

I asked him if there were any people who were Jewish and actively gay.

The rabbi pushed his lunch plate away, now just a pile of skin and bones and puddles of sauce.

Then he told me about Rabbi Steve Greenberg, an Orthodox rabbi who was now out as gay, but still an Orthodox rabbi, and who was trying to prove that being gay was acceptable under Jewish law.

His wife put a hand over her mouth, trying not to laugh.

"What?" I said. *"What?"* Before I moved to San Francisco, I had such the persuasively nasal whine.

"He wasn't always so gay," she said, looking over at her husband.

"One of our friends," he said, "was the last woman that Rabbi Greenberg dated before he came out as gay."

"Which would be," she amended, doing the math, "the last woman he dated, period."

Now Rabbi Greenberg was about to speak on the week's parsha, a chapter of Torah that focused on the Jews escaping from Egypt. It had nothing at all to do with Gay Shabbos except for the eschatological idea that you can speak about the Torah portion and relate it to anything.

But he didn't. He didn't make that cheesy leap from Torah times to how-can-we-be-better-Jews, reducing the Torah to some Hallmark card blurb. He talked about the Torah, and he talked about Moses in the wilderness,

Relate it to anything. This has been put to the test more times than I can comfortably relate. Probably the most out-of-control rendition, and I don't remember how the rabbi got from tab A to slot B, came from one rabbi who turned the story of Balaam, in which a donkey saves its master from being fried by angelic lightning bolts, into a moralistic fable where you have to turn and say, "I was wrong. I am sorry." That was at summer camp, and then the rabbi made the whole camp repeat that together: "I was wrong. I am sorry."

and how Miriam and Aaron sang the Song at the Sea as they crossed and the waters parted, and he talked about Nachshon ben Aminadav being the first person to cross the Red Sea, even though God hadn't split it yet. Rabbi Greenberg said how amazing it was that Nachshon put that much trust in God, and we should all be willing to do that.

After his sermon, he sat down, nodded respectfully to Rabbi Mendy, and squeezed the hand of the man sitting next to him. That was the man with the preppy sweaters, the shaliach tzibur from last night.

Jacob leaned into my ear. "Are they boyfriends?" he asked.

"You'd think so," I whispered back.

When services ended, Gabriel asked me how I could pray alongside homosexuals if I was such a righteous Jew. "What, like you can't?" I said, blown away. Jacob was after me, too. He wanted to keep talking about girls and music and did I think his band should write a song about being gay and Orthodox? "But you like *girls*," I said. "That would be the irony," said Jacob, smiling cleverly. I set them on each other. I ran up to Steve Greenberg, feeling like such a fanboy. I mean, I'd done Internet searches on him before.

I opened my mouth to introduce myself. Gushage fell out. "It's so cool that you're Orthodox and you can do this and you can take your Orthodoxy on your own terms and you still want to serve God and do mitzvos and I've read your stuff and I can't believe anything exists like what you write and your sermon today didn't even *talk* about queer issues and it was so insightful." It really was.

Rabbi Steve Greenberg introduced me to his partner. (That was his word: *"This is my partner,"* he said to me, cool and businesslike. *Partner* was the perfect word for it: not only because their twin *V*-neck sweaters made them look like uniformed astronauts. It sounded crisp. East Coast. Professional, but with a wink to those of us Who Knew.) His partner, the shaliach tzibur, was also named Steve. I got paralyzed by confusion for a second. Why was the first thing I thought of, *I wonder if he ever gets confused at home?*

I reached over and shook the other Steve's hand. Between us, Rabbi Steve Greenberg was smiling in that cou
pley I'm-so-proud-of-my-boyfriend way. "Steve is an opera singer," he said. I pictured Rabbi Rasnikov thinking of reasons to argue with accepting him as shaliach, and Rabbi Steve Greenberg saying, *He. Sings. PROFESSIONALLY.*

I *liked* this dude.

There was that moment of awkwardness when we weren't sure if the conversation was transferring between me and Steve the Shaliach, but then I asked Rabbi Greenberg a question about his sermon, and we started talking.

We talked. We talked through lunch, after lunch, through dessert and midafternoon and the meat chollint, the first time Rabbi Mendy and his wife had ever cooked a meat chollint for a synagogue lunch. "Usually there's so many vegetarians," said Mendy, "but today we figured we would get a big turnout of lots of very frum Jews, and you know how frum Jews love meat!" He emptied the ladle into Tzvi's bowl. Tzvi attacked it. Mendy looked so happy to be serving everyone that I almost felt guilty being a vegetarian. "Rabbi," Mendy said, leaning over to Rabbi Greenberg, "you're not a vegetarian, are you?"

"No, sir," he said, raising up his bowl to be ladled. And as soon as the steamy melting hunks of flesh were in front of him, spoon in hand and meat in mouth, he continued talking.

I didn't realize who Sandi Dubowski was until lunch was almost over. The l'chaims made their way around, a big pitcher of vodka was passed around with a stack of small plastic kiddish cups. Rabbi Rasnikov was going around the room, meeting everyone, blessing them, and then toasting them. He was having more l'chaims than everyone else put together. The rabbi pulled this one guy out of his chair, *Price Is Right*–style, and yanked him close in a chesty bear hug. The guy was a kid, almost my age, wearing tzitzis and a big white knitted yarmulke that came down to his ears, with a small, close-trimmed blond beard. His face was childlike, big eyes and cheeks. He was the kind of boy that my grandparents wanted me to play with—friendly, but easily nervous. When Rabbi Rasnikov made him stand, his hands balled into little fists, thumbs tucked inside.

"Friends," Rabbi Rasnikov said. "Friends. This man is the reason we all got here."

Jacob nudged me. "You're the reason I got here. You woke me up."

"Is that Sandi?" I asked. "Sandi Dubowski?"

"Beats me," said Jacob.

Sandi waved, grinned, tried to sit back down. Rabbi Rasnikov wasn't taking it. He pulled Sandi back up and made him do another l'chaim.

"Sandi," the rabbi said. "Simcha," he said, "can I use your Hebrew name?"

Sandi—*Simcha*—nodded his approval.

"Simcha, the name of your film is *Trembling Before G-d.* And it is my hope today that we can all tremble together a little."

He started clapping his hands and singing a raging niggun, *ai yai yai*'ing it to high heaven. The two rab-bis-in-training picked up the tune immediately, and then so did Mendy and Tzvi and Avraham. A second later, everyone was singing. Sandi/Simcha started to clap, and laugh, and Jacob, shoving his fifth or sixth l'chaim of the afternoon in the air with a flourish (the rabbi: "It's okay, it's for religious purposes, just don't tell your parents"), harmonized away to infinity.

Rabbi Greenberg and I were still talking. We really did talk through the entire meal, the whole afternoon. I don't remember what we said to each other. I mean, part of it, I do, and other parts of it was just stuff that I asked him about, little questions about x and y and was he related to Blu Greenberg, the famous Orthodox feminist theorist, and her husband Yitz ("He's my rebbe! Actually, they're both my rebbes." Me: "You can have more than one rebbe?" Him: "I'm poly-rebbeous") and how it was to live in New York surrounded by people who hated you. "They don't hate me," he told me, "they hate an idea. And what I have to do is show them that that idea isn't what they think it is, that I'm not a bad Jew, or a bad person, because of it." When it was time to go, I was flustered and speechless, the way you are when you meet a girl and you don't know how to ask for her number and you're hoping in your head that these are not the last five seconds of time you're gonna spend together. He didn't have a congregation in New York, and, as the only out gay Orthodox rabbi, he was too famous to just look up in the phone book. I felt like I was spending the last minutes of my life with my movie-star boyfriend.

"So, uh, how do I find you again?"

There. Those were the words. Molly Ringwald in *Sixteen Candles,* Jennifer Grey in *Ferris Bueller's Day Off,* the hot girl with the Thor helmet in *Adventures in Babysitting.* I was becoming an '80s swooning-girl icon, and it was all because of a gay Orthodox rabbi.

"Email me," he said. "Sandi has a link to my address on the movie website. Tell me when you're in New York, and we'll have you for Shabbos."

A week later, I performed at the opening of the San Francisco Queer Center. My friend Jerrica, the queer issues editor of the local Jewish paper, hooked me up with the gig. Neither of us knew if I should do it—I mean, I was mostly only queer by association—but the director came to one of my shows and listened to me talk like a girl and said I'd be just fine. I was on the bill with the biggest queer names in the city. Former porn-star-slash-sexologist Annie Sprinkle. Deep Dickollective, the gay hip-hop group that the *New York Times* had just profiled. Jacob said that he was bringing his whole posse from school. This was one of my first non-bar shows, and because they were all fifteen, it was the first time they could see me perform. It was the first time that Anastasia could get in too. She was nineteen, and even though she was a world away from Jacob's friends (paying rent! working a real job! living three thousand miles from home!) it still felt a little bit illicit to be hooking up with someone who didn't break the bar-age barrier.

Backstage, in the green room, a skinny biker with a silver goatee and bomber jacket introduced himself to me. He took my hand and pumped it with a surprising strength, and he started asking me questions. "I recognized you right away," he told me. "I saw you at Gay Shabbos."

"You mean Shabbos Without Borders," I said absently.

"What?"

"Nothing."

"Yes, well, anyway. I saw you there, and it struck me that night. I've been thinking about producing a film, and I thought you and your boyfriend—if he is your boyfriend—I thought you two would fit brilliantly."

"My boyfriend?"

"That short gentleman with the beard. He looked kind of like a hippie in a tuxedo...."

Jacob.

I almost started laughing. Then I remembered that I was trespassing, and I felt like a complete cultural monster, just the white man smashin' down one more culture.

I tried to explain. "Neither of us is gay."

"That's okay. It would just be one scene, him going down on you, or the other way around, fooling around in a bathroom, whatever you wanted."

"But we're not gay."

He smiled as if I was speaking another language. "I mean, anal would be fine—but only if you were both comfortable with it."

"And Jacob is underage."

"Oh." That stumped him.

He thanked me for talking to him. I thanked him for coming to Shabbos. Feeling a little surge of the Chabad missionary in myself, I told him we had services every Saturday morning and he should come by, because there was lunch afterward and we were always looking for a minyan man.

"Maybe I'll be your minyan man some time," he told me.

We both moved on.

The scene that night was hard core San Francisco: not gay so much as alien. People wore shirts made of tin foil and colored tissue paper, dresses that Björk would wear, boots that rose high enough to be pants. I was wearing a little-boy rugby shirt with superhero stripes on the shoulder, it made me look like a girl with no boobs.

I tumbled through the crowd, watching the drag queens, the leather daddies with slaves on chains, the straight yuppie socialites. Hot, hot girls in black-haired wigs toted around trays of champagne, and I couldn't drink it because it wasn't kosher. I started being careful about kashrus before I started drinking alcohol. In that moment, I realized how I had no idea what champagne tasted like, but I still loved the way it looked, watching the universe inverted and bubbled out through the golden liquid and the twisted glass stems. Dizzily tripping around the sleek gray spaceship-like interior of the Queer Center, I realized why drug addicts call that high hallucinatory feeling *tripping*. I really felt like I was in another universe. Nothing around me was familiar.

I ducked around the corner and slipped into an art installation. Actually it was a bunch of movies—or, like that porn director would say, a bunch of *films*. Two movies were playing, but each movie was being broadcast on three or four screens, showing the same thing from different angles. One was a misty, surreal progression of blurred curves that might or might not be human bodies twisting into each other. You could see a sphere shaking, twisting, slipping into a cupped resting spot that looked vaguely like a hand. There was a soundtrack that sounded like static moaning.

I wasn't sure how much I wanted to see of it. I mean, I was an artist, I was supposed to be open-minded. And I wasn't about to freak out over a gay sex scene. Images of sex weren't so proper to look at, if you were being tznius about it. There was nothing officially forbidden about watching scenes on television in the Talmud, but I was feeling a little uncomfortable. It probably had to do with my hanging around dykes all the time and being uncomfortable about being a boy, male privilege and rape

Television in the Talmud. Well, duh, Matt. Although it doesn't forbid porn outright, voyeurism is pretty strictly discouraged, because the idea is that sex is supposed to focus on the people having it. But the closest passage I can find that actually forbids porn and erotica is one that discourages men from looking directly at an erogenous zone because it could, um, make their children go blind.

fantasies and stuff. I wasn't even that fond of looking at my own penis, let alone movies about other people's penises. I started to wonder how much of my own cursing and flaunting and talking about sex onstage was overdoing it. I didn't think I was sticking my sexuality in anybody's face. I didn't really *want* to stick my sexuality in anybody's face.

And then I spotted Gabriel.

I don't know what he was doing there. I didn't know how he was still in San Francisco or how he wound up in the Castro District or what he was doing in the middle of a deserted art installation watching hairy-chested nekkid men get it on. His eyes were wide behind his thick eyebrows and his mouth was one-quarter open, gaping, breathing heavily. Not in a disgusting way, more like an unbelievableness. I wanted to run up to him. I wanted to call him out on being so condescending to Jacob, and about looking at porn in public, and why was he going to show up to a gay Orthodox Shabbos and not be *out* about it, and was he even gay anyway?

And then I realized: *It didn't matter.* It didn't matter if anyone is gay, or if they hang out in gay places constantly like I did, or if they're the most pious person in the world who feels justified in treating teen Orthodox-outside-the-box kids like shit. We all had our own onuses to carry, and we all had our own fish to fry, and sometimes we just needed to go ahead, fry those bad fish, get salmonella poisoning, and start all over again. Most Orthodox Jews recite Vidui, the confessional prayer, on Yom Kippur, but Chabad says it each morning, as though we really *do* get the chance to be born again every day.

At that moment, I totally understood why.

I ran upstairs, almost plowing over Stella and her friend Hava, who were about to enter the room.

"What's in there?" asked Hava.

"Dude, isn't it almost time for you to go on?" said Stella.

I shot both of their questions a noncommittal "Probably!" I flew up the stairs, straightened my tzitzis, entered the room, and heard M.C. Fairy Butch announcing my name.

The microphone stared at me. The crowd, two hundred people gone suddenly, unnaturally silent, stared at me. From the side of the stage I could see the producer and the M.C., glancing at each other, glancing at the audience.

And me without a set list.

I opened my mouth. I felt it fill with silence. I let the silence drift out.

I ripped out "Dick," the poem about my best friend getting sexually assaulted when we were fifteen, and I did it without thinking about it. I was not ready for this. I didn't even know it was going to happen.

"My sex drive disappeared / the way your appetite disappears / when someone vomits on the table," I said. "You could say / I got sick of it / before I started / I started / to talk and think and act like a girl / picking up speech patterns / the way boys pick up the jackets / that girls drop on purpose. The way girls learn / to make boys work for them / I learned how to make girls / hide me away."

I gripped the mic. My voice coasted between a scream and a whisper. I tried to bounce my hand in the air and keep it steady like a rapper pantomiming a turntable scratch, but I was trembling like nobody's business. I did "Shrink," my poem about being too skinny, and "I'd Rather Be a Dyke," which was kind of a hip-hop song, and it finally got people laughing after all that dread silence. You should never start off a show with a serious poem. You look all vulnerable and the audience gets afraid that you're going to break into a million pieces. And I closed with "Orthodox Girls," which I hadn't expected to do at all, but everyone was so jumpy and happy and I wanted to bust loose and celebrate.

I ran offstage with people after me, flattering in the biggest way. Jacob jumped on my back and started shouting and I whirled him around and wrapped my arms around and hugged him and Darcy. I was sweaty and smelly and gross but they were okay with it. People were asking if they could buy my chapbook and I was like, *yes please,* and then I looked over to the door because when I'm onstage my mind is racing in a million different directions at once, and I remembered that in the middle of my last poem, I'd seen Anastasia appear in the doorway.

She was still standing there. Leaning against a wall, wearing a pixie dress made out of tissue paper and zebra-striped cat ears, one strand of hair over her left eye. Her roommate Bijal, a straitlaced prep girl in a turtleneck and Prada sandals, stood behind her, eyeing the crowd with one nervous hand ticking at her neck.

"It's good to see you," whispered Anastasia.

"Glad you could make it," I whispered back.

Then I ran away.

That night I shared a dressing room with an entire troupe of drag queens, not the kind of queens who look more like women than women do, but the dreamlike, surreal drag queens, the ones with powdered, glittered beards, musclemen who looked like the kids who used to kick my ass in junior high. I dove out of my rugby shirt and into a nondescript concert shirt (Sleater-Kinney, The Bad One Tour 2000) that wasn't so sweat-inflicted and didn't make my stomach and torso look like a perfect size-zero teenage girl's.

I slung it on and jumped back into the party. I stepped outside the dressing room. The crowd swallowed me.

On the balcony atop the Queer Center, Jacob chatted

up some bull dykes, comparing stories about rock shows and independent movies. Everything felt volatile, like it was about to explode. Anastasia and I stood against the frosted glass panels, holding hands, and it felt like the biggest thing in the universe. I came out as straight on-stage that night, I wasn't ashamed of it or anything, but I hadn't held hands with someone in public in a year. I wasn't used to it. I felt like I was dangling on the edge of the building, about to fall.

That was when she kissed me. Her arms and mouth caught me at the point of a *V* shape. My back pressed flat against the glass wall. Our lips dove into each other's and our tongues made *J*'s and hooked, the slight bumps of her taste buds, the silk of her palm ground hard against my skull and pulled it into hers. When I was on stage, every-thing felt real. This felt like performing.

I left the building on Anastasia's arm, not sure where we were going next, except that her roommate had a car and we could pretty much go anywhere.

I passed the film director on the way out. I slipped one hand on his shoulder and whispered that he really *must* come to services at Rabbi Mendy's synagogue sometime. Doing synagogue outreach, setting people up. Maybe I would be a good Chabadnik after all.

11

intimate photography

I broke up with Anastasia. I rebounded with a tour. She rebounded with a porn film. The whole time we'd been dating, I kept expecting my friends to call me out—an Orthodox Jew hooking up with a teenage pagan lesbian—but no one ever did. I started to bug them about it. "It's against Jewish law, and she isn't even supposed to like me, and it doesn't make sense anyway," I complained. "And don't you think I'm taking advantage of her?"

"No," said my best friend Erin—late one night, when all our phone conversations took place so it was free on her cell phone. She had just moved to Hollywood and didn't know anybody yet and spent her free time consoling me. "It's good for you. You needed to get laid."

Getting laid was the one thing we never did. I was inexperienced and scared and afraid of commitment. Anastasia was over the whole sex-with-boys thing. Actually, she wanted complete nonmonogamy. Despite her in-your-face 'tude and radical live-by-the-guitar punk street musician lifestyle, she was a hippie at heart. She wanted us to—in her words—"share our love with others." I told her we could. I just couldn't take her sharing it with me. Sometimes the smallest things kill the biggest romances. Half a year of my life, and all of a sudden, quick as cotton, it was over, kaput.

So I flew back to Philadelphia. I'd had my ticket for a while. American Indians say, you never plan a vision quest, you just *go*. It's not something you pack food for, you don't tell your friends, *See you next week, tell Phred I'm sorry I'm missing his birthday BBQ but I have to go on a vision quest.*

No: Like fasting or praying or ritual slaughter, vision quests are not experiences you can fuck around with. When you find yourself in the desert, going without water for three days and somehow you're not dead, then you can safely say that you are on a vision quest.

And that's how it happened. I'd been planning this tour forever. But only in the air, in my actual airplane seat that an actual college had paid for, did I realize that my month-long jaunt was going to be an actual vision quest.

For four weeks, I rode up and down the coast, in Greyhound buses and strangers' cars, meeting the college liaisons whose middle and last names I knew by heart after emailing them constantly for months. In person they were usually timid, welcoming people, those underweight college administrators who are convinced that they're helping the world by organizing educational-slash-*hip* programs for students, God bless their souls. They took me to dinner in the schools' meager kosher dining halls, then I climbed on stages (or pedestals or podiums or fireplaces) and performed my poetry. People kept expecting me to have reading glasses and a slim volume of sonnets. I grabbed the mic, yelled my lyrics out, sang them like an '80s synth-pop song you refuse to stop loving. I jumped and danced and ballyhooed and did splits across the room.

One night in Providence, I managed to convince this very nice (but skeptical) dykey bandanna girl to put me with the musical acts instead of the poets, because the spoken-word segment was on Saturday afternoon, during Shabbos, and this band I loved, the Butchies, was playing, and I was more like rock and roll than poetry and could I *please* play Saturday night and, finally, she relented.

They held the concert in the university's main auditorium. Queer girls from Boston and New York drove up. There was a girl punk band, a Dixieland drag queen band, me, and the Butchies. The Butchies played furious electronic rock, Sonic Youth guitar screaming, disco- fast drums. Each of their songs was a different time Anastasia and I had gone to some queer bar or open mic or performance event, made private eyes at each other from across the room, and ran home to her Victorian in the Lower Haight to kiss horizontally all night long, our stereos screaming with rock songs so her housemates wouldn't hear. She always made me choose the music, I think, so she couldn't be responsible when her housemates complained. For so long after that, the music bore her residue, the whole experience, it was all tied to Anastasia. My past was being absorbed by her. So many make-out sessions I'd shared with Ani DiFranco and Corin from Sleater-Kinney and Kaia from the Butchies. They could sing about love and hurt and loneliness like nobody else. They sang about girls and they sounded so hurt and pure, the way that only a girl could sing about girls.

I went on right before the Butchies. They set up on the back half of the stage. Kaia was tuning her guitar right behind me. I had the first ten feet of the stage and I was using it fully, running, jumping, stage diving onto the moon-shaped black monitors. I did "I'd Rather Be a Dyke"—"Because every boy's a whore at heart / and every girl is horny / and if I was a lesbian / then I could always score me"—and, in one verse, I threw in a shout-out to the Butchies' drummer. I did "Rock Me Till We're Old and Boring" and I jumped off the stage, one hand slugging the microphone down my mouth and into my throat, one arm outstretched into the air, reaching for the chandelier and the ceiling and the stars. Like I could almost touch forever. Like I was capturing the memories associated with the Butchies, rubbing out every regret-inflicted kiss, rewriting the memories as my own.

I'd borrowed Anastasia's Butchies CD a few months ago, and she never asked for it back. I still have it. It skips a little during the jam-out song about Gertrude Stein, reminding me that Gertrude Stein would never not return an ex's CD, or maybe that Gertrude Stein would never fall into a mess like this in the first place.

I remembered the night this all started, that first night that we made out, somewhere in that gray area between Rosh HaShana and Yom Kippur: "But aren't you gay?" I asked, concerned, as we lay together in bed the way we always did, when Anastasia's tame goodnight kiss lingered on my cheek, and drifted to my lips, pried them open and dove down my throat like a red-hot doctor's shot that burned my tonsils and pulled me flat against her body, skilletlike and smoking. My hands lingered on her hips, at her waist, nervous and afraid to do the things my body was telling me to do.

Anastasia shrugged, the aftermath of the kiss calm and serene. "I guess so. But I like *you*," she said. She ran her hand along the inside curve of my arm as if she was weighing me against the night air. "Are you allowed to do this? I mean, with the Orthodox stuff and all?"

"Don't worry about that," I assured her. "The important thing is to make sure you're feeling okay about it."

This is how I am. In relationships, in real life, in business—forget about me, I just want to make sure everyone else is okay.

So I made sure Anastasia was okay. With her sexuality. With monogamy. When I found out she was a stripper, I was such a feel-good San Francisco boyfriend. I was brilliant.

By which I mean, I was ridiculous.

"If you need any costumes, my friend Bruce does wardrobes at the Opera House," I offered. People told me that stripping was a lifestyle. I thought they meant like an ethnicity, like Anastasia had somehow converted from Christianity to stripper.

Let me tell you how it happened. Anastasia went through jobs like most people go through tube socks. She kept showing up late to the bakery job that started at sunrise. The well-paying Fisherman's Wharf family restaurant where she was a waitress closed without warning. One day she showed up for a lunch shift, and the doors and windows were boarded up. Her last job, secretary to a Palestinian exporter, lasted until her boss started coming onto her and left informational pamphlets on polygamy and religious conversion on her desk. Nine dollars an hour wasn't worth it. For five bucks more, she could have conversations about music and feminist theory with a bunch of other girls, standing behind glass, and occasionally she would have to rip off her clothes and grind.

Only, she didn't tell me. One night we were lying on my bed, watching a movie neither of us really cared about, and she asked, "What would you think if I stripped?"

I said it would be kind of gross.

"Gross how?" Anastasia looked disturbed.

I didn't think about the answer before I said it. I have this habit where, the less attention I'm paying, the more academic and well-thought-out I sound. I said, "Gross, like, right now we're sharing all our orgasms with each other. We know the tilt of each other's chins and our bodies are on the same rhythm. It seems kind of philosophically fucked-up to take your sexuality and just, like, fling it into the universe."

I felt like I was supposed to feel proprietary rights on her. It made me uncomfortable and I hated it. She liked me because I never acted like a typical guy. Right then I was feeling like such a typical guy. Jealous and angry and left out and I didn't know what to say and I didn't want to just kiss her and let it go.

I kissed her. I let it go.

I couldn't sleep for hours. I tried writing. I tried drawing. I wasn't anti-stripper. I really wasn't. I'd never been to a strip club, but I know people who had. Some of my best friends were strippers. I mean—I lived in San Francisco. My housemate Veronica had stripped for two years at the Lusty Lady, the unionized strip club in North Beach. I played pickup basketball in a mostly-girls league in the Castro. Half of them worked at the Lusty, too.

Some of them liked it. Some of them did it for the money. A surprising number were incorporating it into

The unionized strip club in North Beach. Now it's a worker-owned co-op, but, you know, this is ancient history. The SEIU, a local umbrella union, helped the strippers there to organize their own union a number of years ago, and since then, they have orchestrated walkouts, protests, and labor negotiations—all remarkable feats for an industry that can charge a standard $100–$500 stage fee for the house before anybody else makes a cent.

masters' and doctoral theses. Veronica was a classically trained dancer who couldn't get a job in the nepotistic San Francisco dance scene. At the Lusty Lady, she got yelled at by her bosses for "dancing too artsy."

I could understand doing it. When Veronica talked about her rich clients, who met with her behind a glass partition in the Private Pleasures booth and dropped $50 bills in the machine for five minutes and just wanted to talk to her, I even got a little jealous. For my friend Pony, a violently red-haired exhibitionist who liked to dance wild and get naked at fag clubs on Market Street, I even thought it was a healthy idea.

But some people like to eat hamburgers, and other people like to kill the cows themselves. I preferred to keep my interest in strippers to the level of cocktail-party stories. I wasn't looking for Extreme Close Up first-person involvement. I mean—I *liked* keeping my sexuality private in my back pocket.

And I liked keeping my nudity under my clothes.

In the morning, Anastasia got up first and, while I wrapped tefillin and prayed, she made tofu scramble. It was like scrambled eggs, but vegan, and it always tasted better because you had to go all out with the spices and use a lot of veggies so the tofu didn't taste all weird. Anastasia always liked the tomatoes chopped fine. I liked them thick. When one of us wanted to get on the other's good side, we swayed the cut that way. Today, the tomatoes were almost whole. We spent most of the meal talking about Purim, the Jewish holiday that was coming up soon. She liked asking me questions and having me give the answers all in Jewish words that she couldn't understand. Abruptly, in the middle of explaining about costumes and drunkenness, I asked, "When do you decide whether to apply for the stripping?"

Horrible grammar. When I'm upset, my diction sounds like my grandparents'.

"I tried out last week," she answered calmly. "I start today, if you're okay with it."

Of course I was okay with it. If she hadn't said that, I would have hit the fan like shit. But she said, *If you're okay.* She was practically *inviting* me to start a war.

And, because she was my girlfriend and because I am sensitive, I surrendered before it started.

The truth is, it wasn't that bad. Some nights she'd work late and we wouldn't see each other at all, which is good for any relationship. And I had club shows at night, hustling my ass at bars like Paradise Lounge, Dalva, and the Hotel Utah, trying to unload CD-Rs and poetry zines for whatever part of $5 people had, trying to piece those $5 bills into my rent. It was a losing battle, but I loved fighting it. And then sometimes she'd come over and be forceful, the way I liked it, a sexual confidence she'd never had before. I thought she'd be too tired of sex to want to be sexy outside of work.

If anything, it made her hornier. Things I was embarrassed to say, she'd coax out of me with a pressure that felt a little too uncomfortably professional. Somehow it seemed natural. I came to San Francisco to write about my terribly conflicting passions, religion and, uh, regular passion. And here I was living it out. I felt on top of the world, like I could do anything.

I couldn't do anything. I was scared, wrecked, a little heartbroken, and more insecure than I'd ever been. Anastasia was the sweetest, most unconditionally loving human being ever. I didn't want to do anything with her but kiss and sleep in a bed together. She was okay with that. Then I wanted more—not everything, but more. She could do that too.

And when the waves receded, and I got freaked out by the sudden zero-to-sixty of my own sexuality, she didn't mind. She was patient and understanding and just waited for me to get my foothold and be normal again. Inside my head, I was going though my own crisis. Nobody had told me how to be Orthodox. Actually, *lots* of people had told me, and I didn't believe any of them. The preppy Modern Orthodox singles in New York, who went on tefillin dates, which is where you go to dinner with someone and bring your tefillin, the prayer gear that Jews only wear during morning prayers. The married people in D.C. who said that waiting was easy, I'd find my beshert in no time. It was easy for them to say, because they were all boring and ordinary. Who wants a professional poet with a penchant for light bondage, punk-rock shows, and vegetarian cooking? Outside the Orthodox world, I was a star. Inside, I was a pariah—or, worse, I was the kid walking home from synagogue to have Shabbos dinner alone. I was a Member of the Tribe in name only.

I kept going, living my life the way I thought I was supposed to. Anastasia was the top and the bottom, the best and worst parts of life. As good as it got. A constant

Beshert. Literally, one true love. There's this Midrash story that, when a baby is born, God matches up that baby with another baby who will one day be its life partner. In the old days, Jews used to plant a tree when a baby was born, and at the wedding, those two trees would be cut down and made into the poles of the couple's *chuppah*, their wedding canopy. These days, a lot of us Orthodox Jews aren't born observant, and many of the ones who are, live in New York, where you can't really plant trees anyway. So we have to do the legwork ourselves—both the wedding canopy and finding our beshert.

Member of the Tribe. Who comes up with this shit? I think the first time I heard this nickname for Jews was from my sister's Conservative Jewish USY youth group. Member of the Tribe—or M.O.T.—is short-speak for exclusivity among Jews, heard most often as: "She/he's okay to date, s/he's a M.O.T."

challenge. My friend Bradley asked, one night at the Paradise Lounge poetry show, "How does it feel to know you're taking home the girl that everyone in the room wants to take home?"

It felt shitty, knowing it wasn't the life I was supposed to live. And it felt brilliant, thinking I was living the life that everyone wanted for themselves.

I know it's not Anastasia's fault. I was kind of an asshole. She was a sneak. For two performing artists, we were about as communicative as a rock. I was deep and withdrawn and pensive. She flirted at anything with a pulse. Finally, I broke up with her.

I called all my friends whom I'd abandoned six months ago after being afraid of sounding like a kvetch about my Anastasia-related problems, and remembered how good it was to have friends who were just straight-up friends. I rediscovered the bars that didn't have rock shows, the ones where you sit and talk and don't have to climb onstage and bare your soul.

We shot the shit. We told dirty jokes. Then we talked about Anastasia, which resulted in talking about nothing, because you couldn't go thirty seconds into the story without realizing how stupidly doomed we were. We were both innocent performers, each looking to get debauched. And, in our own ways, we both did.

So we hung out, my friends and I. It was a week or two of functioning on the purely basic level of social hibernation, and then I left on tour.

When I got back, the city felt alien again. Not the kind of post-breakup alien, where you crawl out of a cocoon and blink your eyes and remember how bright the sunshine is. I mean the other kind of alien, like in the Disney movie *Flight of the Navigator,* where the kid gets on a spacecraft for a five-minute drive and gets off and finds out that eight years have passed. When you're on tour, performing the same poems every night to crowds of faceless people, the world stands still for you. When I got back, my friends had new girlfriends, and some had new jobs—and then my friend Kassy had started calling herself Rocco and growing hair on her chest. I realized that the world was still spinning, it was just me who was standing still.

My roommate Veronica said Anastasia didn't have a new girlfriend. I made the rounds of Hey-I'm-Back phone calls, cautiously adding her number as number five or six on my list.

Anastasia sounded rushed. I asked if I was interrupting something.

"I'm about to go to work," she said. "Want to meet up afterward?"

I'd never been to the Lusty Lady, but I walked by it constantly. City Lights Bookstore was right around the corner. The #12 bus went straight from my house to the Lusty Lady. I hopped out the bus's back door and hopped straight into a demonstration.

Starving Strippers Have No Ass to Shake!!!
2! 4! 6! 8! Pay Us More to Masturbate!!!
Bad Girls Like Good Contracts!!!

I stood across the street and watched the circle of protest, a gathering of ten or fifteen strippers dwarfed by twenty or thirty photographers, videocameras, and on-the-spot reporters. It wasn't technically a strike, it was a Worker's Action, which meant the girls were still working, and they protested when they were off-duty.

When the protest broke down. Pony ran across the street to hug me. "Matthue! You've come to stand in solidarity!" She jumped on me and hugged me.

I stumbled backward. She weighed almost nothing,

like a child, all skin and bones and breasts. I caught her in my hands, spinning her around as I seized my balance. Pony wore a Catholic schoolgirl skirt short enough to see her ass, a black vinyl bustier, and a T-shirt pulled over it that said LUSTY LADIES NEED A LIVING WAGE. Sparkly red barrettes made her hair look disheveled and windswept.

"What the hell are you doing here?" she asked brightly.

I shrugged. I was just hanging out.

Anastasia flitted out from the double doors nonchalantly, swaying a Dalmatian-patterned handbag off her shoulder. Her hair was freshly cut, pixielike, dyed glaringly blond. She swung her hips independently of the rest of her body. She walked quickly, half jogging, in slow motion, like the last day of school in a 1980s movie.

She spotted me at once and ran over, a chaste kiss on my cheek, fingers lingering too long as she hugged me around the waist, drifting over the curve of my ass. She tugged on my belt and leaned into me, smiling hi to Pony. "Protest good?" she asked, chirpily, as if it was a normal water-cooler conversation.

Pony beamed breezily back, all water-cooler herself.

Someone yanked Pony's arm. CNN wanted to ask more questions for another sound bite. Pony gave the best sound bites; everything she said sounded like a motto.

Anastasia fixed her eyes on me. "Good seeing you, kid."

"Good seeing you, Mom."

"Where should we go?"

We went to Kavarna, a daytime brewery frequented by the girls who worked in the North Beach strip clubs. Anastasia got a cup of coffee as big as her head. I got orange juice. I needed all the vitamins I could get.

We talked. It was awkward at first, then gradually grew

easier, like being stuck with someone you don't know on a long car ride. At first it seemed like anything was too painful to talk about. She'd been seeing people, of course, but nobody current and nobody serious. Finally I asked about the song we wrote together. I'd heard the album version when I visited her producer in New York. She'd gotten another poet to record stream-of-consciousness spoken word under the guitar solo.

"Lucky Dave played me the version with the guitar solo," I said. "It sucks."

"I know." Anastasia stirred the coffee with her finger. It was still steaming.

"Did the poetry kid say 'marshmallow soul flakes'?"

"I *told* you," she said. "It was late at night."

"'My marshmallow soul flakes on your graham-cracker crunch body.'" I had my beatnik-poetry voice in full effect.

"He did *not* say that!" Anastasia protested. Coffee burbled up her nose.

"'Our lip-smacking s'mores of love….'"

"It is *not!*"

"S'mores of Love it *is.*"

"Can't be. There's no chocolate in the song."

Anastasia's face was painted dead serious. Sometimes, she could be a total hardass; she didn't always realize when I was joking. All my real close friends are hardasses. If someone lets me get away with shit, it's only because they're sick of arguing with me.

"I missed you, rock star," she said, almost a moan, her head tumbling into her upturned palms.

"Geez. I thought you never would."

Our hands touched, and we hugged with them, squeezing our fingers together. It was a light hug, like sorbet, palette-cleansing and platonic. The check came. Anastasia paid for both of us, out of a thick handful of crumpled one-dollar bills. For the first time in a while, it didn't feel so bad.

Watching her walk away, this squiggly little ass that I might never touch again, it seemed weird to be resigned. It seemed weird to be in sole possession of my body again.

12

single is hard

Girl watching with girls wasn't doing it for me that night. I had run into Box's friend Meghan on Mission Street earlier that day. She'd told me that Box was supposed to come by the Lex for a tranny boy scene party, and so I showed up to spy on him, but nobody was there, not even Meghan. Sitting alone at the bar felt like moping in an old yearbook. The few girls I did recognize that night were on the prowl. I rolled up in a booth with my beer and avoided them. I didn't want to kill their game. I was still weary from last night, battling it out on the phone with Anastasia. Battling out our friendship. I still loved her. I didn't want her and I felt uneasy about everything we'd done together, but when I thought about the way she clung to me, I still wanted her to be able to.

Why don't I have a cell phone? I asked myself. Oh yeah. Because I was poor and couldn't afford it and I refused to make money any other way than as a professional poet.

I hit the Phone Booth, the sleazy neighborhood bar where my friends hung out. Nobody was there, either, but a crowd of hipsters so hip they would have knocked sunglasses right off the Fonz.

I took a right on 24th Street, headed home, but not really. That week was one of those Indian summers in San Francisco. Everyone was so alive. Yuppie parents were walking their palm-size children home from church and Sunday dinner, the kids in Barbie-size dresses and tuxedos. The goths on 24th Street were dressed in their almost-clothes, more holes than fabric, who didn't say hi to you but ran their long-nailed hands down your chest appreciatively, creepy and erotic.

A few blocks down I ran into Becky, the bartender from Brainwash Café where I used to do poetry. She asked why I hadn't come by. I said to her how I hadn't been feeling like open mics lately. In the aftermath of Anastasia, I was just not wanting to split myself that wide open.

"Dude," she said, "Robin Williams was there. His son was performing."

Robin Williams was San Francisco's only bona fide, A-list celebrity. We had Danielle Steele, too, the romance novelist, but nobody knew what she looked like. Everyone who'd lived in San Francisco longer than me had their own Robin Williams story.

"Damn," I gushed, a little longer and a little less detached than I wanted to be. "What was he doing?"

Becky told me how his son was doing performance poetry. They sat through all the acts and then at the end, he wrote his name down on a piece of paper and performed.

"Robin Williams or his son?" I asked.

"His son," she said, no less buoyed. "And then Robin went up to Wendell and Anastasia and a bunch of the other poetry people and asked them a bunch of questions."

"No shit! Did he take down their numbers or something? Are they going to get recording contracts?"

Becky shot up her hands. "Whoa hoa," she exhaled. "Down, boy, down. I don't think any of those kids are that good, I don't think he's gonna call his agent up or anything."

Yeah, I thought, overconfident and fuming. But if I'd been there, he would have.

The next night I'm supposed to go out again, but I don't know, drinks at the Phone Booth don't appeal to me in the same way. Am I getting more mature? Or am I just getting depressed? I'm standing in the middle of the intersection at 24th and Mission, one foot on each side of the yellow line, and having a moment of realization. I don't want to have a moment of realization. I want to be dumb for a while. Please?

I decide to leave it up to providence. So I jump on the first bus that comes by. It takes me across town, through neighborhoods I don't recognize at all, but one way or another I end up at the Kaufmanns'.

The door is ajar, and I push it open, calling out names. Nobody's home but I can hear a fire sizzle in the kitchen. I go in and investigate.

Deena is back in America, and she's frying a fish.

For the longest time, neither of us says anything. There are two stools by the stove, both empty. I commandeer one and perch on it, hooked back like a vulture, watching the fish sizzle with a morbid fascination. Little chunks of muscle sizzle and sear and start to brown. Of all the vegetarians I know, I've never met one as fascinated by meat as I am. I wonder what would happen if I stuck my finger in that pot, still attached to my body. I wonder if it would turn the same brilliant pink as that fish flesh.

Deena walks over from the oven with a spatula, plunging it in the pan, scrambling the hunks of fish. "The Talmud tells us that righteous people are regenerated into fish," she says, as if it's the most natural thing in the world to talk about.

"Oh," I echo her, mystified.

With a spatula, she presses the fish deeper into the oil. It sizzles, and a cloud of vapor rises from the cast iron.

"So, well, isn't there something, like, bad or wrong or maybe potentially offensive about eating righteous people for an appetizer?" I ask her.

"No, silly," she says. "How else can you absorb their ideas and thoughts and feelings?" With her bare fingers, she scoops up the smallest piece of salmon, places it between her lips, and sucks, thoughtfully, on its juices for a second. "There," she says. "I think this is a fish from a good time."

One by one, people drift into the dining room. The Kaufmann family and the teachers from the neighborhood Hebrew School, just off work. They're all imported from New York City, where they grew up living among thousands of Hasidic Jews. They're not used to this town, its isolation and alienation. And they don't dress like Deena, in her saris and flowy white Berkeley clothes. They wear leather skirts, knee-high boots, each one a little bit more frighteningly hot than the last. If any of them would talk to me, I'd date them in a second. If Deena looked at me twice, I'd ask her to marry me, and I was thinking all this on the rebound but I'm saying it in print, now, and believing it every bit as much.

They're so used to these dinners. Little parties, parties without beer or sexual tension—dinner parties, I think adults call them. Chana was leaving tomorrow, and she sits at the head of the table, her plate heaped high with salmon and rice pilaf. "Salmon is Chana's favorite," Deena whispers to me. "I couldn't *not* make it for her last night." They're so used to being around everyone at once, this far from Brooklyn, where they all have to stick together because for them there's no halfway involvement in the secular world. Everyone buzzes with jealousy for Chana, going back to Brooklyn to be back home. Deena's whispering in my ear. I quote one Hasidic rabbi back at her: "No matter where I go, it is always Jerusalem." It's so good to see her. I've changed so much in the past year. I want to tell her everything I've felt, ask her how much of it is wrong. But how would I feel about her telling me about the pleasures of meat?

Instead I go home, stay up all night, waiting for Anastasia to maybe knock on my door and poke her head in sheepishly and crawl into bed with me. She doesn't. At last the sun comes up and the sky turns a woozy shade of compromise and, in that bright gray that lights up my room enough to read, the world feels sufficiently safe for me to fall asleep. I wake up much later, in the middle of genuine morning, when my room is blazing and the sky is filled with sun.

I came to the Kaufmann house again that Shabbos. Usually I gave myself a week to recover, but showing up at the doorway twice in three days—that carved picture of the Rebbe, the doorbell that played the "Mazel Tov" song— it felt like such a routine that I wondered if I'd ever left. I thought it would feel empty without Chana, who did most of the cooking and always forced the Chabad boys

No matter where I go, it is always Jerusalem. Rabbi Nachman of Breslov, in *Likutei Mahoran.*

to sing, but, like an ant colony, when one dies, the rest swarm in and take over. Deena took care of dinner. Shira shepherded the boys. Shabbos felt like it always did there, a routine, but one that made you feel good about your-self, like flossing.

Even Jacob showed up. A few months ago, Jacob be-came super ultra hardcore, to the point where he decided to go to a Chabad yeshiva in New York. He came back after a week, clean-shaven and not wearing a yarmulke, and stopped visiting the Kaufmann house completely. He sometimes showed up at my house before activist dem-onstrations and punk-rock shows, sometimes to convince me to come with him, sometimes just to talk. I think his stopping being religious made him closer to me than ever, because he knew I gave it up, once, too. I told him stories about my teenagerhood being secular, thinking maybe that he'd get inspired to give all that shit up too and be-come religious again.

But that night he was at the Kaufmanns', praying in his usual treble-soaked voice, flirting with the Chabad girls as if he'd never been gone. He invited them to his concert. "You should come, too, Matthue," he told me. "Maybe you can write it up for *Rolling Stone*."

Shabbos went out late the next night, and we piled into the Kaufmann family car and drove to the concert. It was at the house of Jacob's friend-slash-co-bandmate, Darren, which was in the closest thing San Francisco had to suburbs. The neighborhood wasn't actually on the edge of town, but it was on top of a mountain, so nobody ever went through there on the way to another neighborhood. The concert consisted of us and five or six of Jacob's friends, packed into a basement, a drum kit in one corner of the room, which Jacob's band didn't use but the opening band did.

The opening band was called Weird Alcatraz. It was

Jacob, along with the other guy in his band and a twelve-year-old kid. They played punk-rock covers of songs by Weird Al Yankovic. Most of Weird Al's songs were themselves parodies of other songs, and Zack slammed the drums and the twelve-year-old skidded his fingers along the guitar, singing nonhits like "Lasagna" and "I Love Rocky Road" and "Ricky." Then their friend Morgan did a solo acoustic set of songs about old Nintendo games. Then Jacob's real band, Up With Hope, Down With Mayonnaise, played.

The key to hyping any concert, and to keeping the enthusiasm up for the main band, is to make the opening bands smaller and less talented, but not in a way that undermines their talent or usurps the evening's main event. Such was the case with Up With Hope. Weird Alcatraz had Jacob rocking out on the drums and Darren playing bass, but all ten of us in the room got a shiver, the tiniest thrill, of seeing Jacob and Darren sitting on their stools with their tiny ukuleles in hand, about to bust out.

They busted out.

Jacob and Darren simultaneously strummed up their ukuleles, jamming like a heavy-metal band making wild feedback noise, but it sounded geeky and cute on their thumb-size guitars. Jacob ran over to the empty drum kit and counted off in his most Springsteen rasp. They both did flying jumps into the air, and started to sing "Robbin' the Bank." During the last verse, they both started to play more softly.

"Are you ready?" Jacob whispered to Darren.

Lasagna. Parody of "La Bamba," originally performed by Richie Valens.
I Love Rocky Road. Parody of "I Love Rock and Roll," originally performed by Joan Jett and the Blackhearts.
Ricky. Parody of "Mickey." I don't know who originally performed this but I think it was a bunch of cheerleaders wearing Mickey Mouse sweaters in the '80s on MTV.

"I'm ready," Darren whispered to Jacob.

Then Jacob made everyone in the room stand up, clap their hands, and sing the chorus with them, "Even you Hasidic girls," said Jacob, clapping his hands above his head, swinging his guitar side to side, "Don't give me none of that stuff about how you're too religious. This is a song about love. This is a song about passion. This is a song about robbing banks."

I looked out of the corner of my eye, trying not to look, trying not to be that kid spying on how religious all the other kids are in the room—but my mouth was wide open, framed in that ovular orgasmic *O*, and so were the Hasidic girls behind me, singing, *"We're robbing the bank, we're robbing the bank, we're rob-ob-obbing the bank"* just like Jacob, even swinging their arms a little in that stupid jigging motion that mothers make when they sing along with their infants.

Maybe you just needed to be there, but in that one sliver of a second of human history, there was pure love in that room. Me and the punk kids and the Hasidic girls, swaying back and forth, the mohawked kids with their arms linked, singing about the day we first donned ski masks, it was so simple and pure and beautiful. It wouldn't last, but nothing did, those days—not even Jacob's band, which would break up when Darren left for college and Jacob couldn't remember the lyrics on his own—but, that night, we walked the girls to the car afterward and the sky above the mountain neighborhood hummed like the feedback from a thousand guitars, and the stars glinted like the batteries were ready to go out, and life in that moment seemed just about perfect.

13

the forest

Early that morning, I started a bonfire on the roof of my apartment building. In the background were the flaccid downtown skyscrapers, dwarfed by Twin Peaks on one side and the Berkeley hills on the other, across the bay. I kindled dryer lint and papers with old poems scrawled in pencil, watched the baby flames lick it up. The smoke was thick black. It looked savage against the perfect blue morning. My fire was miniature but it roared in its little box, fierce and wild. I threw bagels and pretzels and moon-shaped slices of rye into the fire, the last traces of bread from my kitchen. Piece by piece, they shrank into black lumps of ash.

I hadn't eaten that morning. I was fasting until nightfall, when we would start the seder, the first meal of Passover.

Jimmy and Miri had rented a shack in the woods, in a yuppie neighborhood that tried desperately to tune out the city. Their shack was actually the servants' quarters to a much larger mansion, five doors down from the house where a famous secular Jewish writer lived. We called it the Yar House—the Hebrew word for *forest*. The one-storey house was buried in the woods behind a huge glass-enclosed building where a bunch of hippie Cal students with parents who were loaded lived.

This was Berkeley.

Berkeley, at first glance, is not where you expect to find a seismic hot-spot of Orthodox Jewish activity. But my friend Steve from Washington had a cousin who used to live out here, whose ex-roommate Tess emailed me about the Berkeley Orthodox community. I kept saying thanks but no thanks.

Berkeley is an innocuous, soft-rock version of San Francisco. The bums are less aggro, the street kids have bigger dreadlocks. It's part college town, part retirement community for old revolutionaries, where white-bearded hippies settled after realizing that the revolution would take more time than they had to give. When I told my mom I was moving to San Francisco, this is the place she must have pictured.

At first I only knew Berkeley by association. Some of C. D.'s friends lived there, mostly conservative middle-aged lesbians and boy computer geeks. Berkeley seemed as exciting as a pocket protector. When I finally said okay to Tess's invitation and found these kids rocking the Friday night service like a speakeasy swing dance, I hated myself for having taken so long. It was my first Shabbos there. Twenty Orthodox kids sat in a wood-shrouded living room draped in tapestries, Shabbos candles burning at every window, the service fluttering from our Xeroxed-and-stapled prayerbooks to our whispering lips. The guys were loosely on one side, the girls loosely on the other. There was no official division—since this wasn't a regular prayer group, we didn't need an official wall between us. No single shaliach tzibur led the service. The guy next to me started the tune for the first prayer. A girl on the other side of the room started humming a lilting, pensive niggun that segued into the second prayer. Nobody complained. Nobody pursed their lips in a stink. In twenty-three years of going to East Coast synagogues I thought I'd seen everything, but I'd never seen people being that chill.

Halfway through the second prayer, someone started banging on his prayerbook—not that single bass-drum whomp like yeshiva boys trying to knock the covers off their books, but actual, talented drums. The next thing I knew, a canopy of girls were spinning in circles, whisking through tunnels of arms, throwing each other in the air. The guys were clapping and singing, long after the songs ran out of words, shouting each *yai dai dai* like their own private national anthem, and I was joining in, too. Were they singing to the tune of a Beach Boys song? Or was it the Cure? How did I get here, anyway?

Berkeley never got better than those Friday nights. The players were so breathtaking, funny and hot and always ready to be your surrogate family. Jimmy and Miri sculpted the Yar House dinners like modeling clay. They invited anybody who would come, but they stacked the odds too. They made sure that Yehezkel, the lapsed yeshiva boy, was there the same week that Deena's ultra-religious sister was in town from New York. They tussled for hours, arguing about which rabbis were the most overbearing. Yosef and his friend Josh happened to show up the same week, childhood friends from Berkeley Community Choir, and they harmonized together on all the Shabbos songs and then sang "Dror

Yikra" over and over until they were stepping over each other's words, singing in the round, and then suddenly the tune matched the Beach Boys' version of "Sloop John B" and then so did the words, that was what they were singing.

At first I felt like I was trespassing. Visiting a stranger's house for Shabbos is cool once or twice, but I was on the fast track to being there every Shabbos. San Francisco was too far to walk from, and there weren't many places that were totally Shabbos observant where I could stay. Then winter ended, spring came, and Jimmy and Miri had one free bedroom. For a second, dreams of being one of the Berkeley kids flashed through my head.

"It's eight hundred dollars," said Jimmy, nonchalantly, to some visiting Jew.

The dreams scrubbed out fast. That was twice what I paid, four times what I could afford, and I would have to take a BART train into the city every night to have some sort of social life, anyway.

BART was my nemesis those days. It cost almost $6 to get to Berkeley from the city on the train, and without a job, even sneaking on got expensive. You still had to pay $1 to sneak on, because you used two separate tickets, one from San Francisco and one from Berkeley. As long as you had two open-ended tickets, and didn't screw yourself up, it was easy to trick the BART machines into thinking that I was two people, one who lived in the city and one who lived in the suburbs. I always used the extra money to buy something rich for the group dinners, huge avocadoes oozing green pus, organic plum tomatoes that Jimmy's girlfriend Caroline loved to pop like cocaine. Then one day, I was early for Shabbos. I called my friend Phred and told him to meet me at the comic book store by BART.

I had stopped wearing my hat constantly. I used to

wear hats all the time, covering my yarmulke, and as I felt people's mean red eyes on me, checking out the punk kid who scammed BART and got caught, I wanted them to be thinking *cheap punk, cheap punk,* and not *cheap Jew, cheap Jew.* I knew they would. In Berkeley, call a rich white man a fag and everyone will pound your ass; call him a cheap, Palestinian-killing kike and people will most likely shrug and pass on.

I wore a hat that day, so there was no excuse, and no scapegoat, except for my stupid-ass self. My farecard beeped when I fed it through the turnstile. The gates did not open. I scratched my ear, like this kind of thing must be a mistake, although of course it wasn't. I knew it wasn't. This wasn't even San Francisco, where you can duck through the orange half-doors and be on the street in ten seconds flat. This is Berkeley, where everyone walks slow, says "excuse me" when they bump into you, and rides the escalators standing still.

The BART worker stalked over. Her swagger and her expression made her look exactly like my second grade teacher, Mrs. Pearlmutter, the one with all the art projects. She ripped my card from my hand. She ran it through the machine, although she knew the score from the second she looked at my face. You don't get away with shit in the suburbs. In Berkeley, you could get fined for stepping on a flower. I told her I lived one stop away, but I was coming from San Francisco, and I had so many BART cards I couldn't keep track.

The BART woman breathed out through her nose.

"You're not a good liar," she said. "You look like a good kid, so I'm not calling the police. But you're a bad liar, so don't try to get out of it."

She made me go to the ticket machine and pay full fare and give her the ticket. I handed it over. She took the ticket and ripped it to shreds.

"I told you," she said, "you're a good kid."

I emerged from that station, cheeks flaring, scalded but unburnt. Outside, the sky was bluer than I remembered it. My veins were still shaking. I walked around the block two or three times before I could think again.

Around the corner I found Phred at the gym where he taught, tying his bags, about to leave. We spent an hour poring through the bargain bins at the comic book store, but even 25-cent *Daredevils* couldn't break me out of the delirious soupy funk of getting caught.

That was the day I was going to meet Jimmy and Miri's new roommate, Tegan. They were being mysteriously vague about her, answering questions like *Where's she from?* with a noncommittal "You'll see!"

I figured that Jimmy and Miri probably wanted to set us up.

My friend Shosh definitely wanted to set us up. She'd been hyping Tegan to me for weeks, this baal teshuva girl from New Jersey who moved to Berkeley last week and had her own highway-to-hell brand of Orthodox Judaism and maybe I could fit into it.

"Really?" I asked Shosh, leaning forward curiously on my forearms.

I always got a little flamey around Shosh. She was a Reconstructionist rabbinical student who was half my friend and half a celebrity. She had published a book on riot-grrrl feminist Judaism. It came out right when I was becoming friends with her and it was confusing to separate the things she told me about herself from the things I read about in her book. Shosh made it all right, though. She had this natural aura that swept away everything. She was one of those women who acts more flamboyant than a gay man. She could talk for hours about Talmudic law—that is, if you didn't mind her interrupting herself with allusions to feminist theory and *The Hitchhiker's*

Guide to the Galaxy. Shosh and Tegan were friends from college and from Jewish movements.

"Movements?"

"Mostly meetings and conferences and stuff," Shosh explained.

I got to the Yar House within a breath of when Passover started. Not to be dramatic, but right before a Jewish holiday starts, everything is dramatic. Racing against the sun. Making sure the food is cooked until that moment where you can't touch it again. We are the original drama queens.

In the house, Jimmy and Yehezkel had covered everything with aluminum foil. Cabinets, counters, tables. The dish rack, even. They were bent over the kitchen table sorting quinoa seeds, checking for traces of wheat. Quinoa is this round, couscous-like grain that's kosher for Passover, the only grain that Ashkenazic Jews like us will eat. The Talmud said that it was kosher, but you had to check every kernel individually for wheat. Their eyes were so close to the table you could barely see them. There must have been, what, a million kernels of quinoa? A square yard's worth, head to head.

Tegan tore into the room, backpack strapped on. She was running to get to her own seder in time, before sunset, even though it didn't start for two hours after that. It was in the city, an hour-long BART ride away.

Tegan's seder, she told me, was being led by antiwar activists and trannies, a San Francisco seder of inclusivity. I got this incredibly vivid mental image of a room where everyone sat on doormats, only they'd call them tapestries, overflowing with karma. Instead of parsley and charoses on the ritual plate, there would be kiwi and hippie fruits and tofu, which was not actually kosher for Passover anyway.

The only grain. Technically, quinoa is a tuber, more closely related to the potato than to pasta.

222

"I just get nervous when people try to make everything political," I said. "My personal freedom from bondage is important, too. Not everything is politics." This year, for me, it was literal, too. I was girlfriendless and commitmentless, floating around Berkeley like a free agent, feeling like I didn't owe anything to anyone. Reducing the seder to a political statement felt a little bit dry.

"You wouldn't say that to the face of a rape victim, would you?" Tegan shot at me.

My face blanched.

Tegan broke into a grin. "Just kidding," she chimed nonchalantly. "I hope I get to see you before the holiday's out. You can have my bed if you want."

She flashed me a smile, which managed to be shy and voluptuous at the same time, and then she was gone.

Passover started on a Wednesday night that year, which meant, since I couldn't travel, I was stuck in Berkeley till after Shabbos ended Saturday night. Those first days of the holiday were magic. I was fluent enough in house mechanics, knowing where dishes went and stuff, that I was almost like a host. Doing chores felt so helpful, like I was ten again. It had been so long since I knew a place well enough to do chores.

Yehezkel, whose family was Sephardic and had all these mystical traditions, picked up matzohs and swung them over our heads like his father used to do. He also sang the Four Questions in Yiddish, and then Keiko,

In Yiddish. Far vos iz di dozike nakht fun peysakh andersh fun ale nekht fun a gants yor? Ale nekht megn mir esn say khomets, say matse, ober halaylo haze—in der doziker nakht—nor matse? Ale nekht esn mir kolerley grintsn, ober halaylo haze—in der doziker nakht—moror—bloys bitere kraytekher? Ale nekht darfn mir nit ayntunken afile eyn mol oykh nit, ober halaylo haze—in der doziker nakht—tunken mir ayn tsvey mol? Ale nekht kenen mir esn say zitsndik glaykh, say ongelent, ober halaylo haze—in der doziker peysakh-nakht—esn mir ale ongelent?

who was from Tokyo, said them in Japanese. Passover is supposed to be the harvest festival, right at the beginning of spring, and there's also the idea of renewal, an end to slavery. That's why we eat parsley, the paschal greens, symbolizing spring and freedom. From one corner, Jimmy started singing a niggun, and Caroline joined in and Miri's yeshiva-bochur cousin started slapping the table in rhythm. The unmistakable smell of pot, half pinewood and half gas-station fumes, drifted across the room. They passed around a bong, water bubbling like a brook, ceramic twisted veins of white and green.

I never smoke, but I was already feeling stoned. Passover is one of those manic Jewish holidays when it's hard to avoid getting trashed. You're not allowed to ingest any bread products all day before the seder, and when your body is starchless and vulnerable, you drink four glasses of wine.

A few hours later, I was woozy and glowing, piles of broken matzoh swimming on the table. The seder ended and most people left, and Yehezkel tried to leave but Jimmy and I pulled him down because we still hadn't sang all the folk songs yet. We sang "Chad Gadya" and then we sang our bad rendition of the Four Questions in Yiddish—Yehezkel refused to correct us—and then, we did four rounds of "Echad Mi Yodea," a Hebrew

In Japanese. Tsumo wa fukkura pan, katai kurakkaa, iroiro taberu noni naze konya dake, naze konya dake hiratai pan shika tabenaino? Nazeka konya, konya dake wa, peshanko pan shika tabenaino. Itsumo wa ii nioi no yasai, kôsô, iroiro taberu noni naze konya dake, naze konya dake nigai yasai wo taberuno? Nazeka konya, konya dake wa nigai yasai wo taberuno. Itsumo wa taberu mono wo shiomizu ni tsukunai noni, ichido mo tukenai noni, naze konya dake, naze konya dake nido mo mizu ni tsukeruno? Nazeka konya, konya dake wa nido mo tsukeruno. Itsumo wa taberu toki, suwattemo, motaretetemo docchi demo iinoni, naze konya dake, naze konyadake motare nagara shika tabenaino? Nazeka konya, konya dake wa motarete taberuno.

counting song that can best be described as the Twelve Days of Passover, only in our version there are thirteen steps—that, plus you sing faster each time until the last verse, where you're skating down the list like a computer virus, reading names as fast as you can spit them out. We did "Echad Mi Yodea" five times before Caroline pulled Jimmy away and Yehezkel snuck out the back door.

I sat at the table alone in a house that wasn't mine, letting the holiday seep in. Then I crawled into Tegan's bed and drifted slowly to sleep. My mind was racing, and the wine in my stomach was turning to sugar, and I didn't want to go to sleep drunk so I kept reciting poems in my head, the ones I was supposed to memorize and never totally could.

I could feel the alcohol dissipating in its slow burn, and just as I was ready to let myself fall asleep, my eyelids heavy and my throat parched, Tegan walked in. She peeled off her shoes and rolled into bed next to me, pulling the blanket hard from my body, eyes closed tight, air pulsing into my neck with quick, hot breaths.

The next morning, I woke up and she was gone, her side of the bed neat, sheets tucked in like nobody had ever been there. The sun was so bright, I could tell that I'd slept through synagogue. I was afraid someone was going to see me and think I was a bad Jew, and either kick me out of the house or demand to know what was up with me and Tegan. I splashed cold water on my face in the bathroom. I could hear Jimmy waking up.

Jimmy and I puzzled together the special Passover service from the enigmatic directions in our prayerbooks. We finished in a flurry, so much faster without the plodding synagogue routines. Then we took a walk.

Jimmy was a park ranger. He was less than a year older than me, but with his well-decorated house and residential neighborhood and actual job, he felt like a different generation. He pointed over to a string of purple vines. "Know what they are?" I shook my head. "Those are marigolds," he said. "They don't look like marigolds, but they are. There are over two hundred kinds of plants that don't exist anywhere but in Berkeley," he told me, and I wondered if my next great love might be with a city. "Want to see them?"

"Yes," I said. "God, yes."

That afternoon I got back from synagogue and found Tegan setting the table for dinner. "What are you doing here?"

She shrugged. "I came back."

"Did you walk? The city's, like, a fifteen-mile walk from here."

Another shrug, even more noncommittal. "I got here," she said.

"Did you get a ride?"

"Do you want to cook?"

We cooked. We worked well together, slicing vegetables, scrambling eggs, spicing everything as a team. Tegan never veered from the recipes. I asked if she thought we should use more olives. She looked at me like, what, could I not read?

Tegan was smooth. Watching her follow those instructions so methodically, slicing artichoke hearts with mathematical precision, then beating the batter hard, like a war, I thought, she probably really *did* walk the fifteen miles from San Francisco. I did the most ridiculous things sometimes for Judaism, walking across town on Shabbos to see a friend instead of picking up the phone. I wondered if she was as extreme and crazy as I was. I wondered if maybe she was even more. The sun started hovering, it was time for afternoon prayers at synagogue. Tegan said she didn't like synagogue so she was going to stay home. I promised to be back in time for dinner.

Turns out I showed up at synagogue earlier than everyone else, almost an hour earlier. But it started late, and there wouldn't be that same frenzied singing as at the Yar House, just a bunch of tired old men in the room, so I left before it started. Walking back to the Yar, though, I could hear the zemiros, the Shabbos songs, floating from down the street. The wisteria reeked of Mizmor Shir. It was loud and it was beautiful.

By the time I came back, all the other guests were already sitting at the table. Among the guests was Keiko, and her mother, who kept asking me questions about this slam thing. That's what she called it: *this slam thing*. Her knowledge of Yiddishkeit was as shaky as Keiko's sudden descent into observance, but she was an actual professional poetry professor.

The second she opened her mouth, I realized how outclassed I was. Shit, I was just a kid writing my thoughts as incomplete sentences. I was not a poet. Everyone at the table started making up haikus, counting on their fingers. Tegan had just learned what a haiku *was* and she was already a better improviser than I was. Spouting haiku on sand and deserts that change to desserts. Keiko took it, changed it to Marco Polo marooned in the China desert, compared them to Moses and the Children of Israel. All I could manage was the desert and the Red Sea.

Keiko's mom nodded, approvingly. "Will you do a performance poem?"

I took a breath.

I launched into one, and then I tried to start up the haiku chain again. But nothing kills conversation like a performance poem. Nobody wanted to dip back into talking normally.

Mizmor Shir. This song/poem/prayer thing. It sounds like what wisteria would sound like as a song. But you probably already guessed that.

These are the things I learn the hard way. I excused myself, ducked into the kitchen, and made everyone tea. Tegan slipped behind me in the kitchen and, working quickly, fixed a plate of Passover cookies and chocolate jelly horrors. Sticking our hands in each other's projects, it felt so weirdly domestic and flirtatious. Neither of us made eye contact. She tried to make me do the poem about Orthodox girls and shomer negiah and how touching is a promise. *Later*, I told her, *later*.

We sat at the dinner table, nibbling on those jelly chocolate things until everyone else made their excuses and drifted off to bed. Tegan pushed with her heels, rocking the legs on my chair, and I did my poem again, finally, letting the words come all quiet, in a whisper, as though I was making them up just then, as though I was talking to her with those words.

And then she went to bed.

"You can follow me if you want," she called over her shoulder, pushing open the door to her room.

And I did, skipping after her like a puppy. As soon as we hit the mattress, we both passed out, dead to the world.

That morning at synagogue, there was a bas mitzvah. I got there just in time to hear the girl's family singing the Song of Songs. The Song of Songs is the erotic poem that King Solomon wrote to the Queen of Sheba, the one where he talks about breasts and clitori in such detail that the standard Artscroll prayerbook refuses to publish a literal translation, instead offering a metaphorical one that translates *breasts* as *Tablets of the Law*. I can only imagine what listening to it does to the brain of someone who speaks Hebrew. I barely understand Hebrew and it

Breasts as Tablets of the Law. Followed by the line: "Your altar and Temple, erect and stately as an ivory tower…." Yes: This is the most popular prayerbook in Orthodox America.

makes me want to cry and come, both at once. Standing in the back of the sanctuary, shoulder to shoulder with my friends, I was thinking, *If I ever get a conventional family and settle down, this is where I want it to happen.* The bas mitzvah girl's mother had a voice like an old bluegrass singer. And, when it ended, we were all yotzei on her.

It took most of the luncheonette outside afterward for me to come down. People walked up to me and I was still shaking. "Good to see you in the neighborhood," everyone told me, approvingly, as if I belonged there. I shook hands. I shoveled fluffy egg cakes into my mouth, one after the other. I waved across the yard to middle-aged couples whose names I had never known, but whose faces were as familiar as last year's pop songs.

Finally Miri and Jimmy and the gang got ready to leave. Jimmy touched my shoulder. *Are you coming for lunch?* he whispered in my ear, and I was like, *Yes, oh please Hashem, yes.* On the way home, Tegan grabbed my arm and whispered in my ear, "Song of Songs got me all aroused, did you get aroused?"

Oh my God. I might be falling for her.

In Berkeley, the macrobiotic vegan vegetable-intensive diet made Passover delicious. We made all these courses that didn't even remind you it was Passover. We had matzoh for that. But as we ate, say, eggplant moussaka or ratatouille or Moroccan cabbage, you didn't even miss the bread part of the meal.

Yotzei on her. It counted.
The luncheonette. The memory that sticks most vividly is of an olive-pesto sauce tossed in with kosher-for-Passover ziti. There were also stuffed zucchini halves, Tam Tam crackers, and of course Passover cookies, which are disgusting in their own way but, when you bite into them, are soft and buttery, a delicate consistency, usually surrounded by chocolate and raspberry jam, which melt in your mouth.

This was Berkeley, though, and everyone had their quirks. One morning Tzippy let out a scream and grabbed Miri's arm, alarmed.

"What is it?"

"I forgot to check for chometz in my dreams!" cried Tzippy, utterly serious. Another time Jimmy was frying this mix of pumpkin and sesame and sunflower seeds and Yehezkel moped in, sleepy like he always was, and grabbed a handful of seeds straight from the pan to munch. "You know sesame seeds are like rice, right? Most Jews don't eat them." Jimmy looked at his pan, up at Yehezkel, then at the pan again, and emptied them straight into the compost bin.

That was the other thing I loved about Berkeley. Being Orthodox wasn't like taking the SATs, where you flunked out if you got an answer wrong. It was uncharted territory that we were all figuring out together.

Back in the city after the holiday, I was reassimilating. Janelle and her girlfriend Erykah were making sure I wasn't sitting at home, and if I was, they pulled me out. One night they took me to a Playboy theme party that was being thrown by a San Francisco–based lesbian porn magazine, and I freaked out because I didn't want to be getting back into that world. They took me along anyway. I spent the night hanging out with models whom everyone else in the room had seen naked, trading knock-knock jokes with them. I decided to make stupid jokes my new obsession, to replace love. My friend Jerrica was there, swishing a cosmopolitan through the crowd like fishing tackle, wearing a paisley smoking jacket and boxers, looking like a young, queer Hugh Heffner. He seized my arm and steered me toward the editor of the magazine, who was twisty and voluptuous in a tight pinstripe suit. The editor was occupied with trying to get into the pants of a woman in a French maid outfit and a sticky orange Afro. "This is Matthue," Jerrica announced, undeterred. "He should write for you."

Caught off guard, the editor spun around and stuck out her hand to me.

"Nice to meet you," she said, switching modes on a dime. "Jerrica has my email. Send me some pitches."

Summer came, and it got colder. The sun was out and the wind was stronger than ever. The dykes in the Mission District drew out their wifebeater shirts and carried dumbbells around on the streets, just to show off their muscles. San Francisco turned into a festival of skin, finely tanned, coming out of our perpetual covers of layers in exhibitionistic glory.

One Friday night I'd decided to stay home because I didn't want to wear out my mooching on the Yar House sofa. I called up my friends and told them I was cooking a free-for-all dinner. I thought everybody would amble over but Phred was sick and Janelle and Erykah were fighting and I don't know where everyone else was, but beer and music were probably involved. I sat at an empty table, eating alone.

I walked over to Box's house.

The red lights were on. I couldn't remember but I thought that meant that Box was disturbable. I leaped on the railing and over to the flowerbed and threw some pebbles at the window. I waited a second, and it slid open. There were sounds of scuffling in the dark, then the door flew open and he stood there, grinning bashfully, in a black velour bathrobe.

Box poured us hot apple cider and we sat in the garden, on the rim of that bathtub that I'd bourgeois-adored when I moved in there so long ago. Then the backyard suddenly felt really small, and I was shivering, so Box ran inside to get me his leather jacket and I followed him in and we poured straight through the house instead, out the front door. Box grabbed his skateboard and I ran down the street alongside him and he made a wide turn onto Valencia and the lights sprang up suddenly. He skated right into the corner store to buy gummy stuff. I waited outside, plastered against the wall, standing as if I was smoking. I stuck my hands into the pockets of Box's leather jacket and felt illimitably cool.

Box glided out on that skateboard. We hit Dolores Park. I don't think I'd ever been there at night. Downtown was just a row of buildings in firefly light. The real expanse was the ocean of houses below it, pointy pueblo Victorians in ghost-lit rows through the Mission. The moon was wild that night. It was fading with a stark intensity. We huddled next to each other at the bottom of the rocket slide, feet up, heads almost in the sandbox. We stared up at the stars. Box passed me a tube of candy called Sluguid that was supposed to taste like vomit but tasted like candy apple relish. Weirdly enough, it was kosher. I sucked Sluguid out of the tube and watched the stars explode.

"Girls suck," said Box.

"Tell me about it," I said.

Box looked over at me. I looked back at him, the tube of Sluguid still in my mouth.

"At least there's Pride," he said.

That year, Gay Pride fell on my birthday. Pride, the perfect time to shed love like an old exoskeleton and pick up a fresh obsession. The weather warmed, quickly and dramatically, and Mission Street began to feel like the Coney Island boardwalk, lined with Italian Ice trucks and curbside basketball games. The concerts and bars, even the small corner dive bars, filled and flowed with unfamiliar faces, new prey for the local cruisers to pick on. My friends changed pitch as Pride neared, giddy or frantic, depending on how many houseguests were coming for the weekend. Everyone was having houseguests. It was the most in-demand time of the year to live in San Francisco.

Of all my friends, the most excited for Pride was Tegan. She wasn't gay, but for Pride, it didn't matter. I wasn't gay either. During Pride, everyone was gay.

The actual Pride Parade happened on Sunday morning. Before that was the Dyke March, which started early Saturday afternoon, while it would still be Shabbos. Tegan asked if she could bring a bunch of friends to stay for Shabbos.

I said sure. We had the biggest couch in the universe in our living room, and it folded out to an even bigger sofabed. It was gratifying that the first guests in the house were Jews coming for Shabbos. I almost felt like bragging. It made me feel like a professional, as if other people trusted my kosherness and my hospitality enough to put themselves under my care. In some perverse, still-illegitimate divine reflex, I was turning into a Silver Spring rabbi.

I just hoped that Pride wouldn't shock them too much.

Batya was the first to arrive, two armloads of vegetables and tofu in tow. I'd never met her before. She was one of Tegan's friends from out of town, a born-and-raised Orthodox girl from New York who was staying in San Francisco for the summer. She had cute little spiky hair and high, thick cheekbones, a posture that sang. At the door she gave me a birthday present, the *On Our Backs Best Erotic Fiction* book, and I was like, "Wait, do you work for *On Our Backs?*" and she was like, "Wait, did you submit a story?" and pretty soon, we'd figured out how I had written a short story with Jews in it, and Batya had been asked to edit my piece. We both acted totally surprised, but come on, of *course* the only two Orthodox Jews working for a lesbian porn magazine would meet eventually.

Batya dumped her food onto the counter. We both watched the bags spill over and cascade onto the floor, a waterfall of round fruits, as well as zucchini and beets and mangoes.

"What should we make?" she asked.

"Whatever you want."

The new house had a big, badass kitchen. It was three times as large as any of our bedrooms. Jacob sometimes came over and skateboarded around it. Counters crawled all along the walls, so much space that I could work on three or four courses at once, bread rising in one corner, chopped piles of bell peppers and squashes like Technicolor snowhills. When Batya came over, I was throwing combinations of vegetables into pots and calling it different things. Despite coming from three generations of professional chefs, my cooking technique is most accurately described as "anything that fits." Batya sat in the corner for a minute watching me wreak vengeance on my vegetables, then asked if she could help. She asked what I was making now. "Spalad," I told her.

"Spalad?"

"It's soup and salad together. You eat it with sporks. Mostly I make chicken salad soup with rice, but you can throw other stuff in if you want."

Batya pushed aside some salting eggplants. She drew a long, narrow, unserrated knife from the array and started

---

Three generations of professional chefs. My great-grandparents owned a kosher catering business in Philadelphia, and if you ask my grandmom, she'll tell you they were the only caterers whose kosher standard everyone trusted.

Chicken salad soup with rice. Only, I used fake chicken.

dicing sushi into strips. We sliced in silence for a minute, then Batya made the first move. She asked how it was to keep Shabbos in a vortex without a million other Jews keeping Shabbos around you.

I said it was tricky at first because, although there were Orthodox Jews all over the place, the last thing I expected to find in the Bay Area was a vibrant observant community.

Batya thought for a second. She told me that at her college, she was only an hour from New York City but it felt like the same thing—doing Shabbos on your own, bringing in non-Jews and Jews who didn't usually keep Shabbos—but, Batya said, she missed having Friday night dinner with people who were doing the whole Shabbos experience, not turning on lights and going out on Saturday morning like it was a regular day. I told her I knew what she meant. I threw all these huge Shabbos dinners and stayed at home when everyone left for the clubs after dessert.

In the middle of letting out our respective histories, we walked over to Jesus Mart, the Latino grocery store where all the price signs say SOLO CRISTO SALVA, and picked up all manner of vegetables, I didn't know what for but I felt confident that the courses would congeal on their own. Batya was nervous and friendly and funny. At the store she bought yogurt with a plain *K* on it, which I

SOLO CRISTO SALVA. "Only Jesus Saves." I used to be afraid to shop there —I wasn't sure if it counted as heresy—but they sold four avocadoes for a dollar and eventually, I asked my rabbi and he said it was okay.

Yogurt with a plain K. Most foods have kosher markings, like a *K* inside a circle or a triangle or a Hebrew letter. And then there are foods with a plain *K.* Since it's legally impossible to trademark a letter, anyone could throw a *K* onto a product's packaging, and while there could be a valid kosher supervision, it is, in practice, more of an eat-at-your-own-risk thing. Some people do, some people don't. I don't, but then again, I'll pretty much acknowledge that I'm a zealot that way.

wouldn't eat but she did. But we talked and she turned out to be really cool—and we both had this thing under our hats, this ambiguously queer thing—and trusting her felt natural. We piled loads of groceries into both our arms and schlepped back home. Within the hour, people flooded my house, and suddenly my living room was full of Jews.

We cooked and ate and sang for hours. All these people I didn't know faded into familiarity. By the end of the night, we were like old friends.

In the morning, we piled into synagogue, where Tirtza and Avraham and all the chomosexuals had friends visiting. The dress code for our synagogue was never very haute—in California, it never is—but today people were in sandals, shorts, sunglasses perched on the edge of their hairlines. Nobody said anything about afternoon plans, but nobody was really hiding it either. I walked with my guests and a bunch of people from synagogue down Church Street through Dolores Park, where they were building a stage and setting up microphones, and my friends and I detached ourselves from the throng of middle-aged gay men and faded into the Dyke March crowd.

The Dyke March was younger, hipper, more dirty and in-your-face and pierced than the standard Pride crowd. Five thousand tattooed dykes scattered among the bright plastic grass in Dolores Park, blocking out the green with their own shades of polka-dot dresses and heavy metal shirts. Tirtza and I walked my guests through the crowd after synagogue. I had never felt so straight, me and a bunch of kids in long pleated skirts and dress suits in the middle of the punk-rock ground-zero of the world. We bumped into Michelle Tea as soon as we got there, of course, standing there like a regular person instead of a venerable rock-and-roll author idol. She had on silver go-go boots, glasses laced with sparkles, a paisley miniskirt and vest. She looked immaculate. "Hey," she said, and I said hey right back.

She remembered me. Michelle Tea actually remembered me. I was so cool.

The Dyke March had a policy of no corporate sponsors, which meant no vendors selling beer, but it also meant a plethora of biker dykes with butchy Elvis hair and studded leather jackets, peeling through the crowd, a flask in each hand. One tough-looking top with tobacco-stained teeth recognized me from a queer poetry reading. She pulled me across two rows deep of shoulder-to-shoulder people, one gnarled hand wrapped around my head. "Hey, you're that kid," she said. "Probably," I said. Other people are better at nonverbal conversations than I am. She offered two flasks, holding both between fingers of the same hand. I took a swig of one. The alcohol burned my mouth, warm and dry on that sunny day. It was so hot but it evaporated all the sweat on my head and my body began to feel cooler.

I started walking around with Tegan and her friends, pushing through the crowd, and we managed to get completely separated within five minutes. I freaked out. I wanted to show Tegan all my gay friends and get compassionate-liberal bonus points. But it was pretty much useless and I decided to ride the wave of the crowd, anyway.

It was still kind of scary, marooned in the throng without a girl as backup. I knew people all over, but there was still the official understanding that biological boys weren't supposed to be at the Dyke March, and I wanted to have a legitimate dyke to defend me. See, I try to be all about keeping it real, but I'm basically a wuss. I drifted between friends of Box and friends of friends

Holding both between fingers of the same hand. I have tried to do this since then. It takes talent.

of Box, letting myself get tossed from conversation to conversation. I spotted Anastasia and ducked back into my own crowd. I was just starting to feel happy and I didn't need anything bringing me back to reality.

My gross friend Bradley, who was a girl, pulled me into the Dyke March. Her grip was stronger than my arms. She was mostly naked, and her breasts were flying everywhere, so that you had to make a conscious effort not to come into contact with them. I kept sidestepping Bradley and I think I hurt her feelings. But she still didn't let go. The ranks of the parade swelled, women of every shape as far as I could see, filling the streets and the sidewalks and undulating in that painfully slow parade pace. Gray-haired, rough-skinned dykes encased in leather kept looking at me like my grandmother does. It was all so big and weird and disorienting, and it made me feel giddy and victorious and like I shouldn't be pushing my luck. Bradley yelled out, "Show us your tits!" at a bunch of grandmotherly women clutching a Parents and Friends of Lesbians and Gays banner. Bradley jiggled hers enthusiastically.

I ducked away. Right behind me was the Lusty Lady convocation, Anastasia's coworkers. I used to be friends with a bunch of them, actual friends. Now they all knew me as that boy who turned Anastasia straight.

I felt one arm grab me, and then another, and they whirled me around, and I found myself face to face with Anastasia. New hair—shorter, bleach blond—and a dress I'd never seen her wear, one that she might have even bought in a store. She probably had money now. She looked really hot.

"Hey," I said. That word—we use it so much, an empty phonetic sound to fill up the blank space of greetings. "I saw you working the crowd today."

"Hey," she said. "I saw you trying not to notice."

The people behind us, realizing we weren't walking any time soon, began to curve around us. After a second there was a solid diamond of marchers, curving around Anastasia's and my bodies, nervously eyeing us as we stood, hands wringing and trying not to intersect with each other, because once we were holding each other's hands, God only knows what we'd pull ourselves into.

"So what were you flyering for?"

"Uh," Anastasia demurred, "you probably don't want to see."

"But I'm *try*ing to be *in*terested in your *life*," I kvetched.

She handed me a flyer. Actually it was a business card. I read the fine print below her stage name. KITTY AND KAT, DISCREET PRIVATE ENTERTAINERS.

"Holy shit," I said. "Are you calling yourself discreet?"

"It was my partner's—it was my coworker's choice," Anastasia said. "She thought it sounded more professional."

I opened my mouth, closed it again. I made a conscious, immediate decision not to involve myself, just then or ever again, in my ex-girlfriend's erotic business affairs. The words hit like that: *Ex. Girl. Friend.* Each hit my stomach harder than the last. I closed my eyes and tried to let the feeling pass.

Anastasia cocked her head to one side like she was trying to see inside my head. She smiled at me, that flirty and curious way that she always did, and she wrapped her hands around my head.

I could feel her breath on my face.

"Anastasia," I said, "please no."

And she pulled her mouth away from mine and rolled her head over, onto my shoulder, scooped me up in a hug.

I'm glad she did. I don't think I could have stood

independently at that second without falling over.

And that was it. A one-second hug, and she was gone. I spun around and didn't see her. I turned halfway and looked down a sidestreet, and there was Anastasia, passing around cards to a group of white-hat prep boys who were checking out the parade of dykes from the sidelines. You know, where the boys were supposed to be. She said something to them and they all looked at her card again and, at once, they all started laughing.

A second later, I got whipped around again. It was Batya, gripping my shoulders, eyes wide and owl-like through her glasses. Did I tell you, she had the cutest spiky hair? On most people, spiky hair looked mod or threatening. On Batya, it looked like Velcro. You wanted to ping it with your finger and see if it sprang back. She had a voice like my mother's, a little overconcerned and way too mature for anyone who hasn't been married for twenty years.

"We've been looking all over for you," she said. "Where have you been? And how the hell did you manage to get worked into the dyke parade?"

The parade swept up Sixteenth Street and turned onto Market, sloping into the Castro District as the sun fell and the sky turned pale with streaks of gray. The parade emptied into the intersection of Market and Castro, where an all-out dance party was going on, DJs on a platform fifteen feet in the air, right next to the traffic lights. It was like San Francisco had gotten a *Queer Eye* makeover. I mean, the stores were always decked-out, but tonight, even the street signs looked fabulous and shimmering. Batya and I fell into the dance party without prodding. Some of the rigid dykes, the Born Dyke Marchers, hung on the edge of the crowd with their DYKE RIGHTS NOW signs, unsure of what to do. Tegan's little ambiguously-gendered friends stood there for a minute with their arms crossed, but gradually, like ice melting, they worked into those college one-two-one-two dance moves. Since when had I learned to dance, gotten to the point I could tell what was dancing and what was only trying? I don't know, but that night it felt like a revelation. The DJ shrilled a St. Germain beat onto the tables and it twinkled on a single sustained note. Batya threw her hands in the air, fingers waving. I rolled my shoulders in place. The drums came back in, and I threw myself down on the ground and Batya leapt back into dancing and even Tegan, mindful of the displaced activists, laughed it up and dove into the music.

Batya gripped my wrist.

"Shabbos is over," she whispered solemnly.

I looked up. Three stars blazed in the sky, more than that. Entire constellations were beginning to glow.

Which meant that—"What time is it?" I asked Tegan at once.

She floundered. "I didn't bring my watch," she said. I turned on the other kids, Tegan's friends. "Do you guys know?"

Not in this dance pit. Angels with mylar wings, boys in shiny shirts, girls with breasts that sparkled. This was the spot I chose to turn twenty-four.

Tegan, Batya, and me, dancing. Hip-hop DJs and techno machines. Tegan, as if she'd been assigned a job, ticking off the minutes until my official birthday, nine o'clock, midnight on the East Coast. I panicked. Was there anything else I had to do before my birthday?

"Is there anything else I have to do before my birthday?" I asked, urgency creeping in.

"Did you get laid?" Batya asked helpfully.

I shook my head. No, but I didn't want to. I was staying a virgin till I got married. Or at least for now, whatever part of my virginity I still had. Frances suggested drugs. I didn't do them either. Jamie told us all the story of when he turned twenty-one and had never eaten a kumquat, and that's what he was doing at the exact moment of his birthday, and I realized I had never eaten a kumquat either, but there was no way I could find one now. The ludicrousness of the idea washed through us, but it felt suddenly important in my mind. The world could blow up again, just like on 9/11—it was still so close to 9/11, and we kept thinking things would blow up—and tonight, half a million people were squeezed into four city blocks, dancing, and we were all queer, the perfect choice for terrorists. I realized then, I hadn't accomplished anything in my last hour of life. I searched faces in the crowd, fully intent on asking people if they were carrying kumquats.

Tegan finally scored a clock and a phone in the same move—from a tall, lanky boy who looked like Perry Farrell and wore black angel wings. They had protested Bush together somewhere. "Eight fifty-nine," she announced proudly.

"Should I just give up my act and have sex?" I asked, half to no one, half to myself.

The boy in angel wings looked delighted, giddy on another plane of existence. I don't think he realized I was even serious. Then he leaned over and gripped my shoulders, his bare chest in my face, and I thought he was going to kiss me. He licked his lips, leaned down, and whispered into my ear.

"Honey," he said, "you don't have to do anything right now. Just stand where you are and dance. It will happen when you're ready. Everything will."

When he said that, I didn't even have to think about dancing. I just *danced*, hard enough so the people around me could feel it, hard enough that we were probably jerking off the seismic fault lines around California, triggering earthquakes like the wings of a butterfly in Indonesia.

I'd typed my parents' number into the boy's cell phone and my parents picked up, half-asleep, delirious with confusion. Where they were—in the time zone I was born in—it was midnight now.

"Happy birthday," I shouted at them through the phone. The DJ spun a song by Björk, and I danced, tossing the phone back to its angel-winged owner, my hands in the air, my hips writhing. I danced harder, shaking my booty against the night.

14

cautious of kashrus

"Batya would be good for you," said Tegan, one Shabbos afternoon a few weeks later. She was lying on her bed and I was staring at a Talmud, absorbed by the curve of the Rashi letters. She was running her nails back and forth on my leg, which for anyone else would be sexual, but I knew the second I touched her back she would snap away. I was staring at the text, unfocusing my eyes until the Aramaic words turned into squiggles, not letters at all but an intricate matte of dots and curves. I was years—*years*—into being Orthodox, and Hebrew still looked alien to me. This book of Talmud was Kiddushin, the one about the laws of marriage. I was having trouble understanding it, on so many different levels. Tegan, perched over my shoulder, seemed like an easier distraction.

"Good for me how?" I asked. "How good for me?"

"She's into Judaism like you are. And she's into all that…alternative stuff."

What Tegan meant by "alternative stuff," I assumed, was queer people. Going to gay clubs and listening to slam poetry and fucking around with the whole thing of being shomer negiah.

You could divide all the Orthodox Jews in Berkeley into two camps—the ones who were shomer negiah and the ones who weren't. Since nobody knew about Anastasia, everyone but Tegan thought I was shomer negiah. And, since Anastasia and I were solidly over, I guess these days I actually *was*.

Most people weren't. Not Justin and Tova, who were both very Orthodox. Everyone trusted their kosher standard, but their Shabbos dinners always ended with Justin and Tova saying goodnight and slipping into the bedroom together. Not Tegan, who made a point of hugging her friends on Shabbos in front of the most religious members of the community.

But Batya.

Batya was definitely not shomer negiah. She was openly bisexual, which was okay because in Berkeley everyone was liberal, but she talked about it constantly, which made people choke on their food. But mostly it was because she worked for the lesbian porn magazine, which might disqualify you for life from being shomer negiah.

"Batya would be good for you," Tegan repeated, oblivious to my lack of reaction. Or maybe she was trying to get a rise out of me. With Tegan, I could never tell.

"Does that mean you don't want to go out with me?" I asked.

Tegan shot an icy glare at me through narrow slits of eyes. I felt her go limp and distant. Wrong thing to say.

"Tonight," I said, quickly. "After Shabbos, we're hanging out, right?" When I stayed at the Yar House,

Tegan and I always hung out after Shabbos. Everyone else was so domestic, Miri would play guitar, Jimmy and Caroline dragged out the LCD projector and they rented movies and sat outside and watched them projected against the side of their house.

"As a matter of fact, no," said Tegan. She swung herself over the edge of the bed, smoothed out her large skirt, and walked out to the kitchen. "I have a date tonight."

I skitted after her. She slid a drawer open and clipped out handfuls of forks and knives. "With who?" I asked.

"Nobody you know," said Tegan. "This guy I work with. He asked me to a movie."

I unloaded a heavy stack of glass plates from the cabinet, sliding them into the crook of my arm. I still couldn't tell if she was serious or not. "A movie? That's, like, crossing over to the dark side," I said.

I added, "Not that there's anything wrong with that," just as Jimmy walked in. Jimmy knew what was up. He said, "Oh good, you guys are taking care of Shalosh Seudos?" Without waiting for an answer, he swiveled around on one foot and retraced his steps right back out.

Shalosh Seudos was the third meal of Shabbos, the time when we satisfy God's commandment to eat bountifully by stuffing our faces an hour or two after our last meal. In Berkeley, Shalosh Seudos turned into an event, everyone from Friday night together again before we went back to the business- and electricity-filled week. For me, it was like Shabbos's last stand. In a couple of hours I'd be chilling at some bar somewhere, shadowing my housemates or writing up a concert for some local newspaper or another. This was the last chance to steep myself in the Old World domesticity with the Yar House kids before I ended up surrounded by the secular world again.

Jimmy backed out of the room, and I turned around

to see Tegan's unearthly big eyes glaring at me.

"What's his name?" I asked.

"Frederick," she said.

It felt like a gut punch. Not only was Tegan not lying, but her date had a name. Names were like daggers. Once people had names, you knew they actually existed. And, God, I wished I spent less time having crushes in my head and more time letting them play out in the outside world.

I clattered plates onto the table, one by one. The fire went out of my head. Maybe Tegan was right.

Maybe I should talk to Batya more.

I don't remember how it happened, but I spent the next Shabbos at Batya's house.

Batya lived in a Berkeley co-op, a big old house that might have been a mansion once, but now twenty-five college kids lived in it. Batya's room, a small purple dorm in the basement, had a bunk bed, a desktop burner, and not much else. She kept a single deep-trowel pan in her underwear drawer so she could make her own kosher food. Her night table held a huge assortment of dildos, vibrators, butt plugs, electric eggs, and things I couldn't even guess how they were supposed to get you off. I looked at the desktop stove in amazement.

"The pan is deep enough so I can fill it with water and boil pasta," Batya told me, like a college lecturer, reaching over to fondle a big red jelly dildo as she talked. "It's really not that hard to keep kosher on your own, you just have to use your imagination. And not mind throwing away plates after every meal." Next to Batya's pot sat a stack of paper plates and plastic silverware, enough for a southern family reunion.

"Cool," I said, mystified. My eyes wandered. "Hey," I said after a second, "why does that dildo have three little penises sticking out of it?"

The dildos were all review samples for Batya's job. She wrote these columns that read: *Hitachi Leaping Rabbit, v. good locomotion, stimulates clitoris effectively and accurately, no G-spot action.* Of the Berkeley kids, Batya was the only one that I didn't have to be squeamish about discussing this stuff with. She was queer and savvy about the queer world, but she knew all the things about Shabbos and God like I did. She knew what shomer negiah meant as well as me, and she knew how to break it even better than I did.

"The ones on the right are muktza," Batya said. "They're the farthest from the bed. That's so on Shabbos, I don't pull out an electric one by accident."

Batya showed me around the house—the yards, the tennis court, the rooms where her friends Frances and Jamie lived, the thatched roof that opened up to a vision of Berkeley as a lush mass of greenery and Hobbit houses. Standing up there was like standing in a movie. If you weren't working four jobs at once, college was like getting to be a millionaire for four years: You never had to show up anywhere, and you got to live in a kickass house that was more like a playpen.

Then Batya brought me into the kitchen, to the walk-in refrigerator where she kept her stuff. If kosher food touches anything that isn't kosher, it becomes unkosher, but there are stories in the Shulchan Aruch about cold meat and cheese touching or bumping together and still remaining okay. Batya had her own shelf in the fridge where she kept a Tupperware container full of her kosher food. "Just in case you need anything," she said. She thudded the latch, a metal arm as long as her waist, shut tight.

Shabbos dinner was being hosted by this kid Jonah

Muktza. Any object that violates the laws of Shabbos, like computers and money and vibrators and other electric appliances.

who just moved into the community. Nobody really knew him, but everyone knew about him. He had a summer sublet in the kosher house at the University of California, a group house that was sponsored by some big Jewish organization, where kids got cheap rent in exchange for keeping the kitchen kosher.

Somebody said he'd grown up Hasidic in Brooklyn. Someone else said he was from the San Francisco Bay Area, that he'd grown up here his whole life and only just decided to become observant. Both stories were doubtful. He had neat, straight hair, a knitted yarmulke that no Hasid would ever wear, and a set of starched button-down shirts that no Berkeley love child would be caught dead in.

That Shabbos, everyone poured into his house. It was called the Bayit, which was the Hebrew word for *house,* because big Jewish organizations with lots of money have no imagination. All the Berkeley Jews were mulling in a glass anteroom, what rich people call a den. We prayed there, all the usual crew and a bunch of people I didn't recognize. Since this wasn't a formal synagogue, we didn't need an actual wall-length mechitza to separate men and women, but there should still be some separation. Somebody dragged in a table, and the few religious kids clustered around it, guys on one side, girls on the other. Everyone else stood in a big clump in the back, freaked out.

We had dinner, and Batya and I only ate the cold

We didn't need an actual wall-length mechitza. According to the Shulchan Aruch, the main code of Jewish law that's a sort of handbook for Orthodox Jews.

There should still be some separation. A point addressed by Rabbi Moshe Feinstein in his collected letters, in which he addresses the problem of synagogues that separate men and women by an open aisle without a barrier.

food. We didn't know if everything was kosher and it was too odd to ask to see every bottle of everything. Jimmy and Miri and Tegan were all there, and they all ate with no problem. But it felt different for them. They lived in Berkeley. They were used to kosher weirdness. Batya and I were East Coast Orthodox. We were paranoid about these things.

Jonah turned out to be cool—cool kosher-wise, but also cool as a person. We had distrusted him because of his wardrobe, the khakis, the way his thin knit yarmulke sat so primly on the periphery of his brow—all those hallmarks of New York that we associated with boringness and religious tedium. But Jonah was so dynamic. He did grow up with a Hasidic father, speaking Hebrew in that thick, glutinous Galician Yiddish accent that dribbled with history. His mother lived in Berkeley, and the secular world ran down his brow in globules, from his decidedly un-Hasidic knit yarmulke (Hasidim only wear black velvet or leather). But most of all, to his musical tastes, which extended to rock bands like Sonic Youth and Bruce Springsteen and Jane's Addiction.

"What do you think of him?" asked Tegan one night.

"I think he's hella all right," I told her.

That night Batya showed me pictures of her high school. She flipped through shots of sports teams and high school clubs, pointing out each of her old friends: She's married, she's engaged, she's married, she's about to have her first kid. Batya was only twenty-two. We were from a culture that might be down with spiky hair and performance poetry and life in the secular world, but we were both still supposed to be married by now.

"What was Anastasia like?" Batya asked, hanging over the edge of her bed. She stared out toward her computer, which sat on her desk. The screen saver kept running all Shabbos long. Her spiky hair dangled toward the floor, moussed in reverse, not looking at me at all. I sat crosslegged on her pillow, perched over her like a vulture. When I spoke, it was in the direction of her breasts.

"She still *is*," I said. "She's loud. Cutesy. Sweet. Sometimes she's almost stupidly sweet. She talks in clichés. She plays the dumbest pop songs."

"Then why were you with her?" Batya's head swung momentarily, just enough to give me a confused glance and then drop back down.

I fell back against the wall. "I don't know. Cause she was a stripper? Because it felt good?" Not even I believed what I said. I sighed. "She's honest. No matter what she was doing, she always did it because she wanted to. Did I ever tell you she was homeless once?"

"Twice," said Batya.

"She didn't need me for anything. She's beautiful and smart and she could have anything she wanted. And all she wanted was me."

"That's not *all* she wanted," Batya said.

I'd told her that tonight Anastasia was out filming a porn movie with her ex-girlfriend. Batya stared at me with big eyes, open and eager, as if she'd listen to me tell her anything.

I reached over her, snatched the yearbook back, and began flipping through it. Pictures of anonymous girl after girl stared at me from the hygienic red drapes of photography day in a school auditorium. I thought about being married to each one of them, imagined what my life would be like. Would we have sex often? What would I buy them for their birthdays?

This *so* wasn't my life.

"Batya," I said. "How am I ever going to date anyone Orthodox?"

"You will," she murmured.

"I know I will. Everyone keeps saying I will. But how do I find her?"

"Oh Matthue," she said, flopping over, staring at me with eyes that were big and sad. "She'll find you. You're yelling loud enough for her to hear, aren't you?"

A few days earlier Batya and I were slumming on Valencia Street, tearing through the specialty magazine stores, the clothes boutiques that neither of us could afford. I kept finding tznius dresses made out of plastic and nylon. Batya kept vetoing them. She'd gone to a yeshiva where girls were allowed to wear pants and she was proud of it. I liked the idea of girls wearing pants. I had this whole Orthodox aesthetic of an eighteenth-century European village, but mod. Women in flapper dresses. Men in pinstripe suits. We were arguing in front of one store when Gravity tripped on the curb and flew into us. Gravity worked for an arts warehouse that was about to go bankrupt and they were having a fund-raiser, she told me, and maybe I could be in it? She wanted to have some up-and-coming writers and then other writers whose names people recognized. Gravity asked me for my number and she strutted away, straight into the writing clinic that was owned by a local novelist who'd blown up, really blown up, like, his life was being made into a Hollywood movie. I turned to Batya and told her how my entire performance poetry career might be the world's most extravagant personal ad. When I stand on stage in front of twenty different people every night and talk about how weird I am, maybe I'm just looking for someone to say, *I'm that weird too.*

"Maybe you'd be better off just asking someone," she'd said.

Batya threw a sheet over her lamp, which made the room dark, and rolled all the way into her bed and under the covers. Without asking where I was going to sleep.

I rolled up next to her on top of the sheets. She wrapped an arm around me and pulled me into her. Batya ran her soft, snaky hands up and down my back, inside my shirt, touching my bare skin, raking me until we drifted off to sleep, her nails against the knobs of my spine.

A few weeks later, Batya came to Shabbos at my house and we went to Rabbi Mendy's for dinner. She kept saying how Chabad was lame, it was only for Jews who didn't know anything about Judaism. I told her Mendy was cooler than that. She showed up wearing a sweater and jeans, and Rabbi Mendy totally read her as a non-observant Jew. Batya waited for the right second in our conversation, then she dropped something about a Talmudic beraisa she'd studied. The rabbi's eyes popped open—he wasn't used to women who were fluent in Talmud—and he said, "But the majority opinion in that section says that midnight is too late to say the evening prayer, although I always thought…." I watched them go at it for the next hour, arguing with the fury and passion of ADD kids who'd just learned how to thumb wrestle. I pecked at the grilled artichoke hearts nebbishly, waiting for a space to say something. It didn't come.

The weeks became bookends for Shabboses, instead of the other way around. Tegan and Batya and their friends became the new Shabbos scene, focused on late nights and parties and having fun—a bar-like, disco-intensive Shabbos experience. We all kept Shabbos, there was never a question about that. But when one of Batya and Frances and Jamie's friends from college threw a party on Friday night, we went to that too.

Everybody lived in the university dorms. Elvin hadn't

gone to school in six years and lived in a dorm. Evie had never gone to school and lived in a dorm, although maybe with her girlfriend. One Friday night, we were all at the Yar and the meal ended early and we left and walked around Berkeley. Telegraph Avenue was crawling with college kids, out on the first warm Friday night of the semester. Streetlights glowed with the soft orange of summer. Kids were running into bars and running out of them. It felt strangely liberating to not be allowed to do that. We walked along the broad sidewalk and I flung my arms out like Leonardo on the *Titanic,* 'cause I really felt like king of the world.

"Zara and Candace are having a kissing party," Batya said, absently, like Zara and Candace had just whispered it in her ear.

We all looked over at Batya.

"I mean," she said, "if you guys want to."

Zara and Candace were students from Batya's college who lived in Berkeley for the summer. Zara had an internship at a queer youth center. She spent eight hours a day having to say no to offers of sex with textbook-cute sixteen-year-old lesbians with pigtails and chestnut cheeks. She'd spent the entire summer being sexually frustrated. Tonight, she was getting it all out.

Jamie was asking which boys from Batya's college were going to be there. Frances didn't say anything, but her stride picked up with a bounce and her hands sank snugly into her pockets. I think she had a crush on Zara or Candace or maybe both of them. Batya technically had a boyfriend, Derek, or actually it was a best friend whom she hooked up with sometimes, but she was supposed to be getting over him. I kept reminding her that she had a job at a lesbian porn magazine and she could get any woman she wanted.

On the way over, Batya couldn't stop talking about

kissing parties. "We had this amazing one in the Bayit at my school last semester," she said, "a hundred and fifty people, and everyone kissed everyone else. They weren't allowed to have kegs in the building, but everybody smuggled something in and they got more alcohol into the building than there ever would be if it was legal. I think the idea of these parties is really freeing. I mean, you don't want to make out with *every* person there, but some people you do it just to be polite, which isn't really cool but it kind of *is*. And then there's the people you don't mind kissing but you'd never kiss if there wasn't a kissing party going on. Like when Tzippy and that girl who was visiting kissed, they went out for three months after that. They were totally prepared not to look at each other again. I mean, they were friendly, but they weren't *friends*, do you know?"

"Mm," I agreed.

"I can't *wait*. I feel so giddy about tonight. I haven't kissed anyone in *weeks*," said Batya. "I really *miss* making out, you know? I think I might be an addict."

"I think I'm shomer negiah," I whispered.

Batya froze.

Jamie and Frances froze. Even Frances's coworker Sudeep, who was from Uzbekistan and didn't know what shomer negiah meant, he froze too.

We stood at the crossroads, not sure if we were supposed to turn. Only Batya knew the directions, and she was the slowest to shrug it off. "Why?" she said to me at last.

I shrugged. "I want to wait till somebody's worth it."

"Until you're *married?*" They all said it at once. It sounded like *death wish*.

"Maybe," I said. "Maybe just till it feels right."

We all kept walking. Frances said, "I can't believe you're going to wait till you're *marri*ed to have *sex* again," and I could have told them that I hadn't had sex yet—maybe I should have—but I didn't.

Zara and Candace lived in an apartment complex that had a door you couldn't open without dialing up on the electronic callbox. The apartment complex looked like a yuppie bungalow village, thatched roofs and high fences twisting with ivy. As Batya and I stood there, not sure what to do, Jamie sank his fingers into the metal gate and lifted himself three feet into the air. His body was big, muscley, with that unformed neckless Silly Putty quality. He scaled the wall in seconds, leaped over, and crashed to the pavement with a thump. A second later, he turned the handle and flung the door open manually.

All was kosher.

We scoured the hallways. Batya was the only one who'd ever been to Candace's apartment, and the only thing she remembered about it was a red poster on the doorway, no floor or room number. We quizzed her. Batya said she remembered there were stairs involved, but she wasn't sure if they went up or down. Finally we found Candace. She was lying in the third-floor hallway, stomach up, lazily shucking a bottle of bourbon around the carpet. "What happened?" Batya gasped, concerned, dropping to the floor like a paramedic.

Candace pointed her beer bottle down the hall. "Zara," she said. "She hijacked my bedroom."

When we celebrate Shabbos, we separate ourselves from time, we move independently from it. Some Orthodox Jews don't wear watches on Shabbos, because it's harder to rest when there's a clock ticking. When Jews invite you to lunch on Shabbos, they don't tell you a time. Synagogue ends, you kibitz, you take your time walking, and, eventually, you show up.

The secular world doesn't work that way. Events have

expiration dates, even late-night parties, and it looked like this show had crashed an hour ago. Candace showed us the rooftop patio, where balloons and cake plates lay scattered over the tables and floor. The turntables were still warm. Under the table, this guy Dee was stretched out with a blanket. He looked up at us like we were angels in his dream. He was crashing with Zara and he fell asleep waiting to get into her room. Dee lived around the corner from me in San Francisco. He was a black goth S/M fag whose name was short for Debauchery. He wore huge metal and leather collars and spikes but when he talked, he sounded like a motherly Martha Stewart.

Dee lived in the absolute most disgusting group house I knew of with about twenty other people. The police kept showing up and threatening to shut them down, but what were they going to do? It was a bunch of kids, twelve or thirteen of them, a different group at any given time. Nobody was older than twenty and, if the police did shut them down, they'd just sleep on the sidewalk outside. Right before the first of every month, Dee threw these huge parties where he raised money to pay rent. People thought Dee was a lazy stoner, but really he was the duct-tape of responsibility that held all the lazy stoners together. He grew up in Compton, in Southern California, as a flaming kid with a fey, burnished voice that could not dip below middle C. In some weird, unspoken way, we felt like soul brothers.

Dee opened his eyes, stretched, and smiled lazily up at us. "Hey kids," he murmured. "Too bad you missed the kissing."

"Shit," said a voice from the doorway. "When did everybody stop kissing?"

It was Zara. She stood in the doorway, naked except for a red Sesame Street sheet. She wore it like a dress, double-tucked under her armpits, held up by her massive breasts.

"When they all left the party," said Dee, yawning again.

Batya let a sigh escape her lips. Everyone shuffled their feet.

Standing in Zara's shadow was a small, fat, adorably fragile girl whose eyes trailed the ground, never looking at anyone above knee level. She touched Zara's arm on the flesh of her elbow and gave her a pleading glance.

"We're. Uhh. Thanks for coming," she said to everyone, vanishing back into the bedroom.

"Nice to see you," whispered the other girl, even quieter. She shot me a quick, embarrassed smile and swept back into the room. I recognized her. She was Dee's roommate, this in-your-face dyke who used to curse out the bike messengers who ran through intersections in our neighborhood.

Dee roused himself. He fished a beer off the stoop, the one bottle among a sea that had been left unopened.

"Well," he said, "you can always keep me company till they fall asleep."

This is the margin of difference in a party night: Batya and I had the same experience of the same exact events, but when we walked home, I was light and happy, and Batya was grumpily unsatisfied.

We shared her bed that night. Lying there, the space of the pillow between our heads, Batya looked at me dead on and asked, "Are you serious about being shomer?"

The fact that she didn't immediately call me out on sleeping in her bed was all Batya—kind, elegant, deferential. She really did take everyone on their own terms. I talked, in my foggy haze, about how shomer negiah literally meant *a guard of your touch,* and I didn't want to stop touching, I just wanted to be more careful about where I put my heart. Batya said that she got an email right before Shabbos. Her best friend, the one who wasn't her boy-friend, had a weekend conference in San Francisco.

I told Batya how nonmonogamy wrecked me. I told her how nonmonogamy was all about making yourself public, and there were parts of me that I wanted to keep private. I said, maybe it was modesty, or maybe it was just that I needed to be in charge of myself again.

Batya turned over, once, then twice, so she was fac-ing me again.

"Making out with people makes me in charge of my-self," she said to me. "When somebody wants me, and it's up to me to decide whether they can have me."

If my Hasidic friends from back East had been there, they'd sock it to us both—officially, God was in charge of both our bodies. But, as sacrilegious as it sounds, God gave us the choice of what to do with our bodies. We can bend our knees and shokel in crazed devotion, or we can get on our knees and fool around with each other. It's one of the paradoxes of Judaism that we believe in free will, which makes it even more meaningful when we decide to serve God without being coerced into it.

The more determined I became to be shomer negiah, the more I thought about sex. It was one of those para-doxes. To keep myself sane, I retreated even further into the queer ghetto near my house. There, I figured, I could always be a cheerleader for my friends to get laid.

That week, everyone showed up at the Yar House for Third Meal, Jimmy's chollint served with salads and some stuffed peppers that Tegan and I made together. All Batya's college friends showed up, and after Shabbos,

Modesty. Being tznius, I mean.

we performed a mellow Havdala—Yehezkel drew out some fresh marijuana and jasmine to use as spices for the service—and, the second we finished singing and the lights came on, everyone whipped out their cell phones. One of Frances's friends scored an invitation to a party in the Mission. Then they were all going to go dancing and crash, some kids at Frances's friend's house and some at mine. It was one of those summer Shabboses that starts late and ends late, and it was almost ten by the time we finished Havdala.

Tegan was brooding in a corner. She had a volunteer job Sunday morning in Berkeley, and she had to be there earlier than the BART trains ran. As everyone else made plans and coordinated beds, Tegan dialed numbers frantically on her cell phone, trying to switch her shift. Everybody was already out for the night.

She yelled, savage and shrill and primal, storming into her room on the hardwood floors and then stomping back out. She saw me, standing in a corner of the hall, waiting with my bag till everyone else was ready to take BART.

"I *hate* living in the suburbs, Matthue," she said. "I swear, God *owes* me for living here."

Tegan begged me to stay in Berkeley that night. She offered to let me crash at the Yar, and I would have— I really would have, I didn't care about one more club night—but I had commitments.

Sunday morning, I told her, I had to meet my tranny basketball group.

Just before she left San Francisco, Batya did an interview with a big-name queer movie star for her magazine, her first cover story. When I showed up to meet Batya, she was still doing the interview. She chewed on a pencil behind the glass windows of the ice cream shop, nodded politely, scribbled furiously when she hit the quote she needed, wagging one finger in the air for the movie star to wait as Batya attacked her notebook with a vengeance.

I sat on the curb outside and waited, listening to my Walkman and singing out loud with the songs. The only person in the restaurant besides them was a boy sitting alone with a cup of coffee, watching Batya and the movie star intently. I mean, of course he was. If you saw a hot Orthodox girl and a lesbian movie star whispering about orgasms and vibrators and fun in the tour bus, you'd probably keep turning around, too.

Batya got up, paid the bill, and they said goodbye outside the café. Batya winked to me and waved as the lesbian movie star walked away. I struggled to my feet and walked over and then the voyeuristic guy came out, wrapped his arms around Batya, and kissed her neck. He looked up, smiled at me, and detached one of his hands to offer for shaking.

"Hi Matthue," she said. "This is Derek."

We walked down to the Castro. The weather was perfect, the kind of warm that didn't make you sweat, and all over the Castro men were dressed for Atlantic City in early summer, Hawaiian shirts and Bermuda shorts, Day-Glo visors like the kind that casinos give away for free. Derek was actually cool. I always want to hate guys that I meet, especially new guys who are hooking up with girls whom I have crushes on, but he stayed mostly out of the exclusive conversation that Batya and I were having, about whether lube needed to be kosher. Whenever I made a point, Batya refuted it by throwing the shomer negiah thing back in my face, saying it the way ten-year-olds call you a dillweed, "Yeah, but you're *shhhho*-mer," as if it had anything to do with the actual argument at hand.

I had nothing to argue back. I don't even know if Derek

knew what *shomer* meant, and I'm sure we were too in-volved to tell him. But I never contradicted her—"Hell *yeah* I'm shomer"—and I remember thinking, *This time it's gonna last.*

We left Derek at the Muni stop on Church Street and went to Safeway. We went on a whole kosher shopping spree. It had been a while since I shopped with someone else who also checked for kosher markings on food. We bought a baguette and tortilla chips and salsa and a six-pack of seltzery Japanese beer and Klondike bars, which I never knew were kosher. In the park, we staked out our own hill, a small one with a single palm tree, and ripped into the baguette and tortillas and salsa and especially the Klondike bars. We drank beer from paper bags. Stuffed and bloated, we lay in the grass. Our bodies formed an *L*, heads nearly touching.

Batya told me that her magazine had offered her a full-time position. I told her that the performance for Grav-ity was official. It was going to be me and three Actual Professional Writers: the memoirist whose book was get-ting turned into a Hollywood movie, this woman who used to tour with Sonic Youth, and Michelle Tea. I told Batya I was scared that I was just there as a token, so

---

This time it's gonna last. Like the Beth Orton song. Sometimes I hear these songs on the radio, old be-bop songs from the '50s and Motown hits from the '70s, and the lyrics could be the dumbest thing in the world but I believe in them all so clearly, the clearest emanation of my belief. Sometimes it's weird, thinking about this whole God thing— do I believe? Do I give as much attention as I should to God, or do I get too wrapped up in the laws?—but then I hear these songs, the ones that force you to bop your head and dance with your shoulders even when you're not thinking about it, and I repeat those choruses to myself, like prayers. How do I believe in God? I believe in God like pop songs. I believe in God like choruses that I don't know what they mean, but I keep singing them.
Heads nearly touching. But not.

Gravity could say they were supporting local youth.

In the park that day, though, I really felt delicate. When you're a doctor or an accountant or a movie star, you have moments, getting hired by a firm or getting cast in a film, when you know you've made it. When your career doesn't fall into those neat holes, you have to kind of negotiate your way into it. I felt like maybe this was it— *It*—the moment in our lives when we decide to be writers. "Are you going to take it?" I asked Batya. I ground the last tortilla chip between my teeth, swallowing uncomfortably because I was still lying down.

"No," Batya said. "I told them, maybe next year. I have to finish my degree, and they don't want me working from across the country."

"Do you think you'll come back?" I asked.

"I dunno," said Batya. "Anything's possible, I guess."

I held one hand in front of my eyes, twisted it against the sky. I tried to see exactly what color my skin was, peach or pink or the golden olive color that my skin got in summer. The blue of the sky was larger than life. It was so unreal, that anything so big could be so blue. The sky is bigger than the world, I realized. I wondered if we were like that, too, and if our bodies were shrink-wrapped inside our personalities, and if, when we looked at each other, what we saw was not our physical bodies at all.

Supporting local youth. "You're lame," Batya said, and to prove it she looked up the other readers' web pages on my computer when we got home and showed me that my site got more visits per day than two of their sites.

15

driving into sunsets

September came. The high holidays moved quickly that year. We prayed swiftly, ardently, remembering how New York caught fire and burned right before Rosh HaShana last year, hoping nothing like that would happen again, thinking how maybe—if we prayed hard enough, did the right combination of bending and bowing and giving thanks—we'd get to December without a bombing. We did. On Yom Kippur I sat at the crest of Dolores Park with Jimmy and Miri and this guy Haskell who had grown up Hasidic, quit as a teenager, and decided to come back for Yom Kippur. We had met on the street and I offered to let him sleep on my couch. He warned me that he wasn't going to speak all Yom Kippur long.

That morning Haskell and I woke up at 4:00 A.M. and drove to Ocean Beach to do mikveh, the Hasidic ritual of dunking your body under the water naked. On that bare empty beach we stripped, ran waist-deep into the freezing morning ocean, and submerged our bodies once, twice, and again. Underneath, the stale noise of the world vanished. We streaked back fast to our clothes pile and flopped on our yarmulkes to say the mikveh prayer. Then we dressed and wrapped tefillin and prayed, facing the sand dunes, shokeling until the sun exploded into existence like a car bomb in front of your school—that surprising.

As we walked back to the car, a woman in a BMW, busy talking on her cell phone, drove straight into me. I don't know how it happened but I jumped up in the air and suddenly I was on top of the hood of her car, on all fours, panting madly and staring at her like a demon. She started crying. It was almost the anniversary of September 11. Nobody was in their right mind.

And then it was night. Up on that hilltop, we watched the planes fly low and the city lights flash. This is what it came to: A year and a half in San Francisco, and I was back to hanging with the straight boys.

Autumn turned to winter. I was practicing poems, honing skills, writing constantly. After the tour, gigs were coming in, poetry was actually starting to pay me money. I photocopied a new zine, drew some pictures in the margins, sold it to anyone who asked. That year Rabbi Rasnikov organized a concert downtown in Union Square for Chanukah, which had always been the biggest Jewish party in San Francisco—hundreds of Jews, maybe even a thousand—all gathered to get down and shake it for the Festival of Lights. Every year they had a celebrity—in the past it had been the owner of Men's Warehouse, but this year they had actually booked Carlos Santana, who showed up and gave a speech about lights and warmth and Kabbala. I was the opening act—or, I was under the condition that I didn't curse or do anything sexual. I wrote a whole slew of poems about playing dreidel and having crushes on girls. From the sidelines, Rabbi Rasnikov watched me, laughing and nibbling on latkes and laughing innocently at my jokes for the first time in what felt like forever.

At the end of December, everyone left town for Christmas, so I bought myself a present. My plan was to come home with a case of beer on Christmas Eve, drink it all, and write for twenty-four hours nonstop. It didn't work. The writing part, anyway. You know how sometimes you want to talk all night and some nights you just want to listen? That morning, I sat down to write and didn't have anything to say. I just wanted someone to talk to me.

I walked through the rain to pick up a video and some rice and beans, and cooked dinner. Standing over the stove with the cordless phone, I called everyone, all the reserve friends who I thought might have stuck around. Nobody picked up. Every person I knew in San Francisco had left town, out to New York or Mexico or the mountains out east or the redwood forest up north. Only my roommate Veronica was here, working double shifts every day at her strip club. Her family only lived a few hours away, in Fresno, but said she'd rather stay here. Veronica said in Fresno she'd just sit home alone, listening to her aunts and cringing, but here, she could take double shifts at the Lusty Lady and pay for the next month of her life.

Now I knew why everyone had left. San Francisco was a town full of single people, and Christmas was the absolute loneliest time of the year to be flying solo.

I closed my eyes and imagined Veronica at work, dancing behind a glass wall, wearing nothing but a Santa Claus hat while broken-down men pumped quarters into slots. That was the closest I got to writing a poem, but I didn't because it was just too sad.

The Chinese video store on 24th Street was open,

and since I don't have a credit card, because no company would trust me with one, I stole Veronica's membership card. I rented *Pecker,* the John Waters movie where a white-trash boy in the Baltimore suburbs gets discovered and becomes a celebrated artist. I was blown away. Ten o'clock that Christmas Eve, I ran to the drugstore and bought myself a camera, the cheapest one they had. Like Pecker, I would take pictures of all the shit I saw and it would turn to brilliant colors, and maybe in New York people would praise my shit and call it beautiful. My best friend Erin called from Hollywood, and I needed to tell her about it.

"New York?" said Erin, disgusted. "Come to Los Angeles instead. It's warmer, and you can hang out with me."

"But I have to *write,*" I kvetched at her. I was so whiny that night.

"Fuck that," said Erin. "Come and see me. We'll have enough adventures to write you a novel."

I contemplated.

All the reasons why I hated Los Angeles sounded like pluses now. Raucous, no-holds-barred dance clubs. Entertainment-industry vultures always looking for the Next Big Thing. In high school, Erin and I used to get into so much trouble together, you could've rewritten the Bible with us as the bad guys.

And at that moment, L.A. started seeming like magic.

"I'll figure it out," I promised her.

I hung up the phone, pulled the afghan on the sofa up to my nose, and listened to the only radio station in town that wasn't playing the Christmas rotation. I fell asleep on the couch waiting for Veronica to come home and watch *Pecker* with me again.

In the morning, Erin called me once more. The noise of the phone woke me straight into a four-alarm headache. The radio was still on, blasting news reports and traffic conditions. Veronica's bed across the hall was still made, not slept in, and I forgot to say Modeh Ani.

"Hold on," I told Erin. I threw the phone in my lap and pushed it hard into the covers and yelled it out. Then I picked up the phone and said, "Yeah, what's up?"

Erin's voice jumped up and down, as though the phone was jostling against her mouth. "I just talked to my sister in Philadelphia. Holy shit, Matt. There's *snow* on the ground."

"Snow?"

"That's what she said. She said it's like a movie. Remember when we used to bury ourselves in snow? Do you remember what that felt like?"

"I don't remember *anything*," I said. "What time is it?"

"You're an idiot. Come to L.A.," Erin said, and hung up.

But I couldn't. My big show was one week away. Famous writers. Rock stars. Me. Five hundred people in the audience. If I left for L.A., I'd cut everything close. When I cut things close, I get too nervous and my heart starts pumping too fast and my nerves throb and I can't stop throwing up. I wanted to be one of those reliable performers who showed up to soundcheck on time, remembered to thank the producers, and never cancelled shows because of emotional crises.

The morning of New Year's Eve, I got a call from my temp agency. I didn't know they knew I was still alive. My temp worker chuckled, as if I was the cutest joker ever. He told me, he figured I was a Jew and so I wouldn't go away for Christmas and could I cover some hours? I said sure. I worked in an old-age home near Ocean Beach, sitting at the front desk, and answering the phone, which never rang. I came home tired, weary, and utterly New Year's planless. Sometimes you've got to trust in God, and some of those times, God just doesn't think you should go out and party.

When I got home, a silver Ford sedan was sitting in the driveway. Veronica didn't have a car. None of our friends drove new cars. Especially not silver family-appropriate cars with a just-washed sheen.

Veronica stepped out of the house, a duffel bag slung over one shoulder. She saw me, reached into her pocket, and pulled out a set of keys. She dangled them from two fingers. She posed like a car-show model on the stoop. She told me she was going down to the town where she grew up near L.A. She said she and her friends Theo and Aubrey were going to spend a white trash New Year's with her high school friends, and did I want a ride?

My backpack was still on my back. My tie dangled, half undone, limp on my chest.

I did, I told her.

To anywhere.

I ran in the house, grabbed a bagel, and while it was toasting, I stuffed some clothes into a bag. I spotted the new zoot suit I bought to wear at my show. I froze. I hesitated.

The toaster went *ding.*

I grabbed the zoot suit, stuffed it into my bag, and ran.

about the author

Born and raised in Philadelphia, Matthue Roth has worked as a baker, a barista, a futurist consultant, and a Hebrew School teacher. He has toured nationally as a performance poet, and has published about a million self-released zines and chapbooks, including *Sometimes I Throw Stuff at This House* (with Phred Chao) and the original *Yom Kippur A Go-Go*. He's been filmed for HBO's *Def Poetry Jam* and appeared in the Cannes International Film Festival. His novel *Never Mind the Goldbergs* was nominated for an ALA Best Book for Young Adults award, and he keeps a secret online diary at www.matthue.com.